ENCYCLOPAEDIA
OF CLASSIC CARS

SALOON CARS 1945-1975

ROB DE LA RIVE BOX

ENCYCLOPAEDIA
OF CLASSIC CARS

SALOON CARS 1945-1975

REBO
PRODUCTIONS

© 1999 Rebo International b.v.
internet: www.rebo-publishers.com - email: info@rebo-publishers.com

© 1999 Published by Rebo Productions Ltd.

text and photographs: Rob de la Rive Box
translation: Stephen Challacombe
production: TextCase, The Netherlands
coverdesign: Minkowsky, buro voor grafische vormgeving, The Netherlands
Layout: Signia, Winschoten, The Netherlands
Typesetting: Hof&Land Typografie, Maarssen, The Netherlands

B0363UK

ISBN 1 84053 103 7

Contents

Foreword

Those in search of a specific make or model should be aware that this book cannot include every make and model manufactured between 1945 and 1975 – indeed the subject is too vast for any one volume. During this period more than 300 car makers still existed, some of which made just a handful of cars in a few models while others produced millions of cars in a wide range of models and variants. Germany alone had thirteen different makers in 1953, which collectively produced 374,837 saloon cars that year, in twenty-two different models. There were a mere two new models from Ford in Germany that year: the Taunus 12M and the 15M. BMW dealers also benefited from two new introductions that year: the 501 and 502. By 1970 the number of car manufacturers in Germany had been reduced to ten but these produced ten times more cars, turning out 3,379,511 saloon cars that year. Ford introduced seven new models in 1970 and BMW brought out six.

Hence a book on the subject has to make choices if it is to remain within manageable proportions. This one aims to provide as wide an impression of the cars of these thirty years and of developments within the car industry. More than 100 different marques of car, which will probably invoke nostalgia for a time when cars were less uniform, are to be found in this encyclopaedia. There are midget cars from the early 1950s that were mainly powered by single or twin-cylinder two-stroke engines, famous for the blue smoke and smell of their exhaust fumes. Such issues were of little concern at the time and no deterrent to people owning these cars. Older readers may recall exchanging a motor-cycle for a small car. Heaters were deemed an unnecessary luxury in those days – after all you were kept dry! The giant American cruisers with masses of chromium plate and the largest possible engine are still with us as collector's cars. Their excessive fuel consumption was of little consequence! The price of petrol (or gasoline) was very cheap in the USA and those who afford such a car in Europe had no need to trouble themselves with the slightly higher running cost.

The cars featured in this book are mainly saloon cars (or sedans as the Americans call them). Sports cars are featured in the companion volume. These are the cars our grandparents and parents drove. Some of them have almost disappeared but others will still be running well into the third millennium because they are cosseted and carefully looked after by their owners.

Many of the models featured will invoke memories of cars in your life or those of parents and grandparents. This is precisely the book's intention – to keep alive memories of the greater diversity of cars of the recent past. These cars were once a part of the daily scene and deserve their place in history.

Rob de la Rive Box

Alfa Romeo

Alfa Romeo managed to survive for many years after its establishment in 1910 by making and selling sports and racing cars. The Italian designers attempted to continue in the same vein after World War II but quickly discovered it was necessary to make cars for a wider public in order to survive.

Alfa only produced the 6C2500 in 1947, which was first introduced in 1939. The car was very expensive, so it could only be afforded by a few enthusiasts. The company changed direction in 1949 under the leadership of Orazio Satta. Satta built a small car

Nicola Romeo.

with a monocoque body that was lighter and cheaper to produce. The engine had four cylinders instead of six, a cylinder head of aluminium, and valves that were operated by twin overhead camshafts. Such features were not offered by the competition.

The resulting car was known as the "1900" because of its cylinder capacity in cubic centimetres, and it was introduced at the Paris motor show or Salon in the autumn of 1949. This car marked the start of a new era for Alfa Romeo. It was not the end of racing cars production, with cars bearing the four-leafed clover emblem continuing to be raced. Alfa Romeo were champion constructors in Formula One and with sports cars on a number of occasions, providing valuable publicity for the marque. The racing cars were subsidised by the profits from saloon cars. Alfa Romeo saloon cars though were much more than a means of getting from A to B. Twin overhead camshafts are commonplace today and even inexpensive cars have four or even more valves per cylinder. In the 1950s and 1960s though this was quite extraordinary. Only high performance cars had overhead camshafts and such cars cost a lot of money. Such technical features were found in cars such as Ferrari, Aston Martin, and Porsche. Alfa Romeo brought them to the general public.

There were saloon and sports car version of almost every model Alfa Romeo produced, such as the Giulia range. These were mechanically similar cars that were produced with racing, sporting, and four-dour saloon bodies. The outstanding 2600 series was launched in the early 1960s. These were beautiful but expensive four-door saloons which included the Pope among their own-

The Guilia was built by Carrozzeria Touring as a four-seater convertible. The car was sold in 1966 and 1967 but only 940 were ever produced.

ers. The 2600 range also included a 2+2 coupe and a convertible built on the same chassis. Carrozzeria Zagato also built a coupé designed with motor-sport in mind.

The first Alfasud was launched in 1971 at the Turin motor show, and was the first Alfa Romeo with front-wheel drive. The Alfasud was designed by Rudolf Hruskadie, a Viennese by birth who achieved fame in Italy. The body-styling was the work of Giorgetto Giugiaro. Alfa Romeo, which was a state enterprise by this time, built a new factory for this car in southern Italy, where unemployment was at its highest. In spite of the good intentions of the Pomigliano d'Arco factory, near Naples, the venture was a fiasco. The 15,000 employees were happy to be paid but far less ready to work and production was frequently sabotaged. The cars built in that first year did great harm to the reputation of the Alfa Romeo name. The problems were eventually sorted out. Since 1973, Alfa Romeo has been part of the Fiat empire, although the workers in the factory at Arese, near Milan, seem almost unaware they are part of a conglomerate and are proud to be working for Alfa Romeo.

The 6C2500 was Alfa Romeo's only saloon in the immediate post-war period. Between 1939-1951, 279 five-seater and 243 seven-seater cars were made. The remainder were coupés and convertibles.

Alfa Romeo 1900

MODEL YEAR: 1950-1958

NUMBER MADE: 19,328

SPECIAL REMARKS: Of the almost 20,000 cars made, 17,423 were four-door saloons. The rest were coupés or convertibles. This proved the overwhelming demand for "ordinary" cars. The 1900 had a four-cylinder engine of 1,884 cc, with twin overhead camshafts, single or twin carburettors, and produced at least 80 bhp at 4,800 rpm.

Alfa Romeo cars

COUNTRY OF ORIGIN: Italy

Alfa Romeo 6C2500

MODEL YEAR: 1939-1952

NUMBER MADE: 1,591

SPECIAL REMARKS: The six-cylinder motor of the 6C2500 was based on the racing engines built by Alfa Romeo before World War II. The engine had twin overhead camshafts with either single or triple Weber carburettors. The 2,443 cc motor used in saloon cars delivered at least 90 bhp at 4,600 rpm.

The Alfa Romeo 1900 started a new era for Alfa Romeo. Its monocoque body made it cheap to build and high output (for Alfa Romeo) was achieved.

The 1900 was succeeded in 1957 by the Alfa Romeo 2000. This had the same four-cylinder motor but this was replaced in 1962 by a 2.6 litre six-cylinder engine to create the 2600, which had the same body. The 2000 had a top speed of 100 mph (160 kph) but the 2600 reached 109 mph (175 kph).

Alfa Romeo 2000

MODEL YEAR: 1957-1969

NUMBER MADE: 2,893

SPECIAL REMARKS: The successor to the four-door 1900 was the 2000. The engine was bored out to 1,975 cc and produced 108 bhp at 5,800 rpm. This power was achieved by increasing the compression ratio and installing twin carburettors. The 2000 had a five-speed gearbox with column change, so that the broad front seat had space for three persons.

Alfa Romeo Giulietta

Alfa Romeo's success started with the Giulietta and was shared by Bertone with his coupé version. The Spyder was designed by Pinanfarina but the saloon was Alfa Romeo's own design.

The Giulietta engine produced 53 bhp at 5,200 rpm. These were not cheap cars though, costing three times as much as a VW Beetle in some European countries.

The dashboard of the Giulietta was equipped with a linear speedometer, which was very modern for the time. The car had an option of two individual seats or a bench at the front. With the column gear-change there was room for three on a bench seat.

MODEL YEAR: 1955-1964

NUMBER MADE: 192,917

SPECIAL REMARKS: The Giulietta was initially built in 1954 as a coupé. Both Alfa Romeo and Bertone made a lot of money with this series which was sold by the thousands. The saloon appeared in 1955 on the same sporting underframe but with four doors and room for six persons. The Giulietta Spyder convertible was introduced in the same year by Pinanfarina.

Alfa Romeo Giulia

MODEL YEAR: 1962-1978

NUMBER MADE: Approx. 500,000

SPECIAL REMARKS: The 1,290 cc engine of the Giulietta had its bore increased to 1,570 cc to give birth to the Giulia. This model too was

The Giulia Super was a saloon car for motor sport. The 1,570 cc engine produced more than 100 bhp, giving a top speed of about 106 mph (175 kph). These cars can be seen racing in their own class at circuits in Europe.

Alfa Romeo launched a mass market car with the Alfasud. More than 1,000,000 cars of this model were sold. Their rarity today is due to the poor quality steel used to build their bodies and structural members. Alfasuds were notorious rust buckets!

produced in a number of versions ranging from motor sport models to family saloon. The top speed was 106 mph (170 kph) and the cars were equipped with disc brakes from 1964 onwards.

Alfetta

MODEL YEAR: 1972-1975

NUMBER MADE: 102,960.

SPECIAL REMARKS: Alfa Romeo were world champion constructors in 1950 and 1951 with the Alfetta Formula One car. The famous name was put into service in 1972 for a good-looking saloon that was also available as a coupé. The car was supplied with 122 bhp by its four-cylinder 1,779 cc engine. The car had a transaxle and disc brakes that were fitted next to the differential.

A 1,779 cc engine delivering 122 bhp at 5,500 rpm throbbed under the bonnet of the 1972 Alfetta. This gave the car a top speed of 112 mph (180 kph), which was quite outstanding for the era.

Alfasud

MODEL YEAR: 1972-1987

NUMBER MADE: More than 1,000,000.

SPECIAL REMARKS: This first small Alfa Romeo had an engine with opposed cylinders (boxer) and front-wheel drive. The cylinder capacity was a choice of 1,186, 1,286, 1,350, and 1,490 cc with power ranging from 63 to 95 bhp, providing a car to meet a wide range of needs. The body was designed by Giugiaro's Italdesign with the technical input from Hruska.

Alvis

The Alvis marque was founded in Coventry in 1920 by T. G. John and G. P. de Freville.

Alvis was taken over by Rover in July 1965 and the final Alvis appeared at the London motor show of that year. The final model was the Alvis TF21 with a six-cylinder engine with triple SU carburettors that developed 150 bhp at 4,750 rpm. With its top speed of 125 mph (200 kph), it was the fastest Alvis ever. When Rover was in turn taken over by Leyland Motors in March 1967, it meant the end of the line for Alvis cars. From then on the name was solely used for military and armoured vehicles, including tanks, which had none of the refinement of the classic Alvis cars.

The first Alvis was a small car with a four-cylinder 1,460 cc engine and an aluminium body. The car was not cheap and the same was true of its successors. The cars were of very high quality though and the engines made by the company itself seem indestructible. In 1928 there were already 6,000 Alvis cars on the road and these were joined that year by a further 800 new ones. Alvis built a new factory in 1937 to produce aircraft engines and then in 1938 a further new engine factory to turn out armoured vehicles with both four-wheel drive and four-wheel steering. The final pre-war Alvis saloon left the Coventry factory in 1939.

During the war, Coventry was heavily bombed and in 1940, the Holyhead Road plant was destroyed. The first post-war car was a TA14 in 1946. The only difference between this car and the 1937 Speed 25 was 16 inch disc wheels in place of the 17 inch spoked wheels of the Speed 25. The first cars to leave the line were all four-door saloons but 1950 saw the appearance once more of Alvis convertibles with the TB14 destined for export to the USA.

The design of Alvis cars was somewhat traditional and conservative which hindered their sales, although in technical terms the cars were excellent. The Swiss coachbuilder Graber had considerable success with this Alvis chassis. He produced special bodies, mainly convertible, on Alvis rolling chassis. Graber was the importer for Switzerland but gradually took on the role of advisor to the company. From 1955, Alvis built bodies in Britain to Graber's design and business started to flourish but the success was short-lived. Alvis threw in the towel in 1965 when they could no longer withstand the competition.

Alvis cars

COUNTRY OF ORIGIN: United Kingdom

Alvis TA14

MODEL YEAR: 1946-1950

NUMBER MADE: Approx. 3,213

SPECIAL REMARKS: The Alvis TA14 only differed from the pre-war Speed 25 by its wheels. Its four-cylinder engine had a capacity of 1,892 cc, delivering 66 bhp at 4,000 rpm.

The 1946 Alvis TA14 was identical to the 1937 Speed 25 except for its disc wheels instead of spokes.

Alvis TC21

MODEL YEAR: 1953-1955

NUMBER MADE: 757

An Alvis TC, as built between 1953-1955.

SPECIAL REMARKS: This was the final Alvis with a "pre-war" body. The engine was a 2,993 cc six-cylinder unit producing 101 bhp at 4,000 rpm.

Alvis TD21

MODEL YEAR: 1956-1963

NUMBER MADE: 1,070

The Alvis TD21 was a fine and quick grand tourer.

SPECIAL REMARKS: The body was designed by Swiss coachbuilder Hermann Graber. Most of the cars were built as convertibles with some coupes.

Alvis TF21

MODEL YEAR: 1963-1967

NUMBER MADE: 106

SPECIAL REMARKS: The Alvis TF21 was both the final model and the fastest. The 3-litre

With a top speed of 125 mph (200 kph) the TF was the fastest Alvis ever made.

overhead valve engine produced 150 bhp at 4,750 rpm giving a top speed in excess of 125 mph (200 kph).

American Motors

The Hudson and Nash companies merged in 1954 to enable them to better withstand competition from the "big three" of General Motors, Ford, and Chrysler. The merger resulted in the American Motors Corporation, or AMC for short. The Hudson and Nash companies had made a great deal of money during the Korean war but this was over by 1954. Hudson lost $10,500,000 that year and although the Nash company made a profit of $14,000,000, it was insignificant from a turnover of $1 billion.

The new basic model was the Rambler, which was a successor to the Nash Rambler. This car was equipped with a panoramic front windscreen. The car was fitted with a Packard V-8 engine because neither Hudson or Nash had their own V-8 power unit. The Ultra-Matic

Nash used colour in an interesting way and this passed to AMC. Cars were often painted two or even three colours.

COUNTRY OF ORIGIN: USA

Rambler American

MODEL YEAR: 1958

NUMBER MADE: 42,196

The 1958 Rambler American was similar to the final 1955 Nash Rambler.

automatic gearbox was also supplied by Packard. AMC was unable to supply its own V-8 engine until 1956. In 1956, the range consisted of the Rambler, Statesman, and Ambassador. The first of two of these were powered by an in line six-cylinder of 3,205 cc as standard but could also be supplied with a 4,097 cc V-8 motor.

The Ambassador was equipped with a 5,359 cc V-8 that produced 258 bhp (SAE) at 4,700 rpm. Enthusiasts were catered for with the Rambler Rebel which was powered by the Ambassador engine. In line with the practice of the Nash company, the bodies were designed by Pinanfarina. Most were sprayed with a duo-tone finish which made them quite striking. Despite all this AMC struggled to make profits. The entire American auto industry went through troubled times in 1956 and AMC lost almost $20,000,000 that year. From 1958 there were no more Hudson or Nash cars; from now on they were simply sold as Rambler. These Ramblers were supplied in a number of different sized models with entirely new bodies and the new cars were an instant success making profits of $60,000,000 for the company.

AMC has produced many unusual cars and copied ideas too from here and there. When Detroit first introduced compacts, AMC already had a small Rambler. When the "pony" cars became popular, AMC brought out the Marlin in 1965 and the Javelin in 1968. This small car maker also had sports cars in its range.

Their Gremlin was barely any longer than the VW Beetle. The car was in reality an AMC Hornet that was chopped off behind the front doors. There was also the Pacer which had a right-hand door that was wider than the left-hand door to make it easier for passengers to get in and out.

SPECIAL REMARKS: Nash sold their final Rambler in 1956 but the model reappeared in 1958 as the AMC Rambler American. The car was available in just one model, a two-door sedan, with a choice of one six-cylinder engine that produced 90 bhp (SAE) at 3,800 rpm.

Ambassador

MODEL YEAR: 1959

NUMBER MADE: 23,799

SPECIAL REMARKS: Of the almost 24,000 Ambassadors, AMC sold 1,477 four-door saloons in 1959. The monocoque body was equipped with a 5,359 cc V-8 engine rated at 274 bhp at 4,700 rpm. The car was supplied as standard with a Flash-O-Matic automatic gearbox but could be supplied with a three-speed manual box on request.

Javelin

MODEL YEAR: 1968-1974

NUMBER MADE: 235,497

The Javelin – this is a 1969 model – was a spacious five-seater available only as a coupe. Customers could choose between a six-cylinder or V-8 engine.

The AMX was the two-seater version of the Javelin. The car was not a huge success because it could be beaten by its rival the popular Corvette.

SPECIAL REMARKS: The Javelin was AMC's response to the Chevrolet Camaro. In 1968, the car was still a "pony car" with a length of 4810 mm (189 in) but had grown into a full-grown horse by 1974 of 4960 mm (195 in). The six-cylinder and V-8 engines varied from 3.8 – 6.6 litres.

Gremlin

MODEL YEAR: 1970-1978

NUMBER MADE: More than 600,000

SPECIAL REMARKS: The Gremlin was to the American students what the Citroën 2CV was for the French. The car was introduced on the first of April in 1970 but not as a joke. This was one of AMC's best-selling cars. The Gremlin had both six cylinder and V-8 engines available. The V-8 engines were 5 litres and delivered 152 brake horsepower.

When sales of the Hornet slumped, Dick Teague chopped the car off behind the front doors, added a simple rear end and the Gremlin was born!

The AMX was only available with a V-8 engine but with a choice of 5,896 cc unit with quadruple carburettors giving 294 bhp at 4,800 rpm, or 6,383 cc motor for 330 bhp at 5,000 rpm.

AMX

MODEL YEAR: 1968-1971

NUMBER MADE: 19,134

SPECIAL REMARKS: The AMX was the two-seater version of the Javelin and quite obviously from the same designer, Dick Teague. The car was only available with 6 or 6.4 litre V-8 engines which produced 294 bhp at 4,800 rpm or 330 bhp (SAE) at 5,000 rpm. The car was dangerously fast at 144 mph (230 kph).

Pacer

MODEL YEAR: 1975-1980

NUMBER MADE: 280,859

SPECIAL REMARKS: The Pacer was a three-doors car with a slightly wider right-hand

The Pacer was the bigger and slightly less idiosyncratic brother of the Gremlin. The right-hand door was somewhat wider than the left one. These cars were also raced in the USA.

The twin screws moved a great deal of water but the lines prevented the Amphicar from having good characteristics through the water.

door than the driver's (left-hand) door. The car was 4360 mm (171 in) long and 1960 mm (77 in) wide. By comparison, a VW Beetle was 4030 mm (158 in) long and 1540 mm (60 in) wide. The car was equipped with a 3.8 or 4.2 litre six-cylinder engine until 1978. Subsequently the car had a 5 litre V-8 motor.

Amphicar

Dreams of cars which as well as being driven can act as a boat or plane are as old as the car itself. Many attempts have been made to build such cars. The German engineer Hans Trippel built amphibious vehicles for the German Wehrmacht and decided to put his skills to use after World War II. Trippel displayed a small amphibious car at the Geneva motor show in 1958 and his eventual

The Amphicar rode too high on its 13 inch wheels to look attractive.

Amphicar was based on this prototype, which was known as Alligator. Trippel planned to sell his unusual car to the Americans and most of the 3,000 cars that were sold ended up in American hands.

The Amphicar had a Triumph Herald engine mounted at the back, driving the rear wheels when on the road. An intermediate gearbox provided drive for twin propellers. When afloat, the car was steered without a rudder by turning the front wheels. The Amphicar had a top speed afloat of $7^1/_2$ mph (12 kph) and 69 mph (110 kph) on the road.

Amphicar cars

COUNTRY OF ORIGIN: Germany

Amphicar

MODEL YEAR: 1961-1968

NUMBER MADE: Approx. 3,000.

SPECIAL REMARKS: An amphibious vehicle is a cross between a boat and a car with the result being a poor boat and a less good car. Trippel's monster was built for the American market.

Armstrong Siddeley

Coventry has sometimes been called Britain's Detroit and indeed the majority of British cars originated from the city. This once included those of Armstrong-Siddeley who built cars between 1919 and 1960 when the company abandoned car production because the public demanded a mass market product that Armstrong-Siddeley were unable to deliver. Armstrong-Siddeley cars were always very special. Even in their most successful days before World War II, the company struggled to produce more than 1,000 cars in a year.

Armstrong-Siddeleys were of similar quality to Humber and Daimler and not much cheaper than a Bentley. Immediately after World War II, the company returned to the market with the Lancaster which was named after the famous bombers which the company had built during the war. In reality the car was an old model from 1939 with a new grill but no-one minded. There was independent suspension of the front wheels with torsion springs, which together with a Wilson pre-selector made the car quite modern. The convertible was named Hurricane and the two-door coupé was a Typhoon.

Before the war, the six-cylinder engine had been 2 litres but this was enlarged to 2.3 litres. The Sapphire was subsequently developed with a cylinder capacity of 3,435 cc. This car had an engine with overhead valves plus twin carburettors and was capable of 100 mph (160 kph). This final model had the customary high standard of internal trim with wood and leather. It was impossible to produce cars of this quality cheaply.

A standard saloon cost about four times as much as a VW Beetle and a seven-seater limousine with manual gearbox was seven times as much and even more with an automatic gearbox. There were Armstrong-Siddeleys for those with less deep pockets powered by 2,290 cc four-cylinder and 2,309 cc six-cylinder engines which were designated "234" and "236". The final number indicated the number of cylinders.

The final and perhaps best Armstrong-Siddeley was the Star Sapphire of which a mere 1,000 were sold. It had a 3,990 cc six-cylinder engine under the bonnet that delivering 165 bhp at 4,250 rpm.

The transmission was through a Borg-Warner automatic gearbox. With its top speed of 106 mph (170 kph), the disc brakes were not an unnecessary luxury. The final car rolled off the Paradise factory in Coventry in July 1960. Its price of £2,489 would have bought a fine country home.

Armstrong-Siddeley cars

Country of origin: United Kingdom

Lancaster

Model year: 1945-1952

Number made: 12,470

Armstrong-Siddeley intended to compete with Rolls Royce with their Star Sapphire. This was unsuccessful. What's in a name?

Armstrong-Siddeley named their first post-war cars after the aircraft which had been built in their factory during the war. This is a Hurricane.

SPECIAL REMARKS: The numbers for this model include Hurricanes and Typhoons. These cars were all built on the same robust chassis and were equipped with six-cylinder engines of either 2 or 2.3 litres.

Sapphire

MODEL YEAR: 1953-1959

NUMBER MADE: 7,207

SPECIAL REMARKS: The Sapphire was supplied with several different engines: six-cylinder ones of 2,309 or 3,435 cc; alternatively four-cylinder ones of 2,290 cc. The power output varied from 122–152 bhp.

Star Sapphire

MODEL YEAR: 1959-1960

NUMBER MADE: 980

SPECIAL REMARKS: The final Armstrong-Siddeley was also the best looking. The Star

A restored 1959 Star Sapphire. The car was too expensive to be able to compete in the market.

Sapphire had every technical innovation the motor industry had up its sleeves. The car was superbly trimmed and finished but cost almost as much as a Bentley. Who would buy an Armstrong Siddeley at such prices?

Audi

The Audi name is one of the oldest German car marques. The company was already making cars in 1910. The name disappeared in 1939 and reappeared in 1965. The designer of the first Audi, August Horch, built his first car in 1900. He left the company in 1909 after a row and started up a new company a year later to build cars. Because he was no longer permitted to use his own name, his son came up with the Audi name which means "listening" in Latin – which is the same meaning as "horch" in German. The new Audi cars were more than equal to Horch cars of the same era. The company was taken over in 1928 by Jörgen Skafte Rasmussen, who owned DKW. Rasmussen formed Auto Union in 1932 with Horch and Wanderer.

The Audi factory ended the war in the Russian zone. Auto Union returned to the German market in 1949 in Düsseldorf with a DKW. The company was purchased by Daimler-Benz in 1956 and then sold on in 1965 to Volkswagen. Within a few months there were new Audi cars in the showrooms. In reality, the first Audis were little more than DKWs with a different name. The important difference though was that the two-stroke motor of DKW had been replaced by a four-stroke developed by Mercedes-Benz. In common with the DKW, the engine powered the front wheels. Audis were of very good quality and captured a large share of the market. The Audi 80 was launched in September 1966, with the 80 representing the horsepower of the engine. This was followed two months later by the 90. A much cheaper version known as the Audi 72 was launched in 1967. The Audi 80 was replaced in December 1968 by the 75. The cheapest model was the Audi 60, which from the spring of 1968 was equipped with a 55 bhp engine. Audi's top model – the Audi 100 – made its appearance in November 1968. The 1,760 cc engine could be supplied with different power outputs from the very beginning. The Audi 100 was equipped with 80, 90, and 100 bhp engines. The Audi 100 S Coupé even had 112 bhp at its disposal.

Audi introduced its four-wheel-drive Quattro in 1980. This car issued in a new motoring era for until then four-wheel drive had been restricted to rugged cross-country vehicles.

Audi cars

COUNTRY OF ORIGIN: Germany

Audi 60

MODEL YEAR: 1965-1972

NUMBER MADE: 216,988

SPECIAL REMARKS: The Audi 60 was the cheapest car the firm offered. The car shared a body with the more powerful and expensive models but its four-cylinder engine was a mere 1,496 cc providing 55 bhp at 4,750 rpm.

A 1968 Audi 60 – this is an "L" for deluxe. The first Audi cars were a DKW F102 with a four-stroke engine, new front, and different back end.

Audi 100

MODEL YEAR: 1968-1976

NUMBER MADE: 827,474

SPECIAL REMARKS: The Audi 100 was the company's leading car. It was successful because of the meagre opposition in the German market in its category.

The Audi 100: ample room for all the family, plenty of luxury and comfort for the experienced motorist and all for half the price of a Mercedes-Benz.

Audi 100 S Coupé

MODEL YEAR: 1971-1976

NUMBER MADE: 30,687

The Audi S Coupé was in a class of its own as a 5-seater capable of 114 mph (183 kph) for a very attractive price. Fuel consumption was 21 mpg (14litres:100km).

SPECIAL REMARKS: The coupé was a two-door Audi 100 with a different roof line. With its length of 4400 mm (173 in) it was 200 mm (7³/₄ in) shorter than the standard saloon and the wheelbase was also shorter by 120 mm (4³/₄ in) at 2560 mm (100 in). The engine was the same as that used in the Audi 100 GL, with a capacity of 1871 cc, producing 112 bhp at 5,800 rpm.

Austin

Herbert Austin did the opposite to many young Australians who went to school and university in Britain. At the age of 16 years,

he left his father's farm at Great Missenden in Buckinghamshire to study at Melbourne University. In Melbourne he met Frederick Wolseley, Irish owner of a precision engineering company, who offered him a job as technical director in his Australian subsidiary, where sheep-shearing machines were made. Austin returned to Britain in 1889, having already built his first car for Wolseley in 1895.

Austin then established his own business in 1904 and he led the company until his death in 1940.

As one of the leading figures of the British motor industry, he was given a peerage, becoming Lord Austin of Longbridge, and also received the OBE, an honorary doctorate in Law, and became a Conservative Member of Parliament.

The one-millionth Austin rolled off the assembly lines in 1947 and the second millionth car in 1952. The company merged with Morris, Riley, Wolseley, and MG to form the British Motor Corporation in 1952. At that time, BMC was the largest car manufacturer not only in Europe, but also in the world. The colossal BMC grew even larger with the addition of Jaguar and Daimler, and by the time Triumph and Rover were amalgamated with the concern it had become the British Leyland Motor Corporation.

*Despite its individual headlights, the Sheerline
A 125 was not an old-fashioned car in its time. It had
independent front suspension and hydraulic brakes.
This is an example from 1950.*

*The Austin A40 Somerset sold 174,306 in
1952-1953. Its 1,200 cc engine produced
43 bhp at 4,300 rpm.*

*The spacious body of the A105 Westminster was designed
by Pininfarina. The A99 Westminster did not have the
coloured body stripe.*

The first post-war Austins were built to pre-war designs. The Eight, Ten, Twelve, and Sixteen still had separate headlights. The 1947 A40 saw a change to modern times with independent front suspension and overhead valve engines.

The A30 appeared in 1951 as a somewhat late replacement for the famous Austin Seven of which 400,000 were sold between 1922-1938. The A30 had a small 803 cc engine of 30 bhp and room for four adults. Austin also built cars for the richest ten percent of the population with cars such as the 1947 Princess which was almost 196 in (5,000 mm) long and had a 4-litre six-cylinder engine producing 137 bhp. This car was of the class of Rolls-Royce and Bentley but cost less than half.

Austin made wide use of Pininfarina in the design of its cars. One notable example that caught the eye with its somewhat rectangular body is the A40 Farina, which was launched at the 1958 Paris motor show.

BMC introduced the Mini (see under Mini) in August 1959 and the Austin Seven 850 shared in its success. A larger version of the

The A60 Cambridge of 1954 had a monocoque body (no chassis). While the A40 had a 1,200 cc (43 bhp) engine, the A50 had a 1,489 cc four-cylinder (51 bhp).

The Austin A40 Sports was aimed at the American market.

There was enough room for the entire family in the A40 Sports which in 1951 still had a separate chassis.

Mini was the 1100/1300 which had 1,098 cc or 1,275 cc engines of 48 or 71 bhp. Austin also made sports cars of real class such as the Austin-Healey of which almost 73,000 were sold. There was also the smaller Austin-Healey Sprite version of which at least 129,347 drove out of the factory.

Austin cars

COUNTRY OF ORIGIN: United Kingdom

Austin A40

MODEL YEAR: 1947-1951

NUMBER MADE: 289,897

SPECIAL REMARKS: The A40 was the first new post-war Austin. The two-door version was named Dorset and the four-door became a Devon. The overhead valve engine was 1,200 cc giving 40 bhp at 4,300 rpm and a top speed of 72 mph (115 kph).

The A40 Devon such as this 1951 example had independent front suspension and an overhead valve engine of 1, 200 cc.

Austin A30

MODEL YEAR: 1951-1956

NUMBER MADE: 222,264

SPECIAL REMARKS: The A30 was the first Austin with a monocoque body and no separate chassis. In spite of its short length of a mere 136 in (3,460 mm), the four-door saloon had space for the entire family. A two-door version appeared in 1953 and an estate car in 1955.

Austin introduced the A30 as a successor for the pre-war Austin Seven. The car was a tremendous success in an era when many changed over to small cars from motorcycles.

Austin A40 Farina

MODEL YEAR: 1958-1967

NUMBER MADE: 342,280

SPECIAL REMARKS: The A40 Farina was designed by Pininfarina. The 948 cc four-cylinder engine produced 35 bhp at 4,250 rpm and achieved a top speed of 69 mph (110

The A40 Farina was named after its designer. The car had a "third door" at the back which is quite commonplace today but exceptional for its day.

kph). There was a "hatchback" rear door and collapsible rear seat that offered a great deal of space in the back.

Austin A60 Cambridge

MODEL YEAR: 1961-1969

NUMBER MADE: Unknown

SPECIAL REMARKS: The Cambridge started in 1957 as the A55 with a 1,489 cc engine. The car got a new body and 1,622 cc four-cylinder engine in 1961. The four-speed gearbox had a floor-mounted gear-change lever but could also be supplied with column change.

Pininfarina increasingly became the consultant for body design for Austin. The Italian company designed the body of the A60 Cambridge. This is a 1963 example.

Austin 1100/1300

MODEL YEAR: 1963-1975

NUMBER MADE: Unknown

SPECIAL REMARKS: The "1100" was the big brother of the Mini and was also available

Although the 1100/1300 was never as admired as the Mini, it still sold more than 1,000,000.

The 1800 was powered by the MGB engine mounted transversely.

with a 1,275 cc engine as the "1300". These cars shared the front-wheel drive/transverse placement of the engine of the Mini and more than 1,000,000 of them were sold.

Austin Allegro

MODEL YEAR: 1973-1982

NUMBER MADE: More than 700,000
SPECIAL REMARKS: Harris Mann designed the body of the Allegro, which succeeded the 1100/1300 series. This car also had front-wheel drive but customers could choose four-cylinder engines ranging from 1,098 cc to 1,748 cc, with power of 44-91 bhp.

The body of the Allegro – this is an estate version – was designed by Harris Mann.

Autobianchi

Edoardo Bianchi was the son of a grocer, who when not yet twenty years old set-up his own workshop to make cycles in 1885. Later, in 1897, he changed direction to making motor-cycles and a year later, Bianchi built

his first car. In the main, the Bianchi cars were somewhat staid but the occasional racing car was also built, though saloon cars remained the company's mainstay. During World War II, the Bianchi company turned our army lorries which was sufficient reason for the Allies to bomb the factory to the ground in 1943. The founder died three years later in 1946, aged 81. His factory had been sufficiently reconstructed for lorries to roll once more off the production line. The company returned to building in 1955, after they had been taken over by Pirelli and Fiat. The first cars left the factory in 1957 bearing the Autobianchi name, although constructed from Fiat 500 parts. Like the Fiat 500, the Bianchina 500 was a four-seater but the body was much more attractive than the Fiat. Autobianchi continued to build special versions of Fiat cars. A fine convertible based on the Fiat 500 was introduced in 1960 and this was followed a few months later by an estate car. This car, known as the Panoramica, had mechanics from the Nuova 500. This Autobianchi provided sufficient space for four adults by increasing the wheelbase of the Fiat 500 Giardiniera estate car from 1,840 to 1,940 mm (72 to 76 in). Other models included the Stellina and Primula. The Stellina was a two-seater sports cars based on the Fiat 600 with a glass-fibre reinforced polyester body. The Primula was launched at the Turin motor show in 1964. The car created considerable

The Bianchi Panoramica had a longer wheelbase and hence more room than the Fiat Giardiniera.

interest and was the first "Fiat" with a third door or hatch-back and with a transverse-mounted engine that drove the front wheels. Fiat bought out Pirelli's interest in 1968 and a year later the first Autobianchi A112 made its appearance. This small family car had a four-cylinder engine with a 903 cc engine that delivered 44 bhp at 6,000 rpm. This Italian "Mini" had a top speed of 91 mph (130 kph). For those who wanted even more power, there was also an Abarth version which reach 94 mph (150 kph).

Autobianchi cars

COUNTRY OF ORIGIN: Italy

Autobianchi Bianchina 500

MODEL YEAR: 1960-1969

NUMBER MADE: Unknown

SPECIAL REMARKS: The Bianchina coupe and convertible was based on the underframe of

Fiat dealers also sold the Autobianchi Bianchina as a coupé and even 2+2.

There was room in the back of the Bianchina 500 with the roof down.

the Fiat 500 Nuova but with a much more attractive body. The Panoramica was the estate car version. The twin-cylinder engine was 479 or 500 cc, giving 17-21 bhp.

Primula

MODEL YEAR: 1964-1970

NUMBER MADE: Unknown

SPECIAL REMARKS: The Primula was the first "Fiat" with a transverse-mounted engine and front-wheel drive. The 1,221 cc engine developed 51-65 bhp. The boot had also been transformed into a third door of a hatch-back.

Autobianchi A112

MODEL YEAR: 1969-1986

NUMBER MADE: 1,254,178

SPECIAL REMARKS: The A112 was a successful competitor in Italy to the Mini. This car had a wheelbase of 2,040 mm (80 in) and overall length of 3,230 mm (127 in), making it slightly bigger than the Mini which had 2,030 mm (80 in) wheelbase and 3,050 mm (120 in) overall length.

The Autobianchi 112 can se be seen driving around. The Abarth version often had a matt-black bonnet lid.

Bentley

Walter Owen Bentley, better known as W.O. was born in London in September 1888. At the age of sixteen, he was apprenticed to the Great Northern Railway Locomotive Works in Doncaster. He founded Bentley Motor Company in 1918, together with his elder brother H.M. Bentley. They built radial engines for the Royal Air Force. After World War I the brothers switched to producing cars and made imposing cars powered by superb 4.5, 6.5, or 8 litre engines. Most of their cars were supplied as sports cars. It is well-known that these cars were virtually unbeatable in their class, so that Bentleys won the Le Mans 24-hour race at least four times in the 1920s.

W.O. was a gifted engineer but a poor businessman so that the company came to the edge of bankruptcy at least three times. On the fourth occasion, the company could only be saved by selling out to Rolls-Royce. W.O. was permitted to stay on to work for Rolls-Royce but he soon decided to quit to join Lagonda, where he felt more at home. W.O. Owen designed a superb 4.5 litre V-12 engine for Lagonda which continued to built after World War II.

W.O. died a poor man in 1971 at 83 years old. He had never been rich and for these reasons the Bentley Owners' Club gave him a cheque shortly after the war and later gave him a second-hand Mini to use. Only 3,061 Bentley cars were built under W.O. Owen's hand and most of these are still running. The same is equally true of course of the higher number of Bentleys built by Rolls-Royce, since these cars are virtually indestructible.

A prototype of the Bentley Mark V1 was built in 1939 and a series of improvements were made during World War II. Once the factory could turn its hands once more to making private cars, the Mark VI rolled from the lines.

The engine of this car was 4,257 cc with power output which Bentley kept secret with the comment that the bhp was "sufficient". This comment was no exaggeration since the engine could propel the almost 2 ton car to a top speed of at least 94 mph (150 kph). Most Bentleys and Rolls-Royces were sold before World War II as rolling chassis on which customers had built the body of their choice. This policy changed after the war and two thirds of Mark VI cars sold had a works four-door body fitted.

The R-type came into being in 1952 by increasing the bore of the Mark VI engine to 4,566 cc. The car's body was virtually identical to its predecessor. Mulliner, which by this time was part of Rolls-Royce, built a fine two-door coupé body on the R-type chassis. This new car was sold as the Bentley Continental Sports Saloon, which had a more highly-tuned engine. The contemporary publicity brochures indicate that the car was capable of 125 mph (200 kph).

The Bentley S Type which succeeded the R-type in 1955 was a considerable improvement. The car had a new, even stronger chas-

W.O. Bentley (1888-1971).

The Bentley S2 was identical to the S1 except for its V-8 engine. This is a Standard Saloon.

The Bentley Mk IV was the first Bentley to be provided with a ready-made works body. This is a 1952 Standard Saloon.

sis, power-assisted steering, and an automatic gearbox available as an optional extra. The customer could also order a body of more modern style. When the Rolls-Royce Silver Cloud II was equipped with a V-8 engine in 1959, the Bentley S2 appeared on the same chassis. The 6,230 cc engine was even quieter, if that is possible, than the six-cylinder predecessors. The four-door saloon and convertible bodies were built of steel but the S2 Continental had an aluminium body.

The final "true" Bentley was the S3, which although technically identical to the Rolls-Royce, still had its own look. Subsequent Bentleys shared their bodies with Rolls-Royce.

The only difference was in the marque badges. The Bentley T1 was the first with a monocoque body and hence no separate chassis. It also had independent suspension all round and disc brakes on all four wheels.

coachbuilders such as Park Ward, James Young, Mulliner, and Pininfarina.

Bentley R

MODEL YEAR: 1952-1955

NUMBER MADE: 2,320

The Bentley Continental R is one of the finest post-war Bentleys, with a body by Mulliner. The car's top speed was 125 mph (200 kph).

SPECIAL REMARKS: The body of the R Type was virtually identical to its predecessor. An automatic gearbox was available as an optional extra.

Bentley S1

MODEL YEAR: 1955-1959

NUMBER MADE: 3,538

Bentley cars

COUNTRY OF ORIGIN: United Kingdom

Bentley Mk VI

MODEL YEAR: 1946-1952

NUMBER MADE: 5,201

SPECIAL REMARKS: Although the Mark VI was available with a works four-door saloon body, the car could still be ordered as a rolling-chassis for the finest creations of

SPECIAL REMARKS: The S1 made its predecessors look old-fashioned, with its entirely new body. Dealers could also offer the car as coupé, Continental, or convertible.

Bentley S2

MODEL YEAR: 1959-1962

NUMBER MADE: 2,310

SPECIAL REMARKS: The big difference between the S1 and S2 was under the bonnet where the trusty six-cylinder had been replaced by a more modern V-8 with a capacity of 6,230 cc.

A 1962 Bentley Continental S2 Coupé with aluminium body by Mulliner.

Bentley S3

MODEL YEAR: 1962-1965

NUMBER MADE: 1,630

Not everyone was pleased with the twin headlights of the S3, which was technically identical with its predecessor.

SPECIAL REMARKS: The S3 was the final model to be instantly recognisable as a Bentley. The subsequent models shared their bodies with Rolls-Royce. A total of 312 were sold of the coupé (or Continental).

Bentley T1

MODEL YEAR: 1965-1977

NUMBER MADE: 1,712

SPECIAL REMARKS: After resisting for a long time, Rolls-Royce and Bentley changed over to monocoque bodies in 1965. The absence of a chassis made the cars lighter, so that they were both faster and less thirsty on fuel.

Bentley entered a new era with the monocoque body of the T1.

BMW

The Bayrischen Flugzeugwerke (Bavarian Aircraft Factory) founded in 1916 to build engines for military aircraft became the Bayrischen Motoren Werke (BMW) or Bavarian Motors Factory in 1922. The company was banned from making aero engines following World War I and turned to making marine engines and motor-cycles. In 1928, BMW took over the Dixi factory in Eisenach which built English Austin Sevens under licence. This BMW-Dixi was a tremendous success and formed the basis for BMW's following models. These included such unforgettable cars as the 327 and 328 sports cars which were built immediately after World War II.

Times were extremely hard for BMW following World War II. The Eisenach factory was

now in the eastern zone and went into full production making the 1939 models. These were first sold as BMW and then later as EMW. The Munich factory had been largely destroyed and the remaining equipment taken as spoils of war by the Americans. BMW was not able to restart making cars until 1952. The first car to come of the new production lines was the superb 501, with enough room for six persons and a 2 litre six-cylinder engine producing 65 bhp. From 1954, the car was also available with a

The BMW 1600-2 was launched at Geneva in 1966. The "2" meant two-doors.

BMW also built sports cars. This is a 2002 Touring which was available with 1.6 or 1.8 litre motors.

BMW persevered with building large cars even though they were difficult to sell. This is the famous BMW 3200 CS.

V-8 engine as a 502. When Mercedes-Benz brought out their 300SL, BMW responded with the 507 sports cars.

The time for big cars had not yet arrived though. In Germany in particular, the demand was for cheap forms of transport such as the Messerschmitt, Heinkel, or Goggomobil. In order to participate in this market, BMW bought the rights from Renzo Rivolta to produce the Isetta in Germany. BMW fitted a single-cylinder motor-cycle engine in the two-seater which although only 245 cc (later 295cc) produced 12 bhp which was sufficient to give a top speed of 53 mph (85 kph).

The Isetta "bubble car" quickly grew in size: first to the 600, with two-cylinder 582 cc engine that produced 20 bhp. This was followed by the 700, which looked like a "real" car and had a 697 cc two-cylinder engine of 30 bhp.

By the 1960s, BMW had the 1500 in their showrooms. This car was the forerunner of today's BMW. The cars became steadily bigger and more powerful: 1,500, 1,600, 1,800, 2,000, 2,500, 2,800, 3,000, 3,200, and 3,500 cc with power up from 80 to 290 bhp.

BMW cars

COUNTRY OF ORIGIN: Germany

BMW 501

MODEL YEAR: 1952-1958

NUMBER MADE: 8,936

The flowing lines of the 501 caused it to be dubbed the "baroque angel" in Germany. The same car fitted with a V-8 engine became the BMW 502.

the 3200 was subsequently developed. The BMW factory only produced saloon versions of these cars but special body firms produced convertibles and coupés.

BMW 503

MODEL YEAR: 1955-1959

NUMBER MADE: 412

The BMW 503 only sold 412 between 1955-1959. There was little demand in those days for expensive cars.

SPECIAL REMARKS: The BMW 501 was a true luxury car, with a 2-litre, six-cylinder engine, that could compete with Mercedes-Benz.

BMW 502

MODEL YEAR: 1954-1963

NUMBER MADE: 13,044

SPECIAL REMARKS: By fitting a V-8 engine, the BMW 501 became the 502, from which

The coachbuilding firm of Baur was responsible for this 1955 BMW 502 coupé.

SPECIAL REMARKS: The BMW 502 was the basis for the 503. The 502's body was designed by Albrecht Count Goertz. It was a fine touring car but very expensive, costing more than eight times as much as a VW of the time.

BMW 507

MODEL YEAR: 1955-1959

NUMBER MADE: 252

SPECIAL REMARKS: Count Goertz was also responsible for designing the BMW 507 which was to compete with the Mercedes-Benz 300SL. This only partially succeeded.

The German designer Count Goertz, who lived in America, was responsible for the look of the BMW 507.

Isetta

MODEL YEAR: 1955-1962

NUMBER MADE: 161,728

SPECIAL REMARKS: The Isetta was developed as a small car for the person who no longer

The BMW Isetta was little more than a motor-cycle with a canopy. This is a 298 cc engine model with 13 bhp.

The Isetta only had one door and that was a small one!

wanted to ride a motor-cycle but did not have enough money for a "real" car. The front of the car was also the only door.

BMW 600

MODEL YEAR: 1957-1959

NUMBER MADE: 34,813

SPECIAL REMARKS: The 600 started to look like a car, having four wheels and two doors. They were not successful because they cost more than a VW Beetle.

The BMW 600 had four wheels and now had two doors – one at the front and the other on the right.

700

MODEL YEAR: 1959-1965

NUMBER MADE: 188,011

SPECIAL REMARKS: The BMW 700 was available as saloon, coupé, and convertible. The latter two models were sold 13,758 times. These were the final BMW cars with air-cooled two-cylinder motor-cycle engines.

The BMW 700 now resembled a true car. It was also available as coupé and cabriolet.

The BMW 2002 ti had a 130 bhp engine and a top speed of 116 mph (185 kph).

BMW 1500

MODEL YEAR: 1961-1966

NUMBER MADE: 23,554

SPECIAL REMARKS: The BMW 1500 heralded a new era for BMW. They had done with miniature cars and now built true cars. The 1500 had a 1,499 cc four-cylinder engine of 75 bhp which gave a top speed of 94 mph (150 kph).

BMW 2002

MODEL YEAR: 1968-1975

NUMBER MADE: Unknown

SPECIAL REMARKS: The four-cylinder engine of the 2002 was 1,990 cc with a power of 100 bhp. The 2002 ti has 130 bhp available, and the 1973 turbo version boasted 170 bhp.

The BMW 2002 was also available from 1969 with an automatic gearbox.

The BMW 2002 Turbo arrived on the market in 1973-1974 – just when no-one wanted a fast and thirsty car. Consequently, only 1,672 were sold in those years.

BMW 2500 CS

MODEL YEAR: 1968-1975

NUMBER MADE: 29,505

SPECIAL REMARKS: The BMW 2500 CS was available with 2.5, 2.8, and 3-litre engines. In 1974, the 2,494 cc six-cylinder engine produced 150 bhp, capable of accelerating the 1,400 kg (3,080 lb) car from 0-60 in 10 seconds (0-100 kph in 10.5 seconds).

The BMW 2500 CS was not only a great car for touring: it was also successful in motor sport.

Bond

The Bond Equipe was a sporting 2+2 with glass-reinforced polyester body and Triumph Herald engine.

Three-wheeled cars have come and gone and almost all of them were survived by the Bond, named after the spiritual father Lawrence Bond. A vehicle bearing this name was displayed in 1949 at a car and motor-cycle show where it attracted interest from both motorists and motor-cyclists. British motor-cyclists who were fed-up with having to cope with the elements on their motor-cycle were able to switch over to these new vehicles with their motor-cycle licence, provided there was no reverse gear. If he was too lazy to push his car back, the price of £295 for the car was increased by £8 10 shillings but then a car licence was needed.

The first Bond cars were two-seaters with an aluminium body and 122 cc Villiers two-stroke engine. The single-cylinder engine drove the single front wheel which also steered the car. The car was not at all bad and a 200 cc version appeared in 1951 that

The earlier Bond cars were clearly three-wheelers. This 1957 car was designed to look like a "real" car.

had a top speed of 47 mph (75 kph). This car also had a pointed nose with a single front wheel which made it instantly recognisable as a three-wheeler. Bond therefore introduced a model in 1953 with a front end that had the appearance of a normal car, with a body of similar width as a four-wheel car and wings that housed no wheels. This car was tremendously successful and Bond sold at least 14,000 of them in 1956.

Meanwhile the quest for greater power also affected Bond and the motors became bigger so that the Bond 875 of 1965 appeared with a Hillman Imp power unit instead of a sputtering two-stroke engine. Bond took the easy root and installed the Hillman engine, complete with gearbox and suspension. Drive was no longer through a single front wheel but through both rear wheels. Bond ceased making cars with two-stroke engines in 1966 and a three-wheeler could be ordered with a Triumph Spitfire engine in 1967. Bond Cars gave the top speed as 79 mph (126 kph) but this must surely have been measured over a dead straight road with no side wind with the car weighing a mere 858 lb (390 kg). The Bond Bug, designed by Tom Karen, appeared in 1970. The car had no doors: instead the entire front and sides of the body could be tilted forward.

Bond also built sports cars, with its Bond Equipe selling 4,500 between 1963 and 1971.

Bond cars

COUNTRY OF ORIGIN: United Kingdom

Bond Minicar

MODEL YEAR: 1948-1950

NUMBER MADE: Unknown

SPECIAL REMARKS: The air-cooled motor-cycle engine produced just 5 bhp so that the top speed was no higher than 40 mph (65 kph).

Bond 875

MODEL YEAR: 1965-1970

NUMBER MADE: 3,431

SPECIAL REMARKS: The Bond 875, with its rear-mounted Hillman Imp engine and polyester body shell, had a top speed of more than 75 mph (120 kph).

Bond Bug

MODEL YEAR: 1970-1974

NUMBER MADE: 2,270

SPECIAL REMARKS: The Bond Bug was sold with two different four-cylinder engines: a 701 cc producing 29 bhp at 5,000 rpm and 748 cc giving 32 bhp at 5,000 rpm.

The Bond Bug did not have doors: instead the entire front, roof, and sides of the car tilted forwards.

Borgward

A new German saloon car was shown at Geneva in March 1949 for the first time. Carl Friedrich Wilhelm Borgward (1880-1963) built the Hansa 1500. This was the first truly new car to be built in Germany since the war. The American style body with the wings incorporated within the general lines resulted from Borgward having studied American publications while being held in a camp for war criminals. The car was a great success. When its production ceased in 1952, more than 22,000 had been sold. The successor was the Hansa 1800 which was also available as a convertible and with a diesel engine.

The Isabella was launched in 1954. This car was built in saloon, coupé, and estate car versions. More than 200,000 of these cars were eventually built.

Carl F.W. Borgward (1890-1963).

The Hansa 1100 was powered by an aluminium water-cooled opposed cylinders motor.

Carl Borgward was the sole owner and shareholder of the company and was quite idiosyncratic. Each of his three makes of Borgward, Lloyd, and Goliath not only had their own dealer networks: each also had its own research and development department. If one make suffered losses, these were made good from the profits elsewhere. It is not really surprising that Borgward's empire failed financially in 1960.

A contributory factor in this failure was Borgward's determination to compete in the same market as Mercedes-Benz, resulting in the development of the Borgward Hansa 2400, launched in 1952, which never shook off its teething problems. Its production was stopped in 1955 after a mere 1,032 had been sold. This was followed by another large Borgward – the 2300 of which 2,500 were sold before the company's bankruptcy.

Borgward did not have unending success with his Goliath cars either. The Goliath was introduced in 1950 with a 700 cc two-stroke engine which was quickly uprated to 900 cc. By the time the car was eventually fitted with an 1,100 cc four-stroke engine, its image had been ruined. Borgward tried to recover by giving the car a new body style and renaming it the Hansa 1100 but it was now too late. A few hundred cars were built from existing parts after the company failed. Borgward had more success with the Lloyd. This midget car was launched in 1950 with a plywood body and twin-cylinder two-stroke engine of 293 cc, producing 10 bhp. The engine grew to 386 cc in 1953 and with it the model name changed from Lloyd 250 to Lloyd 400.

The Lloyd 600 had a steel body and twin-cylinder four-stroke engine of 596 cc. A deluxe version of this car appeared in 1957 under the name Alexander. The final Lloyd

made was the Arabella, which had a four-cylinder "boxer" engine of opposed twin cylinders with a capacity of 897 cc. However, the company collapsed before this car was ready for the market. Much was written at the time about the collapse of the Borgward concern, which cost thousands of workers their job. The bankruptcy might well have been prevented but this would have required a different course of action by the City of Bremen and a less stubborn approach by Carl Borgward.

Borgward cars

COUNTRY OF ORIGIN: Germany

Hansa 1500

MODEL YEAR: 1949-1952

NUMBER MADE: 22,504

SPECIAL REMARKS: The Hansa 1500 was a modern car in both appearance and mechanically. The 1,498 cc four cylinder engine delivered 48 bhp at 4,800 rpm.

The Borgward Hansa 1500 was a great sensation when it was launched in Geneva in 1949. It was the first German car with an American style body.

Hansa 2400

MODEL YEAR: 1952-1955

NUMBER MADE: 1,032

SPECIAL REMARKS: This was the first luxury Borgward with a six-cylinder engine of 2,337 cc and 82 bhp. Electrically-operated windows in the doors were standard; automatic transmission was available as an option.

Hansa Isabella

MODEL YEAR: 1954-1961

NUMBER MADE: 202,862

SPECIAL REMARKS: This was the best of the bunch! The Hansa Isabella was a virtually indestructible car with a two-door monocoque body and enough space for five adults. The

Borgward earned his page in the history books with the Isabella.

This is the Isabella 2+2 coupé which cost in the region of three VW Beetles!

four cylinder engine was 1,493 cc and delivered 60 bhp in standard form or 75 bhp at 5,200 rpm in the TS version.

Hansa 2300

MODEL YEAR: 1959-1961

NUMBER MADE: 2,587

SPECIAL REMARKS: The big Borgward cost Carl Borgward his company. This is such a shame for it was a fine car, complete with pneumatic suspension. The six-cylinder engine produced 100 bhp and had a top speed of 62mph (100 kph).

Goliath 700

MODEL YEAR: 1950-1957

NUMBER MADE: 36,296

SPECIAL REMARKS: The Goliath had a modern body yet was powered by an old-fashioned twin-cylinder two-stroke engine, which was front-mounted. There were also 26 sports cars built with Rometsch bodies.

Goliath/Hansa 1100

MODEL YEAR: 1957-1963

NUMBER MADE
14,908 and 27,751

SPECIAL REMARKS: The 1000 was the final Goliath and it was subsequently renamed Hansa when confidence was lost in the marque. The Hansa version can be recognised by the fins on the rear wings which were then in vogue.

Lloyd 300

MODEL YEAR: 1950-1952

NUMBER MADE: 18,087

SPECIAL REMARKS: The German nickname for this car implied it was held together with sticking plasters. The body was made of three-ply covered with leather and the car was powered by a 293 cc twin-cylinder engine that produced 10 bhp and could reach 47 mph (75 kph).

The Lloyd 300 had a plywood body that was partially covered with leather. Fuel consumption of two-stroke mixture was 50 miles per gallon (six litres per 100 km).

Lloyd 600

MODEL YEAR: 1955-1961

NUMBER MADE: 36,296

It is obvious that the Lloyd is fitted with swing axles when viewed from the rear.

SPECIAL REMARKS: The final Lloyd 600 and Alexander models had a steel body and four-stroke engine. This engine gained an overhead camshaft in 1957, producing 25 instead of 19 bhp.

The dashboard of the Lloyd 600: a speedometer, a couple of switches, and an ashtray!

Once a four-stroke engine was installed in the Lloyd 600, it could reach 63 mph (100 kph).

Lloyd Arabella

MODEL YEAR: 1959-1963

NUMBER MADE: 47,042

SPECIAL REMARKS: The Arabella was one of the causes of Borgward's failure. The car was a constant source of problems and the cost of guarantee work grew out of control. The engine had four cylinders that produced 34 and subsequently 45 bhp at 5,300 rpm.

Bristol

The Bristol aircraft factory was established in 1910. During World War II, the factory produced the famous Bristol Blenheim bombers. Towards the end of the war, the government advised the Bristol board to seek a different line to ensure peace-time employment for their workers.

The chief engineer, Roy Fadden was asked to investigate the potential of the car market and found openings there. The first Bristol could be seen driving on the winding country roads in 1944 but it took until 1947 before a Bristol went into production and was shown at Geneva. It was a four-seater saloon with superb aerodynamic aluminium body and a six-cylinder BMW engine that was made in Britain under licence.

A second model appeared in 1949: the Bristol 401, which was equipped with a body by Touring of Milan. The construction used a patented lightweight system in which the aluminium skin was attached to thin steel tubes. These Bristol cars were sporting thoroughbreds that had speed enough for the circuit but were better suited to long journeys. They were also extremely expensive and small numbers were produced as 2+2 coupés and convertibles. The first four-door family car was not introduced until October 1954 when the 405 was launched at the Paris motor show.

Bristol used the old 1,971 cc BMW engine up to 1958 but with the Bristol 406, they introduced the 2,216 cc six-cylinder engine. The 406 was the final Bristol with a six-cylinder engine. Subsequent models, from the 407 in 1961 onwards, had American Chrysler V-8 engines. The 406 had a 5,130 cc motor that produced 253 bhp, the Bristol 409 was equipped with a 5,211 cc unit, and the 411 had a 6,277 cc V-8 engine. Buyers of the Bristol 412 could choose V-8 motors of 5,898 or 6,556 cc.

Bristol still build superlative sporting cars with classic lines and huge American engines.

The Bristol 403 was built from 1953-1955. This coupé had a top speed of 103 mph.

Bristol cars

Bristol 400

MODEL YEAR: 1947-1950

NUMBER MADE: 700

SPECIAL REMARKS: The Bristol 400 was powered by a BMW engine that was made in Britain under licence. The engine had been used before World War II in the Frazer-Nash. Power output was slightly more than 80 bhp at 4,500 rpm.

Bristols like this 1940 type 400 quickly earned the nickname "Business Express" as fast cars for successful businessmen.

Many Bristols were sold as rolling chassis. This is a 400 with a Pininfarina body.

Bristol 401/402/403

MODEL YEAR: 1949-1953

NUMBER MADE: 650

SPECIAL REMARKS: The bodies of the 401 coupé and 402 convertible (only 20 made)

This 1951 401 was equipped with a body by the Swiss special bodyshop of Beutler of Thun.

were designed by Carrozzeria Touring. A higher-powered version with 107 bhp motor was the 403 of which 281 were made.

Bristol 404/405

MODEL YEAR: 1954-1957

NUMBER MADE: 52

SPECIAL REMARKS: The Bristol 404 had a new-style of body with an unusual position-

The deeply-recessed radiator grill was unusual at the time for the Bristol 404 and 405.

The 405 was the only four-door Bristol. The sales figures prove there was demand for this type of car.

ing (for the time) of the radiator grill. The 405 (265 made) had a longer wheelbase and four doors. Only 43 404 convertibles were built.

Bristol 406

MODEL YEAR: 1958-1961

NUMBER MADE: 174

SPECIAL REMARKS: The 406 was a 404 with a more highly-powered engine. Overdrive and disc brakes were standard equipment.

Bristol 407

MODEL YEAR: 1961-1963

NUMBER MADE: 88

Some of the 88 Bristol 407 model were sold as rolling chassis to various body specialists. This aluminium body is by Zagato of Italy.

SPECIAL REMARKS: The 407 was the first Bristol with a Chrysler V-8 engine. This necessitated adapting the chassis and front suspension but was a considerable improvement.

Bristol 408/409

MODEL YEAR: 1964-1965 and 1966-1967

NUMBER MADE: 83 and 74

SPECIAL REMARKS: The Bristol 408 was a 407 with twin headlights and a new grille. The succeeding 409 had better brakes and an alternator.

Bristol 410

MODEL YEAR: 1967-1969

NUMBER MADE: 79

SPECIAL REMARKS: The 410 was an improved version of the 409. The 5,211 cc V-8 engine produced 254 bhp at 4,400 rpm. The car now had separate braking circuits. The 411 had the same body but with a larger 6,277 cc engine, producing 340 bhp at 5,200 rpm.

Bristol 411

MODEL YEAR: 1969-1976

NUMBER MADE: 287

Although the Bristol 411 was described as a sports coupé, it had room for five persons.

SPECIAL REMARKS: The Bristol 411 was first shown at the London motor show in 1969. The car had a Chrysler V-8 engine that produced 340 bhp at 5,200 rpm, with a top speed of 137 mph (220 kph).

Zagato designed the Bristol 412 and also built the bodies, using aluminium sheet.

Bristol 412

MODEL YEAR: 1975-1982

NUMBER MADE: Unknown

SPECIAL REMARKS: Bristol attempted to reach a new target group with the 412, which had a "Targa" body – a convertible with fixed roll-over bar.

Bugatti

The Paris motor show of 1951 saw the first Bugatti to be shown for a long time. The first post-war cars closely resembled those which had made the marque famous before the war and they were made in the same factory in Mulhouse where all the famous examples of the Bugatti marque had been made.

There was one major difference though: the founder Ettore Bugatti was unable to be present, having died in 1947. The Bugatti 101 was the responsibility of the youngest son, Roland Bugatti and Pierre Marco, who had worked for the company since 1919 and worked his way up to general manager.

The type 101 was a clear successor to the Type 57 with a straight-eight 3.2 litre engine with twin-overhead camshafts. The engine could also be equipped with a Rootes compressor (turbocharger) which raised the output from 160 to 200 bhp. Pre-war Bugattis had been renowned for their sporting successes but had not been able to achieve performance levels such as these. However, this was no longer exceptional in 1951, with a Ferrari engine delivering greater bhp, while a Jaguar XK 120 equalled the performance but at half the price! Technically, the rest of the car was nothing exceptional. For example, the Bugatti still had a fixed front axle, albeit highly polished. Consequently there was no demand for the car and the factory ceased production. In 1955 attempts were made to

Ghia built this two-seater for the American designer Virgil Exner, on the running gear of the Bugatti Type 101.

produce a Grand Prix car but this never got beyond the prototype. The factory closed for good in 1956 and was taken over by Hispano-Suiza. It was the end of the line for one of the great pre-war marques.

Bugatti cars

COUNTRY OF ORIGIN: France

Bugatti Type 101

MODEL YEAR: 1951-1954

NUMBER MADE: 7

Most of the Type 101 Bugattis had Gangloff bodies. This is a convertible by that designer.

SPECIAL REMARKS: The Type 101 was an attempt by Bugatti to rekindle its pre-war successes. The car was too expensive and too dated mechanically to make any impression.

Buick

David Dunbar Buick was a plumber by trade when he developed a means of bonding porcelain to metal. This invention was tremendously important for industries making products for the kitchen and bathroom and Buick could probably have made much more money for his patent than the $100,000 which he received. He used this money to establish Buick Auto Vim and Power Company, from which the Buick Motor Company was formed in 1903.

Buick had little success with his cars and hence he was pleased to sell the company in 1904 to James H. Whiting. The president of the new company was William Crapo Durant who succeeded in making Buick profitable and in establishing the basis of General Motors.

Buick re-emerged in the car market after World War II in 1946 with the final pre-war model, in common with most other manufacturers. The firm had an advantage though since it had launched a new model in 1942 which consequently stood out positively from the competition. Buick sold more than 156,000 of them in 1946 and the demand steadily increased with 404,675 Buicks being sold in 1951.

The 1948 Buick Roadmaster was at the time the most expensive Buick, with a convertible costing $2,837. The eight-cylinder engine was 5,249 cc, producing 145 bhp at 3,600 rpm.

The old straight-eight cylinder engine was replaced in 1953 by a new V-8 engine which was installed in the 1953–54 Buicks. Buick achieved third place in the US car market in 1955 by selling 781,296 cars. When the eight millionth Buick rolled off the line on April 5, 1955, it was also the three-and-a-half millionth post-war Buick!

Buick introduced a compact car in 1961. This Buick Special had a 3.5 litre aluminium V-8 that was also fitted to Oldsmobiles and used to the modern day by Rover. Buick returned to their trusted cast-iron V-6 engine in 1962.

Because the demand for sporting cars increased, resulting in good sales for Chevrolet's Impala and Ford's Thunderbird, Buick answered with the Riviera. This car had a 6.5 litre V-8 engine that was uprated to 7 litres in 1966 to produce 340 bhp (SAE). The Riviera was given a new body in 1971 which people either loved or hated. The car was designed by Donald Lasky and provided seating for five. The car was eye-catching from every angle but most impressive was the rear-end "boat tail". There was a 7,468 cc V-8 engine beneath the "hood" or bonnet delivering 269 bhp to the rear wheels. This was the most expensive Buick in the range that year and the car was only available with Turbo-Hydra-Matic transmission. Buick customers in 1975 could choose from nine different basic models from the small 3.8 litre Skyhawk to the 7.5 litre Riviera. Today's Buick range looks very different. In 1997 the smallest car was the Skylark with a 2,392 cc engine and the Riviera had a 3,791 cc V-6 engine. How times change!

Buick cars

COUNTRY OF ORIGIN: USA

Buick Super (1947)

MODEL YEAR: 1947-1948

NUMBER MADE: 277,134

SPECIAL REMARKS: Because Buick had introduced an entirely new model in 1942, it was

simple for them after the war to pick up the reins. The engine was a straight eight-cylinder overhead valve unit which did only 10 miles per gallon (30 litres per 100 km).

Buick Super (1951)

MODEL YEAR: 1951

NUMBER MADE: 169,226

SPECIAL REMARKS: The almost 170,000 Buick Supers sold in 1951 included 92,886 four-door sedans (or saloons) and a mere 8,116 convertibles. The 4,315 cc straight-eight engine produced 129 bhp at 3,600 rpm.

The motor in the 1947 Buick Super was a 4,067 cc straight eight-cylinder. This engine made almost no noise but was very thirsty.

A 1951 Buick Super. Note how the bonnet (or hood) hinges to either right or left.

Buick Roadmaster Skylark

MODEL YEAR: 1953-1954

NUMBER MADE: Unknown

SPECIAL REMARKS: Back in 1953, the Roadmaster Skylark was the most expensive

The Buick Roadmaster Skylark was the toast of 1953. The design by Harley Earl included wire wheels and a lower roof-line than other convertibles.

Buick could proudly announce in 1962 that heating, external mirror, cigar lighter, and electrically-operated windscreen wipers were standard equipment!

Buick in the range. The Skylark was a special convertible with wire wheels and every imaginable accessory that Buick could offer. The car was only made in 1953 and 1954.

Buick Century

MODEL YEAR: 1957

NUMBER MADE: 65,964

Of the 65,964 Buick Century cars sold in 1957, 10,186 were estate cars. The 6 litre V-8 engine produced 253 bhp at 4,400 rpm.

SPECIAL REMARKS: The Buick Century closely resembled the Buick Special but could be recognised by the four false nacelles at the rear of each front wing. The V-8 engine's capacity was 5,957 cc, producing 253 bhp at 4,400 rpm.

Buick Special Deluxe

MODEL YEAR: 1962

NUMBER MADE: 50,292

There was a choice of 3,247 cc V-6 or 4,923 cc V-8 engine for the 1962 Buick Special. The Deluxe shown was only sold with the V-8 unit.

SPECIAL REMARKS: The Special was Buick's compact car. They sold a total of 110,790 of them in 1962, with just under half being the Deluxe model. The Deluxe model had additional accessories, such as an ashtray for rear passengers and carpet on the floor.

Buick Riviera

MODEL YEAR: 1971-1973

NUMBER MADE: 101,618

SPECIAL REMARKS: This coupé had a wheelbase of 122 in (3,100 mm) and an overall length of 217 in (5,520 mm). Despite weighing more than 4,400 lb (2,000 kg) the car's top speed was 130 mph (210 kph).

The 5-seater Buick Riviera coupé was surely one of the best looking cars to come out of Detroit in 1971.

Striking characteristics of the Riviera were the high rear wings and pointed rear end, dubbed "boat-tail".

Buick GS

MODEL YEAR: 1972

NUMBER MADE: 8,575

SPECIAL REMARKS: GS stood for Grand Sport:

the car was a sporting version of the Skylark that was intended to compete with the "muscular" cars of Buick's competitors.
There were both coupés and convertibles sold as GS 350 and GS 455. The numbers indicated the cylinder capacity in cubic inches.

The Buick GS (this is a 1971 model) was Buick's answer to the "muscular" cars. There was a choice of two V-8 engines: 5,724 cc/193 bhp or 7,468 cc/228 bhp at 4,000 rpm.

Cadillac

Henry Martyn Leland began his adventure with automobiles in 1901 by making engines for Oldsmobile and a year later started to build cars. These created a sensation under the Cadillac name. One of these cars was exhibited at the Motor Show in New York in 1903 and was an immediate success. Orders were taken during the show for 2,000 cars, which was more than the small company could build.

Cadillacs have never been cheap cars. A seven-seater limousine in 1906 cost $5,000: a considerable sum considering the two-seater "Curved Dash" Oldsmobile cost a mere $650. General Motors was formed in 1908 by William Durant, based on Buick and Oldsmobile; Oakland and Cadillac joined in 1909.

Durant needed a prestige car marque for his company and therefore accepted the asking price of $4.5 million. This was the biggest business deal that had ever taken place in Detroit. Cadillac was always one stage ahead of their competitors.

hey built four-cylinder engines in 1905 while others still made do with two cylinders. Cadillac also introduced V-8 engines to the market in 1915 and the factory was the first in 1930 with a V-16 engine. While all other US manufacturers still only made open cars, Cadillac came out in 1910 with a fully enclosed body. The electrical starter motor was invented for General Motors by Charles Kettering and was first installed in 1912 in a Cadillac. The marque was the first, in 1929, with a synchronised mesh gearbox and the short-stroke V-8 with high compression and five main bearings set an example for all modern US automobiles.

Cadillac continues to fill the roll given it by Durant in 1909 as the prestige marque of General Motors to compete with Ford's Lincoln and Chrysler's Imperial. Increasing numbers of heads of state, industrialists, and film stars bought Cadillacs.

In December 1941, the final pre-war Cadillac rolled of the production lines to be replaced two months later by the first M-5 tanks and aero engines for the American military. Cadillac's war ended on 17 October, 1945 when they were able to restart production of private cars. Late in 1949, the millionth car rolled off the lines and by 1956 the factory produced more than 150,000 cars in one year for the first time.

Cadillac fitted all its cars from 1954 onwards with power steering which was much appreciated by women drivers who had found it difficult to park the heavy cars. Air conditioning quickly became nothing extraordinary and cruise control followed in 1959. This was also the year in which under chief designer Harley Earl the tail fins reached their greatest heights.

The Eldorado appeared in 1967 with front-wheel drive and two years later the front wheels were equipped with disc brakes. Cadillac was also well able to compete in the

Chief designer at GM, Steven Earl, liked the tail fins on the P38 Lightning fighter and decided to add them to his cars in 1948.

A 1948 Cadillac dashboard: simple but effective.

Tail fins reached their greatest height in 1959 and began to shrink from 1960.

Cadillac only offered the Series 62 as a convertible in 1946, when 1,342 were sold.

quest for horsepower. The 1970 Eldorado had the biggest engine ever mass produced in Detroit: 8,194 cc giving 406 bhp at 4,400 rpm!

The top speed was in the region of 125 mph (200 kph) with fuel consumption of 12 miles to the gallon (1 litre to 4 km). Safety became a major consideration and from 1972 all cars were fitted with safety belts (although they had been installed by Saab ten years earlier).

The first air bags followed in 1974. A major newcomer to Cadillac was the Seville which was the size of a European car, measuring 204 in (5,180 mm) from bumper to bumper compared with 205 in (5,220 mm) for the Jaguar XJ6 and 195 in (4,950 mm) of the Mercedes 450 SEL. The engine size was not much reduced though at 5,737 cc. Nor was this a cheaper car, costing in the United States fifty per cent more than a Cadillac de Ville.

SPECIAL REMARKS: The body of the "62" was identical to the Oldsmobiles and Buicks of that year. The V-8 engine's capacity was 5,675 cc, producing 156 bhp at 3,400 rpm.

Cadillac Series 62 (1948)

MODEL YEAR: 1948

NUMBER MADE: 34,213

SPECIAL REMARKS: Cadillac was the first of the GM marques to introduce a new body in 1948. Little was changed with the engine but this was less essential.

Cadillac Eldorado (1953)

MODEL YEAR: 1953

NUMBER MADE: 8,367

SPECIAL REMARKS: The Hydra-Matic automatic transmission was standard equipment on this car, together with leather interior trim and chromium-plated wire wheels.

The 1953 Eldorado still had modest tail fins. Its 5,424 cc V-8 produced 212 bhp.

Cadillac cars

COUNTRY OF ORIGIN: USA

Cadillac Series 62 (1946)

MODEL YEAR: 1946

NUMBER MADE: 18,566

By 1957 the tail fins had assumed large proportions. This is a Coupe de Ville.

Cadillac Coupe de Ville (1953)

MODEL YEAR: 1953

NUMBER MADE: 14,550

SPECIAL REMARKS: Coupe de Ville was the fancy name given to Cadillac's two-door coupé. With more people choosing air conditioning they also switched from convertible to coupé.

Cadillac Coupe de Ville (1957)

MODEL YEAR: 1957

NUMBER MADE: 23,813

SPECIAL REMARKS: The Cadillac range received a new, lower chassis in 1957.

Driver's view of a 1957 Coupe de Ville. Here too there was masses of chrome.

The Eldorado Brougham was built by hand and available in a choice of 15 colours and at least 44 interior trims.

Cadillac Eldorado Brougham

MODEL YEAR: 1958

NUMBER MADE: 304

SPECIAL REMARKS: The final Eldorado Broughams were built in Detroit in 1958. Henceforth, Cadillac's special cars were built by Pininfarina in Italy.

Cadillac Series 62 Convertible

MODEL YEAR: 1959

NUMBER MADE: 11,130

The side windows of the 1959 convertible were also electrically-operated.

SPECIAL REMARKS: There were completely new bodies in 1959 and the V-8 engine now has 6,384 cc capacity, producing 330 bhp at 4,800 rpm.

The 1969 Eldorado was launched on 26 September 1968. There was a selection of 21 colours and at least 205 interior trim choices.

The 1969 Eldorado was 221 in (5,610 mm) long and weighed 4,719 lb (2,145 kg).

Cadillac Eldorado (1969)

MODEL YEAR: 1969

NUMBER MADE: 23,333

SPECIAL REMARKS: The 1969 Eldorado had a short chassis and had front-wheel drive. There was room for six persons in this car that was only sold as a two-door coupé.

Cadillac Seville

MODEL YEAR: 1975

NUMBER MADE: 16,355

SPECIAL REMARKS: The Seville was Cadillac's attempt to compete with the expensive imported cars. It was only partially successful because at $12,479, the car was extremely expensive.

The 1975 Seville was intended to take on Jaguar and Mercedes. Its was a similar size but much more expensive.

Checker

Anyone who visited New York in the sixties or seventies must undoubtedly know Checker from the famous yellow taxis. These were indestructible cars which were commonly driven more than 600,000 miles or 1,000,000 km. The first taxi was made by the Checker Cab Manufacturing Company in 1923. They have never been wholly up-to-date but certainly very tough. Up to 1960 they had six-cylinder side-valve engines made by Continental who then produced slightly more modern overhead valve engines. Checkers were first sold as private cars in 1959 but

The yellow Checker taxi was a regular sight on the streets of New York. This is a 1971 example.

This Marathon estate car cost $3,200 in 1965 when Checker built 6,136 cars of which 5,206 were supplied as taxis.

The unusual Checker minibus had six or eight doors. The vehicle was only sold to American hotels which used the limousine to collect guests from airports. It was a major attraction in Europe.

Checker Marathon

MODEL YEAR: 1961-1982

NUMBER MADE: Unknown

SPECIAL REMARKS: The Marathon was the deluxe version of the Superba. Only cars for the private market were sold under this name.

Chevrolet

were never very successful. The Continental engine was replaced in 1964 by a Chrysler engine: at first the customary six-cylinder but from 1971 the cars were also available with a V-8 engine.

Checker cars

COUNTRY OF ORIGIN: USA

Checker Superba

MODEL YEAR: 1960-1964

NUMBER MADE: Unknown

SPECIAL REMARKS: The Superba was the first Checker available to the general public. Its 3.7 litre six-cylinder overhead valve Continental engine delivered 124 bhp.

There are varying stories behind the foundation of each automobile marque. Sometimes it is one of constant success but there are stories with sad endings. One such is that of Louis Chevrolet who was born on Christmas Day 1878 at La Chaux de Fonds in Switzerland. When he was twenty-one, Louis left home for France where he became a cycle maker. By way of Paris and Canada, Chevrolet found his way to New York where he was employed as a mechanic by Fiat.

Chevrolet's boss made a racing car available to him and he quickly made a name for himself as a racing driver. The founder of General Motors, William C. Durant offered him a place in his Buick racing team and Louis' brother Arthur, who had also come to America, was employed by Durant as his personal chauffeur.

Louis Chevrolet (1878-1941).

With Durant's help, the Chevrolet brothers started their own car factory in a building left empty by Buick. Their first prototype left the factory on 3 November 1911. By the end of 1912 they had sold 2,999 Chevrolets. As a result of a row with Durant, Chevrolet sold his shares in the company for a mere trifle and then started to build racing cars under the Frontenac name. The cars appear to have been very successful but Chevrolet underestimated his former employer. Once the Frontenac name became famous in the United States, Durant built sedan cars under the name in Canada, where Chevrolet had failed to register the marque.

Louis Chevrolet died on 6 June 1941 as a poor and forgotten man.

The first post-war Chevrolets exited the factory on 3 October 1945. They looked identical to the 1941 models but had been given new names. The 1941 Master range and Deluxe became the Stylemaster and Fleetmaster.

These cars still had six-cylinder overhead valve engines of 3.5 litres and power of 91 bhp at 3,300 rpm. Because these cars were heavy four-door cars weighing 3,238 lb (1,472 kg), fuel consumption was of the order of 18 miles per gallon (1 litre per 6 km).

The cars were not changed in 1947 or 1948 because they sold like hot cakes. It was not until January 1949 that Chevrolet introduced a new model to the press at the Waldorf Astoria in New York. The car was the same length as its predecessor but had a12 in (300 mm) shorter wheelbase. The bonnet or hood had also been shortened but the boot or trunk was now deeper. The wings had become an integral part of the body. This car too was given a new names: the Stylemaster became the Special Series and the Fleetmaster was named Deluxe. The cars were a great success and for the first time since 1927, Chevrolet made over 100,000 cars in a year.

The innovation of 1950 was the Powerglide automatic transmission with two gear ratios. The automatic gearbox was very successful and of the 827,317 Chevrolets in 1952 that left the factory, 289,733 had the automatic box. Its was about this time that Detroit began the "chrome war". The more chromium plate the merrier so that small decorative trims became huge glimmering swathes of bodywork. Enormous quantities of chromium-plated parts were incorporated on every car. There was no stopping Harley Earl, General Motor's chief designer. It was soon being said: "Chrome is God and Harley Earl its prophet." Chromium plate remained in vogue until Pontiac brought out their Grand Prix in the sixties, expressly without any chrome. This car was a best seller. There were celebrations at General Motors on 23 November 1953 when the 50 millionth General Motors car rolled off the production line. Its was a 1954 model Chevrolet BelAir, painted pink.

Chevrolets had a new body every two or three years or at the very least a revamp every year with a different grill. The panorama windscreens came and went again when sufficient people had bashed their knees as a result. The cars also bore tail fins but these were more restrained than with other makes and perhaps more attractive as a result. With or without fins, 1958 was an excellent year for Chevrolet. They sold 1,255,935 cars which was 250,000 more than Ford and 29.5 per of the total US market.

In 1959 there were 600,000 smaller cars imported into the USA, which used less gasoline and were easier to find parking spaces for. Detroit decided it too must build them, and called them compacts. Ford had its Falcon, Chrysler the Valiant, and Chevrolet the Corvair.

These cars spelled disaster though for the American auto industry. The Corvair was

technically quite interesting with its air-cooled aluminium boxer engine mounted in the rear. The fact that the engine was in the back was the car's undoing. The centre of gravity was far too near the rear of the car and this caused oversteer and many accidents.

After the consumer activist Ralph Nader published his book *Unsafe at any speed* in which he focused attention on the Corvair, Chevrolet were confronted with hundreds of legal actions by dissatisfied Corvair owners who had crashed their car. Chevrolet won all the actions but the bad publicity had ruined any chance of success for the car and production stopped in 1969. It was not until the summer of 1972 that the National Highway Safety Administration was able to prove that the accidents had nothing to do with the Corvair and that the car was as safe as any other. Unfortunately this news came too late.

The demand for compacts reduced in 1961 so that Chevrolet introduced an in-between model, the Chevy II. This car was available with a four or six-cylinder engine and from 1964 a V-8 was also possible. The car was successful and in its first year sold 386,507, with 59,900 of them being estates. The Chevy II was nothing out of the ordinary but although less striking than the Ford Falcon, it cost less than $2,000 making it cheaper than the Corvair.
The Chevy II became less popular from 1964 on (it became known as the Nova from 1969) because of the introduction of the Chevelle which filled the gap between the Chevy II and the big Chevrolet.
The car was slightly larger and more spacious than the Chevy II/Nova and had a choice of four engines. Customers could choose from two six-cylinder and two V-8 engine motors. Another excellent year for Chevrolet was

1965 when they again sold over 2,000,000 cars of the following types:

Corvair	235,528
Chevy II	122,080
Chevelle	344,100
Biscayne	145,300
BelAir	271,400
Impala	1,046,500
Corvette	23,600
	2,188,508

Chevrolet attempted to take a share of the market created by the Ford Mustang with the Camaro. It was a sporty car that was suitable for the family driver who could no longer drive a Corvette. The Camaro has a mono-coque body plus a wide choice of engines. There were two six cylinder motors of 3,768 and 4,094 cc and no fewer than six V-8 units ranging from 5,354-6,489 cc.

The Ford Thunderbird also caused a response from GM: the result was the Monte Carlo which was launched in 1970. It was based on the running gear of the 1969 Pontiac Grand Prix and was 9 in (230 mm) longer than the Chevelle. Here too there were three V-8 engines to choose from: 5,733, 6,570, and 7,443 cc in five power ratings from 235-365 bhp.

Chevrolet was always busy with its small car project, resulting in the Vega compact in 1971. This car had a four-cylinder aluminium engine with overhead camshaft of 2,287 cc, producing 81 bhp at 4,400 rpm. The Vega was a small car of 169 in (4310 mm), weighing just 2,211 lb (1,005 kg) but had a top speed of 94 mph (150 kph). The Vega filled the gap in the market once more.

The horizontal fins of the 1958 Chevrolet BelAir Impala were very striking.

Chevrolet was number one in Detroit again in 1975. They sold 1,707,528 of their Vega, Nova, Camaro, Chevelle, Monte Carlo, BelAir, Impala, Caprice, and Corvette models.

Chevrolet cars

COUNTRY OF ORIGIN: USA

Chevrolet Stylemaster

MODEL YEAR: 1948

NUMBER MADE: 171,593

Of the 171,000 Stylemasters which left the factory in 1948, 48,456 were four-door sedans. The rest were two-door coupés and sedans.

SPECIAL REMARKS: The Stylemaster was the cheapest Chevrolet in 1948. Under the bonnet was a 3,547 cc overhead valve engine which produced 91 bhp at 3,300 rpm.

Chevrolet Special Series

MODEL YEAR: 1950

NUMBER MADE: 261,812

SPECIAL REMARKS: Of the 260,000 cars, 66,959 were Fleetline models which had a streamlined rear end which became known as "fastback".

There were 43,682 Fleetlines with a two-door body sold in 1950. The engine was a 3.5 litre six-cylinder which produced 94 bhp.

Chevrolet BelAir

MODEL YEAR: 1955

NUMBER MADE: 770,955

This 1955 model BelAir came off the production line at Flint, Michigan on 23 November 1954 to be the 50 millionth Chevrolet since 1911.

SPECIAL REMARKS: The 1955 BelAir had a 4,342 cc V-8 engine that in US market models produced 164 bhp (SAE) at 4,400 rpm. Export models only produced 152 bhp at 4,400 rpm.

Chevrolet Impala

MODEL YEAR: 1958

NUMBER MADE: Unknown

SPECIAL REMARKS: The Impala was the more expensive version of the BelAir, which was already one of the most expensive cars. The Impala was only available as a coupé or convertible, the latter of which cost $2,841.

Chevrolet sold 254,571 Corvairs in 1963. Of these, only 7,472 Monza Spider Convertibles were sold.

Corvair Monza Spider

MODEL YEAR: 1963

NUMBER MADE: 19,099

SPECIAL REMARKS: The Corvair was an interesting car that technically-speaking towered above the Ford Falcon or Plymouth Valiant. Its aluminium boxer engine of 2,287 cc pro-

The interior of a Monza Spider.

With a turbo operated by the exhaust gases, the Corvair engine produced 152 bhp (SAE) to give a top speed of 100 mph (160 kph).

The 1962 Chevy II was available as a two-door or four-door, convertible (with six-cylinder engine) and also as an estate.

duced 81 bhp at 4,400 rpm. With turbo this increased to 150 bhp (SAE) at 4,600 rpm.

Chevy II

MODEL YEAR: 1962

NUMBER MADE: 386,507

SPECIAL REMARKS: The main attraction of the Chevy II was that it was cheap. This was the principal reason why it sold so well. In its first year of 1962 it was offered with a 2,519 cc four-cylinder or 3,186 cc six-cylinder engine.

Chevelle

MODEL YEAR: 1964

NUMBER MADE: 338,286

SPECIAL REMARKS: Of this total units, 142,034 had 3,185 cc six-cylinder engines and the rest were produced with 4,637 cc V-8 motors. The Chevelle's engines also grew larger and larger so that by 1970 it could be ordered with a 7,443 cc V-8.

Chevrolet Camaro

MODEL YEAR: 1969

NUMBER MADE: 230,799

SPECIAL REMARKS: Chevrolet introduced the Camaro in 1967 as a competitor to the Ford Mustang. Although successful, it could not beat the Mustang which sold 472,121 units in 1967.

Only 16,519 Camaro convertibles were sold in 1969, and of these only a few were equipped with the "SS package" and a 350 cubic inch V-8 engine.

With its 97 in (2470 mm) wheelbase and 175 in (4460 mm) overall length, the 1971 Vega 2300 was similar in size to European cars.

The 1974 Monte Carlo had a top speed of 112-131 mph (180-210 kph) depending on the engine fitted.

Chevrolet Monza 2+2

MODEL YEAR: 1975

NUMBER MADE: 66,615

SPECIAL REMARKS: Chevrolet rolled out the famous Monza name in the autumn of 1974 for a sporting 2+2 on the Vega chassis with a four-cylinder 2.3 litre engine or six-cylinder 4.3 litre V-8 unit.

Chevrolet Nova

MODEL YEAR: 1975

NUMBER MADE: 272,982

SPECIAL REMARKS: Half of the 1975 Nova cars sold had six-cylinder engines. Police forces preferred the V-8, especially the 5.7

The lightweight Monza (2,761 lb/1,255 kg) had a top speed of 112 mph (180 kph) with its 4,301 cc V-8 that produced 112 bhp at 3,600 rpm.

Chevrolet Monte Carlo

MODEL YEAR: 1974

NUMBER MADE: 312,217

SPECIAL REMARKS: Every Monte Carlo had a V-8 engine: customers could choose in 1974 from five engines from 5.7-7.4 litres. These were all two-door coupés on the Chevelle chassis.

Chevrolet Vega

MODEL YEAR: 1971

NUMBER MADE: 269,900

SPECIAL REMARKS: In 1971, Chevrolet introduced the new Vega sub compact. It had an aluminium four-cylinder engine of 2.3 litres that produced 90 bhp at 4.600 rpm.

litre unit. When fitted with the quadruple Rochester carburettor, this motor produced 157 bhp at 3,800 rpm.

Chrysler

CHRYSLER

The life of Walter Percy Chrysler was full of variety. He was born on a Kansas farm in Ellis but farming held no interest for him so he joined the Union Pacific Railroad. He cleaned locomotives, became a mechanic, and subsequently a director of American Locomotive. Chrysler bought his first car in 1905. It was a Locomobile. Then in 1912 he went to work at General Motors where he worked his way up to become president and overall head of Buick. Chrysler departed General Motors in 1916 following an argument about the ailing Willys-Overland. He sorted out that company's problems for a salary of $1 million per annum and when that company was fit to continue on its own he did the same for Maxwell until establishing his own company in 1924.

Chrysler delivered their final pre-war car in February 1942 and then turned its lines over to making tanks and army trucks. The company built 25,000 tanks, 60,000 40 mm cannons, 18,413 B-29 bomber engines, and 29,000 ship engines.

Towards the end of 1945 thoughts could return to buildings cars but the cars were identical, except for a new grille, to those of 1942. The "Town & Country" range that was introduced in 1946 were noteworthy for incorporating wood trim on coupés and convertibles. Wood trim itself was nothing new for Chrysler or the other makers but before the war it had been restricted to estate cars (known as station wagons in the US). The cars remained unaltered until the summer holiday of 1948. Chrysler had six basic models on offer: Windsor, Royal, Saratoga, New Yorker, Crown Imperial, and Town & Country. Little was changed in the engine department either. The six-cylinder motor was still 4,106 cc producing 116 bhp at 3,600 rpm and the straight-eight 5,300 cc engine produced 135 bhp at 3,400 rpm. In contrast the chassis was entirely new with a 4 in (100 mm) longer wheelbase. The wheelbase of the six-cylinder engined cars were 125 in (3,180 mm) for the Royal and 135 in (3,430 mm) for the Windsor. The eight-cylinder cars were 131 in (3,340 mm) for the New Yorker and 145 in (3,690 mm) between the wheel centres. A Town & Country-style station wagon was added to the Royal range in 1949, offering enough room for nine persons.

Chrysler sold 167,316 cars in 1950, a total they had not reached since 1928. The following year Chrysler introduced its 5,426 "Firepower" V-8 engine with a capacity of 5,426 cc. This engine, with hemispherical ignition

Walter Percy Chrysler (1875-1940).

The Crown Imperial had space for eight persons: three at the front, three behind, and two fold-down seats between the front and back seats.

A 1946 Town & Country convertible. The "Woody" could also be ordered as a fixed-head coupé after 23 May 1950.

chambers in the cylinder head, was to spark off the "horsepower war" that broke out between the Detroit marques.

The models had their bodies changed and the engines enlarged every couple of years. A highlight of 1955 was the Chrysler 300, esigned by Virgil Exner. It was based on the Windsor Deluxe chassis with a V-8 engine that had a compression ratio of 8.5:1 with twin quadruple jet carburettors, and power of 304 bhp resulting in a top speed of 125 mph (200 kph). This made the Chrysler 300 the fastest US production car and subsequently it became a racing car after achieving 145 mph (232 kph) while attempting to break a record.

A small V-8, known as the "Spitfire", replaced the six-cylinder Chrysler engine in 1955. A 4,925 cc version was installed in the Windsor that produced 191 bhp. The output of the "small" engine was increased to 289 bhp by increasing the bore to 5,801 cc in 1957.

The fortunes of the US automobile industry were like a yo-yo in the fifties with a good year often being succeeded by a bad one. For example, 1957 was an excellent year but 1958 was extremely poor as the following figures illustrate.

	1957	*1958*
Chevrolet	1,522,536	1,255,935
Ford	1,522,408	1,038,560
Chrysler	118,733	49,513
Imperial*	37,946	13,673

* Imperial, Dodge, Plymouth, and De Soto became separate marques from Chrysler in 1955.

This was Chrysler's worse year since 1938 and marked the company's first post-war loss.

From 1952, all Chryslers had the same 125 in (3,200 mm wheelbase) but in 1958 the customer was given a choice of two sizes: 122 in (3,100 mm) for Windsors and 125 in (3,200 mm) for other models except the Imperial which had a 129 in (3,280 mm) wheelbase and was 225 in (5,730 mm) long overall. Once again the engines had been uprated with the "small" Windsor yielding 294 bhp, the Saratoga 314, the New Yorker and Imperial more than 350, and the 300 D even 390 bhp. If customers wanted more power from the 300 D, it was also available as an optional extra with fuel injection.

The lowest priced Chrysler in 1962 was the Newport which had a 5,907 cc V-8 that produced 269 bhp. This model was available in four sedan versions plus two estate variants. The demand for low-priced cars is borne out by the sales figures:

Newport 4-door sedan	34,370
Four-door coupé	7,789
Two-door coupé	9,405
Two-door convertible	2,135

The Saratoga and Windsor were no longer made which reduced the range to four basic

models: the Newport, the 300 (which replaced the Windsor), the New Yorker, and the 300 H. In addition, there was also the Imperial range.

The 300 K returned in 1964, after a one year's absence. The engines once more had increased their power. The "Short Ram" V-8 was 6,769 cc with twin quadruple chamber Carter carburettors and power of 395 bhp which made a top speed of 137 mph (220 kph) possible.

Chrysler broke through the 200,000 car barrier in 1965 for the first time with 224,061 units. The company had overtaken Cadillac and was now the tenth most important manufacturer. The cars were given new bodies with an investment by Chrysler of $300 million. The cars were longer and far more attractive than their predecessors. Because of the success of 1965, the bodies remained unchanged in 1966 for the simple reason that Chrysler was able to sell all that it could make. The Chrysler 300 gained a few more bits of chrome bright-work but that was the sum of it. This car was available with a choice of V-8 engines: 6,286 cc for 330 bhp at 4,800 rpm or 7,206 cc for 370 bhp at 4,600 rpm.

Sales dived once more in 1970 but the entire automobile industry suffered the same fate. Chrysler made "only" 158,614 cars but Imperial suffered far worse, making a mere 10,111 cars. In 1971, the new Newport Royal range was introduced. This was then Chrysler's cheapest car. The few hundred dollars savings against the previous Newport range cars was achieved by using a smaller 5,897 cc engine instead of the 6,555 cc V-8 and by lowering the standard of interior trim.

When the Arab oil producers turned off the supply of oil in 1974, Chrysler suffered badly. Although its cars were all completely new models that year they sold only fifty per cent of the previous year's volume. Things got even worse in 1975 and the future looked very bleak with bankruptcy in sight until Lee Iacocca took over running Chrysler and got rid of the losses in much the same manner Walter Chrysler had done with Willys Overland 75 years earlier.

Chrysler cars

COUNTRY OF ORIGIN: USA

Chrysler Crown Imperial

MODEL YEAR: 1946

NUMBER MADE: Unknown

SPECIAL REMARKS: The number of cars built in 1946 is unknown but cannot have been many since only 750 were sold up to 1948. These cars were equipped with 5,229 cc straight-eight cylinder engines on a long chassis with a 145 in (3,700 mm) wheelbase.

Chrysler New Yorker

MODEL YEAR: 1946

NUMBER MADE: Unknown

SPECIAL REMARKS: The New Yorker had the same straight-eight engine as the Imperial. The 137 bhp at 3,400 were sufficient for a top speed of 94 mph (150 kph).

The 1975 New Yorker was only available as a Brougham. The car was 227 in (5,770 mm) long and did not fit most garages.

The 1955 Windsor was available as a 2-door or 4-door sedan and also as convertible or Town & Country estate.

Chrysler Windsor

MODEL YEAR: 1955

NUMBER MADE: 98,874

SPECIAL REMARKS: The Windsor was the cheapest Chrysler. In 1955, the car as only available with the new V-8 engine, with the six-cylinder no longer being made.

Chrysler Imperial (1956)

MODEL YEAR: 1956

NUMBER MADE: 10,458

The high rear wings were a feature of the 1956 Imperial. Its V-8 was powerful enough to reach 109 mph (175 kph).

SPECIAL REMARKS: The 1956 Imperial could be ordered in three body types: four-door sedan, two-door coupé, and four-door coupé. Their 5,801 cc V-8 engines produced 284 bhp at 4,600 rpm.

Chrysler Newport

Half of all Chryslers sold in 1962 were four-door Newports.

MODEL YEAR: 1962

NUMBER MADE: 83,120

SPECIAL REMARKS: Of this total, the majority (54,813) were sold with four-door bodies, making it the best selling Chrysler. In USA the car cost $2,964.

Chrysler 300 (1964)

MODEL YEAR: 1964

NUMBER MADE: 26,887

SPECIAL REMARKS: The 300 range resembled the 300 Letter range which was known as 300-K in 1964. These cars had a 365 instead of 395 bhp engine and cost about ten per cent less.

Chrysler 300 (1966)

MODEL YEAR: 1966

NUMBER MADE: 49,598

SPECIAL REMARKS: The 1966 300 had clearly been given a facelift. There was a new grille

Chrysler made 2,026 convertibles of the 1964 300 range. These cost $4,320.

In common with all the cars of the 300 range, this two-door coupé had two bucket seats at the front. In the rear was a bench seat for three.

Only 577 were built of this 1967 Imperial convertible. The 7,206 cc V-8 produced 355 bhp at 4,400 rpm, giving a top speed in the region of 125 mph (200 kph).

and extra chrome between the wings and doors. At 222 in (5,640 mm) long, these cars were Chrysler's longest.

Imperial

MODEL YEAR: 1967

NUMBER MADE: 2,770

SPECIAL REMARKS: The Chrysler 300 was a long car but the Imperial was even longer. In 1967 it unitary body was 227 in (5,710 mm) with a wheelbase of 127 in (3,230 mm).

Chrysler Newport Royal

MODEL YEAR: 1971

NUMBER MADE: 33,350

Although the 1971 Newport Royal was a new model, it appeared the following year with a virtually new body (1972 model illustrated). The Newport Royal had disappeared by 1973, when the cheapest Chrysler model was a plain Newport.

SPECIAL REMARKS: This model was launched in 1971 and production ceased in 1973. The car was $100 cheaper than the standard Newport with the savings being due to a "smaller" 5,897 cc V-8 engine specially developed for this car.

Citroën

The grandfather of the founder of Citroën was born Roelof Limoenman in the Netherlands but changed his name from "lemon man" in Dutch to Citroen, which is French for "lemon".

When his son Levis Bernard Citroen established himself in Paris, he added the emphasis above the "e" to ensure a French pronunciation of the name. Levis had five children, with the second named André Gustav. This son began to build cars in 1919 and became extremely rich. So rich indeed that although he gave money away with great largesse and also gambled, it hardly dented his fortune. The fortunes changed though when he developed his Traction Avant. This car was the source of much trouble in 1934 and led to Citroën becoming bankrupt and dying penniless on 5 July 1935, abandoned by his former "friends". Unfortunately André Gustav was unable to live to see his Traction Avant become one of the most acclaimed cars of its age. It continued in production until 1957!

Citroën produced their first post-war car in June 1945. This was a Traction Avant, which was largely made of parts which had survived the war. The post-war car is distinguished from the pre-war version by the nacelles in the bonnet which replaced the air inlet flaps. The car was available in three versions: the Légère (or "Light") Large, and 15 Six models. The first two had 1,911 cc four-cylinder engines, producing 56 bhp at 3,600, while the Six had a 2,867 cc six-cylinder overhead valve engine, producing 77 bhp at 3,800 rpm. Production ran in fits and starts that first year because of shortages of materials. At the end of the financial year, 1,525 cars had been built. In common with the pre-war Traction Avants, which first left the factory in 1934, the post-war cars were continuously improved. The power was slightly increased and in 1952 the body was given a facelift with a new boot added. Prior to this, the spare wheel was screwed on to the outside of the boot. The Familiale, which had existed before the war, re-appeared in 1953 with a 3,270 mm (129 in) wheelbase compared with the 2,910 mm (114 in) of the Légère and 3,090 mm (121 in) of the 15 Six. This car had room for eight persons, three of which had folding seats between the fixed front and back seats.

Citroën introduced another innovation in April 1954, with their hydro-pneumatic suspension dampers on the rear wheels of the 15 Six. The final 3,079 units of this cars were equipped with the new system, acting as a test bed for the sensational Citroën DS which replaced the Traction Avant.

The final Traction Avant rolled off the line at the Quai de Javel on 18 July 1954, 23 years, 4 months, and 15 days after production started. Of the 759,111 Traction Avants made, 700,961 were built in France, 31,750 at the Belgian factory at Forest, and 26,400 were made at Slough, England.

A strange looking prototype was first seen in Citroën's Paris factory in 1938. It was the subsequently famous (or infamous) Deux Chevaux or 2CV, with four doors, and room for four persons and their luggage. The car was equipped with a 375 cc twin-cylinder engine which drove the front wheels. The war and other reasons delayed the cars launch for ten years until October 1948 at the Paris motor show. Ugly as the car was, it was a tremendous success and people had to wait two years to buy one. When launched, the car had the same 375 cc capacity as the prototype which produced a modest 9 bhp at 3,500 rpm. There were plenty of French who were quite happy with the top speed of 40 mph (65 kph).

By 1952, Citroën was building enough Deux-Chevaux to export some of them. In Holland, where they first appeared outside France, they were quickly dubbed the "Ugly Duckling". The size of the engine was regularly enlarged: in 1954 to 421 cc for 12.5 bhp and in 1961 Citroën's engineers managed to coax 14 bhp from the same engine capacity. The speedometer was awkwardly placed beneath one corner of the windscreen because it also operated the windscreen wipers! The speedometer was moved to above the steering column in 1962 and wipers with electric motors were installed. More importantly, a fuel gauge was added for the first time. Until then the 2CV driver had to use a dipstick to check the fuel in the tank but this entailed having to wave the dipstick in the air to allow the petrol on the dipstick to evaporate!

An extremely unusual version of the Deux-Chevaux was the 2CV Sahara, which had two engines! One drove the front wheels and the rear engine powered the back wheels. The driver could choose to drive with one or two engines. The Deux-Chevaux had its twentieth birthday in 1968, during which time more than 2,500,000 had been sold. In 1968, the 2CV had yet another facelift and the 425 cc engine produced 16.4 bhp which permitted a top speed of almost 60 mph (100 kph) at which speed it did 60 miles to the gallon (1 litre per 20 km). The biggest changes came in 1970 when two different models were offered: the 2CV4 with a 431 cc engine and a top speed of 59 mph (100 kph) and the 2CV6 with a 597 cc engine that delivered 28 bhp and a top speed of 69 mph (110 kph). It was decided in 1990 that the 2CV must die. It was not possible to build the car to conform to the environmental demands of various countries and the car was considered far too noisy. A total of 3,868,631 were built. The final 2CV rolled of the production line at Malgualde in Portugal in July 1990.

The Citroën Ami 6 was launched at the Paris motor show in 1961. It was a larger version of the 2CV but not much better looking than the original. The four-door car was powered by an air-cooled opposed twin-cylinder engine of 602 cc that produced 22 bhp initially but finally in 1969 yielded 32 bhp. The successor was the Ami 8 which had the same 32 bhp boxer engine but a new body.

The Citroën Dyane was launched in August 1967 to fill the gap between the 2CV and the

At the end of 1962 the Traction Avant had an enlarged boot-lid which doubled the luggage space.

Ami 6. This car had the air-cooled 425 cc twin-cylinder engine of the 2CV that produced 18.5 bhp at 4,750 rpm. This was increased in 1975 to 32 bhp at 5,750 rpm.

Let us return though from the "toys" to the "real" cars. Citroën had enough experience of their hydro-pneumatic suspension system by 1955 to incorporate it in their newest car. The Citroën DS was launched at the Paris motor show in October 1955 with much razzmatazz and it was the star of the show. The DS was a worthy successor to the Traction Avant.

The DS19 was every bit as fascinating in both mechanical terms and appearance as the Traction Avant had been in 1934.

Under the bonnet, there was not just an engine, but an entire hydraulic installation. This not only operated the suspension but also assisted the steering and brakes, operated the automatic transmission, and changed the gears. The car was powered by the 1,911 cc four-cylinder engine from the Légère, which delivered 62 bhp. There were disc brakes on the front wheels. In the autumn of 1965, the Citroën ID appeared, which was a simpler version of the DS. The left foot was needed once again for the clutch and there was no power assistance for the steering.

After Citroën took over the Italian firm of Maserati the Citroën SM or Citroën Maserati deluxe sporting coupé was created, combining the technical strengths of both companies. Maserati produced the 2,675 cc V-6 engine with four overhead camshafts that developed 170 bhp, while the suspension, steering, and disc brakes were of Citroën origin.

The Citroën GS was a smaller version of the DS. It was launched in 1970, equipped with the same unique suspension. This car had disc brakes all round and an air-cooled boxer engine of 1,015, 1,129, 1,222, or 1,299 cc. The GS was produced up to 1980 in a number of different variants.

It was not easy for Citroën to follow the great successes of the Traction Avant, 2CV, DS, and GS. Whether their designers have done so is a question of personal taste. The CX appeared in 1974, looking rather like a larger GS. The engine was now transverse mounted under the bonnet and was available with turbo and also with a diesel. The engine capacity grew from 1,885 to 2,500 cc with power increasing from 102-170 bhp.

Citroën cars

COUNTRY OF ORIGIN: France

Citroën 11CV

MODEL YEAR: 1934-1957

NUMBER MADE: 759,111

The windscreen wipers of the 11CV moved to the bottom of the windscreen in June 1952. This is an 11 Normale. The 1,911 cc engine produced 56 bhp at 3,800 rpm.

SPECIAL REMARKS: The post-war 11CV was virtually identical to the pre-war car. The 1,911 cc four-cylinder engine produced 56 bhp initially and from 1953 59 bhp at 4,000 rpm.

Citroën 15 Six

MODEL YEAR: 1938-1955

NUMBER MADE: 47,670

SPECIAL REMARKS: This was a superb car. The big 2,867 cc motor ran almost silently, producing 77 bhp for a top speed of 84 mph (135 kph).

Citroën 2CV

MODEL YEAR: 1949-1990

NUMBER MADE: 3,868,631

SPECIAL REMARKS: The first 2CVs were truly primitive cars. Gradually they acquired a bit more finesse and more powerful engines. But the early Deux-Chevaux were much prized and are now collector's cars.

The first Deux-Chevaux were certainly no racing cars. The 375 cc engine delivered a meagre 9 bhp at 3,500 rpm which struggled to reach a top speed of 40 mph (65 kph).

Even the emergence of the Dyane 6 in 1967 could not push the 2CV from the showrooms. The newcomer managed to sell almost 1,500,000.

Citroën Ami 6

MODEL YEAR: 1961-1969

NUMBER MADE: 1,039,384

SPECIAL REMARKS: The Ami 6 was based on the running gear of the 2CV but had a different body. The inward slanting rear window was an unusual feature.

Citroën Ami 8

MODEL YEAR: 1969-1979

NUMBER MADE: 755,955

SPECIAL REMARKS: The difference between the Ami 6 and 8 was the body which in the 8 had a more conventional rear window. The Ami 8 also had a more powerful 32 bhp boxer engine. The small car of 3,980 mm (156 in) was spacious for its size.

The Ami 6 was intended for those who did not like to drive such an ugly car as the 2CV. The rear window was like that of the Ford Anglia.

Citroën Dyane

MODEL YEAR: 1967-1984

NUMBER MADE: 1,443,583

SPECIAL REMARKS: The Dyane should have replaced the 2CV with its headlights incorporated into the wings and "more attractive" body but it failed to topple the 2CV, even though it sold quite well. The Dyane ceased production six years earlier than its "predecessor".

Citroën DS

MODEL YEAR: 1955-1974

NUMBER MADE: 1,455,746 (including ID)

SPECIAL REMARKS: The DS also grew during its lifetime. The DS21 has a 2,175 cc engine of 109 bhp at 5,250 rpm. The 2,347 cc engine

The DS23 Pallas was the top of the DS range. This model was produced from September 1972 until April 1975.

The headlights were sited behind glass from September 1967 and the more expensive models had spotlamps that turned with the steering. The final standard convertibles were made in the autumn of 1971. After this they were solely made to special order.

of the DS23 produced 141 bhp at 5,500 rpm. This version had a top speed of 119 mph (190 kph).

Citroën ID

MODEL YEAR: 1957-1967

NUMBER MADE: See DS

SPECIAL REMARKS: The ID had the same body as the DS but was a more basically equipped model. There was a manual gearbox and no hydraulic gadgetry. Citroën also economised on the interior trim and dashboard.

After Citroën acquired a major shareholding in Maserati the SM or Citroën Maserati was developed as a joint project. The engine and gearbox were Maserati, while the steering, suspension, and many other technical features were from Citroën.

Citroën SM (Citroën Maserati)

MODEL YEAR: 1970-1975

NUMBER MADE: 12,920

SPECIAL REMARKS: The letters SM stood for Sa Majesté in the same way DS meant Déesse or goddess. This coupé was an example of what Italian and French technology could offer and that was quite something!

Citroën GS

MODEL YEAR: 1970-1980

NUMBER MADE: 1,707,257

Special remarks: Of the total number of DS cars built there were 360,005 estate cars and ideas from these were incorporated in the smaller GS but with a simpler air-cooled boxer engine.

Although the GS was built as a middle-of-the-range car it contained many of the gizmos from the DS, such as the suspension and a braking system with disc brakes all round.

The CX was the successor to the DS and was built from 1974-1985. It resembled an enlarged GS but was almost identical mechanically to the DS.

Citroën CX

MODEL YEAR: 1974-1985

NUMBER MADE: 1,034,489 (to 1989)

SPECIAL REMARKS: The CX was significantly less spectacular than its predecessor, the DS. The transverse-mounted four-cylinder engine was also available as an economical diesel.

Crosley

America has always been the land of the big car and is always likely to remain so. Even though Detroit has and does build "compact" cars, these are generally bigger than those from Europe and Japan. It is the exception though that proves the rule and Crosley built cars that would be regarded as small outside USA.

Powel Crosley built cars as early as 1909 and 1913 but these were and remained proto-types. Crosley had no shortage of money for in 1922 he was the world's biggest producer of radios but his dream was a car with his name on the radiator grille. A third attempt at a car finally resulted in 1939 in the Crosley, which was a small car with a 12 bhp twin-cylinder engine. Before the Americans entered the war, Crosley had sold 5,000 of these cars. The car re-emerged in 1946 and the factory continued building small cars until 1952. The cars had a monocoque aluminium body and a 725 cc engine that produced 27 bhp. This was a four-cylinder engine with an overhead camshaft that was easily more highly tuned. Various builders of performance cars in Italy proved this possi-

The Crosley Dashboard. It was no coincidence that a radio was included since Powel Crosley was still the world's biggest radio manufacturer after World War II.

ible. The external appearance of the car was changed regularly and customers were able to choose from several body types. There was a sedan, estate, and even a sports car. This latter model was named The Hotshot. It was an open two-seater without doors and with a windscreen that could be laid flat on the bonnet. The Hotshot even had disc brakes which was quite unusual for 1950. A Crosley competed in the 1951 Le Mans 24 hour race driven by George Schraft and Bill Stiles but their race was soon over when the dynamo mounting bracket broke.

Crosley sold his factory in 1952 for $63,400 to General Tire who stopped production that same year. Crosley made no money from his cars. Shortly before his death in 1961 he admitted that his "hobby" had cost him $3 million.

Crosley cars

COUNTRY OF ORIGIN: USA

Sedan Deluxe

MODEL YEAR: 1946-1952

NUMBER MADE: 81,746 (of which 5,757 before World War II)

SPECIAL REMARKS: The Crosley with its length of 150 in (3,820 mm) was 9³/₄ in (250 mm) shorter than the VW Beetle. Its top speed of 75 mph (120 kph) was in reality dangerously fast.

The Crosley had an aluminium body and space for 4 persons.

Daf

Brothers Huub and Wim van Doorne set up their workshop in Eindhoven, the Netherlands on 1 April 1928 and built their first trailer that same year. The name Daf originated from Van Doorne's Aanhangwagen Fabriek (aanhangwagen is Dutch for trailer and fabriek means factory. Soon the factory employed more than a hundred personnel.

A new factory to build trucks was constructed in 1950 and the first prototype car was made in 1957. This Daf 600 was exhibited at the Dutch motor show in 1958 but newspapers and magazines had heralded its arrival for so long that the public was tremendously disappointed when confronted with an plain, ordinary, somewhat small car. The four-seater had two doors and an air-cooled twin-cylinder boxer engine of 590 cc that produced 22 bhp at 4,000 rpm. The car weighed 575 kg (1,265 lb) and had a top speed of under 56 mph (90 kph). That would have been that had the car not also been equipped with an unusual transmission system. There was no gearbox; the car was equipped instead with a new form of transmission called Variomatic which was a Daf invention.
This powered the rear wheels by rubber drive belts which were operated by the engine vacuum. The system had the same advantages as an automatic gearbox but could drive as fast in reverse as forwards. The standard Daf 600 cost slightly less than Dfl 4,000 (about £500 at that time) which was reason enough for 3,000 people to order one then and there at the show. It was the cheapest car with an automatic transmission system for which countless inexperienced drivers had been waiting.

These people had to wait a while longer though for the first cars were not delivered until 23 March 1959. Times were good for Daf and they built 20,000 cars in 1962.
The Daf 600 was succeeded by the 750 with a 750 cc engine, producing 30 bhp. The deluxe version was named Daffodil. This car was replaced in 1967 by the Daf 33.

Daf established a name as the car for older and timid drivers and the cars were often seen as an obstacle on the road. To improve this image, Daf set up a rally and race department. Formula 3 cars appeared on the circuits with Variomatic transmission and rallies without a Daf competing soon became unthinkable.

Giovanni Michelotti designed a more attractive body for the car which resulted in the Daf 44 which was bigger and faster than its forerunners but also a good deal more expensive. The 44 was succeeded by the Daf 55 which was powered by an 1,100 cc Renault engine. A Daf 55 coupé obtained a creditable seventeenth place in the London–Sydney Marathon.

Late in 1972, Volvo took a major stake in Daf which enabled production to be stepped up. Daf built 82,500 cars in 1971 and by 1973 this was almost 99,000. By January 1974, Volvo possessed 75 per cent of the shares in Daf with important consequences for the company's policy. The Daf 33 ceased production, the Daf 44 became Daf 46, and the Daf 66 was renamed Volvo 66. The replacement car to these was the Volvo 343.

Early Dafs such as this 1964 Daffodil can be spotted by the sloping bonnet line.

Daf cars

COUNTRY OF ORIGIN: The Netherlands

Daf 600

MODEL YEAR: 1959-1963

NUMBER MADE: 312,367 (includes Daf 750 & 33)

SPECIAL REMARKS: The Daf was the ideal second car or ideal transport for the district nurse. The engine was rather noisy but no-one seemed to mind.

Daf 750

MODEL YEAR: 1961-1963

NUMBER MADE: 312,367 (includes Daf 600 & 33)

SPECIAL REMARKS: When people started to complain that Dafs failed to get to the top of Alpine roads pulling caravans, the Daf 750 was introduced with more powerful 26 bhp engine. On the flat this could reach 69 mph (110 kph).

Daf 33

MODEL YEAR: 1967-1974

NUMBER MADE: 312,367 (includes Daf 600 & 750)

SPECIAL REMARKS: When the Daf 44 emerged, the Daffodil was renamed Daf 33. This model had an engine that delivered 28 bhp at 4,200 rpm. The Daf 33 had sufficient room for the entire family and with the estate version there was even room for the family's dog.

When Daf decided to use numbers instead of names, the Daffodil became the Daf 33. This is a 1972 example.

The Daf 46 replaced the 44. It had a twin-cylinder 844 cc engine that gave 34 bhp at 4,500 rpm. The Daf 46 had a top speed of 75 mph (120 kph).

Daf 44

MODEL YEAR: 1966-1974

NUMBER MADE: 167,905

SPECIAL REMARKS: A new and larger body was designed by Italian specialist Michelotti for the Daf 44. The twin-cylinder engine was now 844 cc, producing 34 bhp at 4,500 rpm. The car was renamed Daf 46 in 1974 and 32,353 of them were sold.

Daf 55

MODEL YEAR: 1967-1972

NUMBER MADE: 164,231

SPECIAL REMARKS: In terms of engine at least, the Daf 55 moved into the medium-sized car bracket. There was a 1,108 cc four-cylinder Renault engine under the bonnet that produced 45 bhp at 5,000 rpm. The 55 was available as saloon, coupé, and estate, all of course with Variomatic transmission.

Daf 66

MODEL YEAR: 1971-1972

NUMBER MADE: 146,297

SPECIAL REMARKS: This was the last true Daf. The model was subsequently to become the Volvo 66. The Volvo was very similar to the Daf model except for a De Dion rear axle and another 2 bhp from the Renault engine.

Daimler

In 1986, Frederick Richard Simms purchased the rights to use Gottlieb Daimler's patents in Britain. Simms principal interest was in Daimler's engines. In 1896, Simms sold his company for £35,000 to Harry J. Lawson who subsequently founded the Daimler Motor Company Ltd in Coventry. A Year later, Daimler started to make cars and its first customer was General Montgomery. Within a short time, the British Royal family regarded Daimler as their supplier of cars. Coventry was bombed regularly during World War II and although some 70 per cent of the factory was destroyed, the factory kept on producing armoured cars, tanks, and aero engines. Daimler celebrated its fiftieth birthday in 1946 by introducing its first post-war cars. There were just two models at that time: the DE27 and DB18. The DE27 had a six-cylinder engine, while the DB18 had a straight-eight motor. The famous pre-war clients though had changed their allegiance to Rolls-Royce.

The banker and chairman of Daimler's board, Sir Bernard Docker, privately arranged with a coachwork firm to develop several new body styles which resulted in the first "Docker" Daimler in 1946. This was certainly not the last. Docker married Lady Norah Collins in 1949 who wanted to make Daimler famous once more. Her unusual cars attracted a great deal of attention at shows. The first car built for her was a coupé that was delivered in June 1950 and in that same autumn a second car was delivered to her. It was a Sedanca de Ville with a straight-eight engine. The most famous "Docker" Daimler though was undoubtedly the "Gold Star" of 1951. Those parts that were chromium-plated on a normal Daimler were gold-plated instead. Inside the car were such details as a golden tea service and silk trimmings. The final "Docker" Daimler was built in 1955. By this time Daimler's management began to realize the cost of these excesses.

Daimler also built relatively small cars, such as the Conquest, which was launched pre-war and thereafter continuously improved. The 2,433 cc engine was uprated in 1954 from 75 to 101 bhp to create the Conquest Century.

From 1956, Daimlers were also available with an automatic gearbox and they were equipped with disc brakes in 1958. A V-8 engine was available to the factory from 1958 and this was first incorporated into the Daimler Majestic. The following year this was to be found in Daimler's biggest pot-war success, the SP 250 (generally known in Britain as the Daimler Dart). This was a two-seater sports car with a glass-fibre reinforced polyester body which was completely at odds with Daimler's general image and range.

Daimler was sold to Jaguar in 1960 and from 1963, the Jaguar Mk II was also sold with "badge engineering" as a Daimler 2.5 litre V-8 saloon. The Daimler Majestic was replaced in 1968 by the Daimler Limousine but this was also built with Jaguar components. This old-fashioned and very conservative model

One of the "Docker" Daimlers of 1954. Hand-painted stars embellished the bodywork.

had sufficient room for eight people. The Daimler 2.5 litre V-8 car was available to order until 1991 but true Daimlers had long since disappeared. Jaguar (and therefore also Daimler) was taken over in 1990 by Ford. The American company was more interested in earning money than tradition so that although the Daimler marque still exists, it is nothing more than a Jaguar with a different emblem. Despite this many British owners who would never buy a Jaguar continue to buy Daimlers because of their associations.

Daimler cars

COUNTRY OF ORIGIN: United Kingdom

Daimler DB18

MODEL YEAR: 1946-1953

NUMBER MADE: 8,223

SPECIAL REMARKS: This model was developed long before World War II but the first post-war cars did not look much more modern. The six-cylinder engine had a capacity of 2,522 cc which developed 86 bhp at 4,300 rpm.

The DB18 was designed in 1939 and retained its old-fashioned style until 1950.

Daimler DE36

MODEL YEAR: 1946-1953

NUMBER MADE: 205

An impressive 1948 DE36 with body by Hooper. There was a gigantic straight-eight engine under the bonnet.

SPECIAL REMARKS: Although the days of the straight-eight engine were long past, Daimler still built them until 1953. The capacity was 5,460 cc and power was 152 bhp at 3,600 rpm. This car was only available to order.

Daimler D18 Sports Special

MODEL YEAR: 1948-1952

A 1952 D18 Sports Special. It was a three-seater with space in the back for the third person.

The dashboard of the Sports Special with lots of wood and dials. Note the gear-selector lever of the Wilson gearbox.

NUMBER MADE: 608

SPECIAL REMARKS: This three-seater was built by the coachwork firm of Barker. The 2,522 cc six-cylinder engine produced 86 bhp at 4,300 rpm which took the car to a top speed of 81 mph (130 kph).

Daimler Conquest Century

MODEL YEAR: 1953-1957

NUMBER MADE: 9,620

The top speed of the Conquest Century was 90 mph (145 kph) so that it was also used in rallies. The car was supplied with an automatic gearbox from 1957 onwards.

SPECIAL REMARKS: This Conquest was not intended to be driven by a chauffeur. It was superbly finished with plenty of leather and chrome.

Daimler Majestic

MODEL YEAR: 1958-1962

The Daimler Majestic was launched in 1960. The standard equipment included Borg-Warner automatic box, leather trim, and thick pile carpet on the floor.

The Daimler Limousine was the final true Daimler. It has a wheelbase of 141 in (3580 mm) and overall length of 226 in (5,740 mm).

NUMBER MADE: 1,490

SPECIAL REMARKS: The Majestic was powered by a 3,794 cc six-cylinder engine which produced 147 bhp at 4,400 rpm.

Daimler Limousine

MODEL YEAR: 1968-1991

NUMBER MADE: Unknown

SPECIAL REMARKS: This eight-seater limousine was powered by a 4.2 litre Jaguar engine which produced enough power to take the heavy 2,140 kg (4,708 lb) car to a top speed of 106 mph (170 kph).

Delahaye

Delahaye was considered one of the most famous car makers in France, being regarded in the same class as Bugatti, Talbot, and

Delage. The cars from the Delahaye factory, which had been in existence since 1894, were expensive and sporty. They were impressively stylish but could also compete in motor sport. A Delahaye won the Monte Carlo Rally in 1937 and 1951. There was little interest after World War II in expensive cars. The public bought either a Renault 4CV or Citroën 2CV and those who had the money preferred a Maserati, Ferrari, or Mercedes. Delahaye was taken over in 1954 by it former rival, Hotchkiss and built four-wheel drive vehicles and trucks until 1956.

In 1946, Delahaye, in common with others, re-introduced its pre-war models. These were the 134 and 135 M which had a four cylinder and six-cylinder engine. These cars still had separate chassis with independent front suspension. The cars were therefore quite up-to-date in technical terms. The cars were sold as rolling chassis just as had been done before the war for specialist coachwork builders to create special bodies. Some superb bodies were created by the likes of Chapron, Letourneur et Marchand, Guilloré, Franay, Saoutchik, and Figoni. The six-cylinder engine in the 135 M developed 100 bhp at 3,800 rpm. The 135 MS had triple carburettors and could rely on 130 bhp and a top speed of 94 mph (150 kph) which was quite something at that time. The right-hand drive cars were supplied with a four-speed gearbox or electro-magnetic Cotal gearbox.

The French singer Charles Trenet had Figoni build this special body in 1949 for a 135 M.

Perhaps the management at Delahaye thought "nothing ventured nothing gained" when they replaced the 134 in 1947 with the 175. This supercar had a six-cylinder 4,455 cc engine that delivered 140 bhp. This was increased to 160 bhp at 4,000 rpm in 1950. The brakes were hydraulically operated and the standard model had a Cotal gearbox. The Delahaye 178 and 180 had a longer wheelbase than the 175 but were built on the same chassis.

The final Delahaye was the 235 in 1951. This had a 3,557 cc six-cylinder engine with power of 150 bhp at 4,200 rpm. This model was unable to prevent the marque's demise. Fewer than 100 cars were sold that year and Delahaye could not survive.

Delahaye cars

The Delahaye 180 was a 170 with a wheelbase of 3330 mm (131 in). This is a 1950 example by Franay with a second windscreen.

COUNTRY OF ORIGIN: France

Delahaye 135 MS

The five-seater body of this 135 MS was built by Hermann Graber in Switzerland.

The rear of the Graber-bodied 1949 135 MS. The tiny rear lights were considered adequate in those times.

MODEL YEAR: 1936-1952

NUMBER MADE: Approx. 2,000

SPECIAL REMARKS: The Delahaye 135 M and MS were cars for the "upper classes". The model was equipped with all manner of special and unusual bodies.

Delahaye 175

MODEL YEAR: 1949-1951

NUMBER MADE: Unknown

This Delahaye 175, with a body by Saoutchik, was shown at the 1949 Paris Motor Show.

SPECIAL REMARKS: The Delahaye 175 had a new chassis, modern suspension, and De Dion rear axle. It was often sold as an open seven-seater to heads of state in African countries.

Delahaye 235

MODEL YEAR: 1951-1955

NUMBER MADE: Fewer than 100

Carrozzeria Ghia in Turin designed and built this special body on a 235 chassis.

SPECIAL REMARKS: The Delahaye 235 had the same wheelbase and six-cylinder overhead valve engine as the 235 MS. The cars were mainly sold as rolling chassis.

De Soto

De Soto closed down after building 2,024,629 cars on 30 November 1960. The death struggle has lasted three years but Chrysler had decided in 1957 to let De Soto come to an end. There was no demand any more for a medium-sized car in America. The market share for this size had been 39 per cent in 1955 but this fell to 31 per cent in 1957 and 26 per cent in 1958. The average American bought either a big American car or a smaller imported one. The compact car had not yet arrived on the scene. De Soto sold 117,747 cars in 1957 but the following year this was a mere 36,556. This fell still further in 1961 to 2,400. Another old marque disappeared.

De Soto was founded on 4 August 1928 by Walter P. Chrysler, and was named after the Spanish explorer Hernando De Soto, who had once been a governor of Cuba. The De Soto marque was to compete with Oldsmobile, Nash, and Pontiac. In the first year this was very successful. The De Soto cars shared their bodies with Plymouth, Dodge, and Chrysler but were much cheaper. The final pre-war car was made on 9 February 1942 and the first post-war one in March 1946. Although the car had new doors, wings, and bumpers, it looked just like the 1942 model. The first post-war models were the Deluxe and Custom. The Deluxe had a 3,580 cc six-cylinder engine of 96 bhp while the Custom's

De Soto
Diplomat

1952

was 3,880 cc and 110 bhp (SAE). The sizes of the cars were also different. The Deluxe had a 117 in (2,970 mm) wheelbase while the Custom was either 121 in (3,080 mm) or 139 in (3,540 mm). The final model was the Suburban which had room for eight people. There were also coupés and convertibles but these were low volume sellers.

The first truly new cars were launched in 1949. They looked shorter and smaller but offered more space because the wheelbase had been extended by 4 in (100 mm). The range was extended in June 1949 with an eight-seater estate.

De Soto had built both six and straight-eight cylinder engines before the war. The first V-8 engine was introduced in 1952. This Firedome V-8 was a modern overhead valve engine that closely resembled Chrysler's FirePower V-8. The engine was 4.5 litres and had a compression ration of 7:1, a twin carburettor, and a hemispherical combustion chamber. The power was at least 162 bhp at 4,400 rpm. The Firedome was one of the most powerful and modern engines of its time. Competitors such as Buick, Pontiac, and Packard only had pre-war straight-eight

engines available. Unfortunately this advantage was not fully pressed home. The V-8 was slightly higher than the straight-eight engines and to prevent creating an entirely new body, the designers had constructed an air vent in the bonnet or hood. This vent was given to both the V-8 models and those with six-cylinder engines so that the V-8 lost its exclusivity.

All the De Soto models were given new names in 1953. The six-cylinder engine models became Powermaster Six and those with the V-8 were Firedome. The eight-seater model with six-cylinder engines only disappeared from the range in 1954. They had to make way for the new Coronada. In the mean time sales fell severely with the books showing only 69,844 cars sold at the end of 1954. The entire De Soto management team was fired and the new management were given a budget of $250 million to put the marque back on top. The designer Virgil Exner came up with some impressive designs. His creations were the Firedome, with a 4,768 cc V-8 engine of 187 bhp and the Fireflite with the same size motor, producing 203 bhp, which were launched on 17 November 1954. All the cars had the same 125 in (3,200 mm) wheelbase and were finished in a two-tone paint job. Customers flocked back in their droves and once more De Soto sold 129,767 cars in 1955. Exner was a celebrated man and was given increasing freedom by the directors. Shortly after this he introduced his first four-door coupé. De Soto did not stay out of the race for more horsepower either: this is why Exner built the Adventurer in 1956 to compete with the Chrysler 300. This new coupé was available in black, white, or red, or any combination of these three colours.

De Soto models have always played with colours. Two tone paint jobs were popular in 1950. This is a 1950 Custom.

The V-8 engine produced no less than 320 bhp, which gave the car a top speed of 144 mph (230 kph). The Adventurer was the most powerful car to come out of Detroit in 1957.

The De Soto models were improved and refined each year. They received twin headlights and fins on the rear wings but none of this prevented the demise of the marque. In 1959 the meagre production volume was too low for a factory of its own for De Soto, so the cars were built on a line in the Chrysler factory. Chrysler's top-of-the-range marque of Imperial moved to the factory where De Soto cars had been built for 23 years. The final De Soto convertibles rolled off the new line in 1959. There were two models in the range in 1960: the Fireflite and the Adventurer.

Both cars were based on the running gear of the Windsor but only 19,41 of them were sold and hence on 30 November 1960, Chrysler decided to cease production of De Soto models.

De Soto sold 700 station wagons in 1950. Of these 600 were with wooden trim and the other 100 had steel rear ends.

De Soto cars

COUNTRY OF ORIGIN: USA

De Soto Deluxe

MODEL YEAR: 1946-1948

NUMBER MADE: 68,094

SPECIAL REMARKS: There was still a side-valve engine in the first post-war De Soto models. This six-cylinder engine had a capacity of 3,858 cc and produced 111 bhp at 3,600 rpm.

De Soto Custom

MODEL YEAR: 1950

NUMBER MADE: 88,321

Both the Deluxe and Custom (illustrated) were launched in 1949. Both cars had new bodies but the Custom had the most chrome.

A 1951 Custom convertible cost $2,862 but a customer had to find $3,047 for an estate.

SPECIAL REMARKS: After getting new bodies in 1949, the models remained unchanged in 1950. The 87 mph (140 kph) Custom had a 125 in (3,180 mm) wheelbase and was 206 in (5,250 mm) long overall.

De Soto Firedome

MODEL YEAR: 1952

NUMBER MADE: 45,830

SPECIAL REMARKS: There was an eight-cylinder engine in the Firedome, for the first time since 1931 but it was a V-8 "hemi", producing 162 bhp at 4,400 rpm, rather than a straight-eight.

De Soto Adventurer

MODEL YEAR: 1957

NUMBER MADE: 1,950

SPECIAL REMARKS: The Adventurer was top-of-the-range for De Soto and was available as a convertible or fixed-head coupé. It was powered by a 5,907 cc V-8 engine that produced 360 bhp through an automatic gearbox.

De Soto Fireflite

MODEL YEAR: 1960

NUMBER MADE: 14,484

SPECIAL REMARKS: The Fireflite was built for the last time in 1960. It was available in three body types: four-door sedan, four-door coupé, and two-door coupé. It 5,907 cc engine produced 299 bhp at 4,600 rpm.

In 1960, the four-door Fireflite was the most expensive but least loved De Soto.

Exner gave the 1960 Fireflite quite exaggerated tail fins.

The dashboard of a 1960 De Soto Fireflite.

De Tomaso

Motor racing was the great passion of Alejandro De Tomaso. He drove in his first race in a Bugatti Type 35 at the age of 17 in his native Argentina. In 1955 he won his class in a 1,000 kilometres race from Buenos Aires, driving a Maserati A6GCS. After this De Tomaso left his homeland for Europe. Here he was employed as a test driver for Osca and met the extremely rich American woman racing driver, Elizabeth Haskell and they became married and entered races together. Since money was available in abundance, the Argentinean decided to build his own cars but De Tomaso was a restless character who had barely completed one project before he wanted to start the next. The list of his prototypes is too long to list here but these included both road cars and Formula One racing cars. He had tremendous success when he managed to sell his design for the Pantera sports car for Ford. De Tomaso also bought and sold numerous car makers and body specialists such as Ghia, Vignale, Maserati, Innocenti, and Benelli.

There were only two saloon cars built under the De Tomaso name: the Deauville and Longchamps. The four-door Deauville was designed by the American Tom Tjaarda, whose father had designed the Lincoln Zephyr for Ford among other notable projects. The bodies of both the Deauville and Longchamps were built by Ghia, where Tjaarda was chief designer. Both De Tomaso saloon cars were powered, as was customary, by American Ford power units, which in this case was a 5,796 cc V-8 that delivered 270 bhp at 5,600 rpm. The Deauville was an expensive car with nothing spared in terms of equipment. There was an automatic gearbox, air-conditioning, a wooden dashboard, and leather upholstery and trim.

The Longchamps had the same mechanical parts as the Deauville and the customer could choose from a Cruise-O-Matic automatic box of five-speed manual gearbox. Both cars were very fast with a top speed in the region of 144 mph (230 kph) but were readily controllable as such speeds.

De Tomaso cars

COUNTRY OF ORIGIN: Italy

De Tomaso Deauville

MODEL YEAR: 1971-1988

NUMBER MADE: 244

The Deauville was De Tomaso's first limousine. The car had to compete with Jaguar and Mercedes but failed in this objective.

SPECIAL REMARKS: De Tomaso had overhead camshaft cylinder heads cast for the prototype of the Deauville but instead used standard Ford engines in the production car.

De Tomaso Longchamps

MODEL YEAR: 1972-1988

NUMBER MADE: 412

The Deauville was superbly finished with abundant leather and wood, with the instrumentation of a sports car.

The Deauville was a spacious 2+2 that was perfect for long, fast journeys.

SPECIAL REMARKS: The Longchamps was launched in 1972 at the Turin motor show. In common with the Deauville, it had the same body/chassis of unitary construction but it still weighed 1,700 kg (3,740 lb).

DKW

Danish engineer J. S. Rasmussen made his fame initially through his motor-cycles, before he built his first car in 1928. This was a small two-seater with a twin-cylinder two-stroke engine and front-wheel drive. This combination of two-stroke power and front-wheel drive were to become associated with DKW until 1966. When the global economic crisis was at its

DKW built 15,193 of this Universal estate between September 1953 and June 1957.

worst, Rasmussen convinced the management of Horch, Audi, and Wanderer to establish the Auto Union. This new company was incorporated on 1 November 1931 in Chemnitz but after World War II most of its factories were in the Russian zone of Germany. The former DKW cars were now built as IFA cars and DKW had to start again from scratch.

The company set itself up in Düsseldorf and it was there that the first DKW saloon car was produced in 1950. The model was known as the Meisterklasse F-89 and was according to the old formula of two-stroke engine and front-wheel drive. The body was of steel and was available in two-door saloon or convertible versions. The sound name established by DKW before the war was now of great importance. Customers queued for the car, even though it was considerably more expensive at 5,830 Deutschmarks than a Volkswagen. In 1950 the factory delivered 1,380 cars and managed ten times as many the following year. The model was only radically modified in 1953, when it was given a

larger rear window, new oval grille, and smaller wheels. The three-cylinder two-stroke 900 cc engine produced 34 bhp which was adequate for a top speed of 75 mph (120 kph). The range was fairly broad in 1954, with a choice of two-door saloon, two or four-seater coupés, two or four-seater convertibles, or two-door estate car, known as Universal.

In 1955, the "Grosser DKW 3=6" was introduced with a body 100 mm (4 in) wider and a 2 bhp increase in engine power. The Monza sports car followed based on the 3=6 model. This was a two-seater coupé with polyester body that was initially made by Dannenhauser & Stauss but subsequently by Wenk, Massholder, and Schenk.

The Auto Union 1000 made its appearance in 1958 with the three-cylinder engine now increased to 1,000 cc and this model was fitted with disc brakes on the front wheels in 1959. There was also a 1000Sp two-seater version of this car for the sports-car enthusiast that was available as coupé or convertible. It closely resembled the 1955–1957 Ford Thunderbird.

In 1957, DKW introduced the Junior but did not start its production until August 1959.

Advertising photograph of the DKW 3=6.

A proud owner of a 1956 DKW F93 which she has restored single-handed.

The Monza was not sold via the DKW dealer network.

The prototype had a three-cylinder 600 cc engine but the production car had a sputtering 750 cc two-stroke. The Junior Deluxe had an 800 cc engine and the successors to the Junior were the 800 cc powered F12 and somewhat simpler F11 with a 750 cc three-cylinder engine. There was also an open roadster version of the F12 but only 3,000 of these were sold.

The final DKW was the F102 which was launched in August 1963. Initially, this was a two-door saloon but a four-door version followed about six months later. These were unremarkable cars that were to form the basis for the subsequent Audis. The bodies and front-wheel drive were retained but the sputtering two-strokes had made way for a four-cylinder four-stroke engine. In other words the cars were no longer a true DKW.

DKW cars

Country of origin: Germany

DKW Meisterklasse F89

Model year: 1950-1954

Number made: 59,475

The F89 Meisterklasse was the first post-war DKW. Karmann built the four seater convertible, while the two-seater version was constructed by Hebmüller.

Special remarks: The mechanical parts of the F89 were identical to the pre-war F8 but no wood was used any more in the body's construction. The convertibles were built by body specialists Karmann (the four-seater) and Hebmüller (two-seater and some two-seater coupés).

DKW Sonderklasse

Model year: 1953-1955

Number made: 55,857

Special remarks: The Sonderklasse was powered by a three-cylinder engine which had undergone development before World War II. The 896 cc engine produced 34 bhp at 4,000 rpm. With a three-speed gearbox, the car was capable of 75 mph (120 kph).

Grosser DKW 3=6

Model year: 1955-1959

Number made: 157,330

Special remarks: There was a bigger 903 cc engine of 38 bhp in the new and larger body, which had windows that open "the wrong way". From 1957, the engine was uprated to 40 bhp at 4,250. The DKW 3=6 was available as saloon, coupé, and estate.

Illustration from an advertisement for the DKW 3=6.

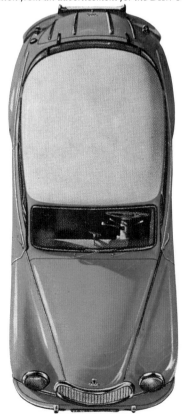

DKW 1000/1000S

MODEL YEAR: 1957-1963

NUMBER MADE: 177,008

SPECIAL REMARKS: This was the final "true" DKW for the enthusiast in terms of the body-style. The power was now 44 bhp at 4,500 rpm and a higher 50 bhp in the S version.

The doors of the DKW 1000 no longer opened "the wrong way". When the side windows were wound down the look was of a fixed-head coupé.

The 1000 Sp clearly imitated the Ford Thunderbird. This is a coupé version.

Only 1,640 convertibles were sold of the 1000 Sp, compared with 5,000 of the coupé.

The DKW Junior, in this case a Deluxe, which can be discerned from the indicators fitted outside the grille.

The S version had a top speed of almost 87 mph (140 kph). The Sp sports car engine produced 55 bhp.

DKW Junior/ Junior Deluxe

MODEL YEAR: 1959-1963

NUMBER MADE: 118,986 & 118,619

SPECIAL REMARKS: DKW entered a new chapter with the Junior. Only the mechanical

The F102 successor to the Junior had a significantly larger body and a 900 cc engine.

The final DKW F102 with its four-stroke engine, was the first post-war Audi.

aspects of the car bore a relationship with previous models. The 741 and 796 cc engines produced 34 bhp but the Deluxe had more torque.

DKW F102

MODEL YEAR: 1964-1966

NUMBER MADE: 52,753

SPECIAL REMARKS: The F102 was the first car with an entirely new body/chassis of unitary construction. The three-cylinder engine was resized to 1,175 cc which increased power to 60 bhp at 4,500 rpm. The DKW F102 could be recognised by its round headlights compared with the rectangular ones of Audi.

Dodge

Brothers John and Horace Dodge built their first car in 1914. The company had a tempestuous time and when both brothers died within a short time of each other in 1927, Dodge were making at least 146,000 cars each year. Those who inherited the company were more interested in money than getting their hands dirty so they sold the company to Walter P. Chrysler for $175 million. This included the car factory, foundry, and steel works.

After World War II Dodge produced a new range of cars based entirely on pre-war models. These cars sold like hot cakes. There were two basic models: the Deluxe and Custom (although the Deluxe was known as the Kingsway outside USA). The Deluxe had a 117 in (2,970 mm) wheelbase and that of the Custom was 119 in (3,040 mm). The Deluxe had a 3,580 cc/96 bhp six-cylinder engine while the Custom's six-cylinder motor was 3,770 cc, developing 104 bhp.
The first truly new models, such as the Mayfarer, Meadowbrook, Coronet, and Wayfarer did not appear until 1949. These were

longer, smaller, and lower than their forerunners. The Wayfarer was an entirely new design. From now on, the cars were given the usual annual facelift. The 1953 models were almost entirely new. The grille had been retained from the 1952 model but the windscreen was now one piece of curved glass, which was described as "panoramic". The cars were still available with the old six-cylinder engine but there was also a V-8 engine in the range. This new 3,954 cc engine, which was named "Red Ram", developed 142 bhp at 4,400 rpm. A further new model, the Dodge Royal that appeared in 1954, was also available with Power-Flite automatic transmission.
The cars got new bodies again in 1955 but the panoramic windscreen had been dropped because although it was visually pleasing, too many people bashed their knee-caps against the corners.

The engines had not been overlooked either: these became bigger and more powerful. There was a successor Super Red Ram of 4,419 cc and 193 bhp and the six-cylinder engine had been increased to deliver 125 bhp. The slogan for these cars in 1957 advertising was "Bigger, more powerful, longer, and lower." The wheelbase had also been increased. In 1957, the range consisted of the Coronet, Royal, and Custom Royal. Within each basic model were a number of options, including a four-door coupé. The four-door estate was now dubbed Sierra and the two-door version was called Suburban. These cars had three bench seats, with the rear bench facing backwards. These seats that looked out the back window were popular with children. The cars gradually became more luxurious. In 1958, 96.4 per cent of all Dodge cars were fitted with an automatic gearbox, 62.5 per cent had power steering, 2.5 per cent had electrically-operated windows, 44.7 per cent a radio, and 4.4 per cent had air conditioning. Fuel injection arrived for the first time in 1958, and this produced at least 333 bhp at 4,800 in a V-8 engine.

Various makers introduced a "compact" car in 1959: the Dodge model was the Dart. which was 208 in (5,290 mm) long with a 118 in (3,000 mm) wheelbase, making it a fairly large car (Mercedes 220 has a 2,750 mm (108 in) wheelbase). The car was significantly cheaper though than a big Dodge. The compacts could be delivered with a 3,682 cc six-cylinder engine or one of three V-8 power units ranging from 5.2-6.3 litres. In spite of the introduction of compact cars, the other 1960 new Dodge models grew bigger. Two new models were added to the range: the Matador, and Polara with wheelbases of 122 in (3,100 mm) and 212 in (5,400 mm) in that order. Dodge sold 356,572 cars in 1960, in twenty different versions ranging from convertible to station wagon.

The following year, a small car, in American terms, was launched, known as the Dodge Lancer. It was "only" 188 in (4,780 mm) long and was powered by either a 2,789 or 3,682 cc six-cylinder engine. The car was not successful and was therefore dropped in 1962. The Lancer was replaced by a new version of the Dart. Dodge did not forget those with a preference for a more sporty car, catering for them with models such as the Charger, a sports coupé with an engine of 425 bhp power output, and the 1970 Dodge Challenger. This latter coupé or convertible, with a choice of six-cylinder or V-8 engines, had to compete with the Chevrolet Camaro and Ford Mustang. Engine capacity varied from 5,210–7,206 cc and top power was in excess of 430 bhp! By 1975, the range consisted of the Dart, Coronet, Charger, and Monaco. Each range had choices of coupé, saloon, and estate, except the Dart. Dodge had stopped building convertibles now that almost every car was equipped with air conditioning.

Dodge cars

COUNTRY OF ORIGIN: USA

The Dodge Custom Town Sedan was a rare car, intended for those who employed a chauffeur. Note how the rear doors open "the wrong way".

Dodge Custom Town Sedan

MODEL YEAR: 1946-1948

NUMBER MADE: Approx. 27,000

SPECIAL REMARKS: The Town Sedan was the "top-of-the-range" model. Its 3,770 cc engine delivered 102 bhp at 3,600 rpm which took it to 75 mph (120 kph).

Dodge Wayfarer

MODEL YEAR: 1949-1952

NUMBER MADE: 217,626

Overall length of the Wayfarer was 196 in (4,980 mm) with a 115 in (2,920 mm) wheelbase. The 3,770 cc six-cylinder engine produced 105 bhp.

SPECIAL REMARKS: The Wayfarer was the cheapest Dodge of its time. The model was available as sedan, coupé, or convertible, all of which had two doors.

Dodge Coronet

MODEL YEAR: 1949-1959

NUMBER MADE: Unknown

SPECIAL REMARKS: In 1949, the Coronet was the most expensive Dodge. By 1954 it fitted between the cheap Meadowbrook and expensive Royal ranges. After 1956, the Coronet became the cheapest car in the range.

In 1953 the Coronet was the finest offering from Dodge. The car had a choice of six-cylinder or V-8 engines.

The Dodge Royal not only had the most powerful engines, it also had every imaginable item of equipment.

Tail fins were in vogue in 1957.

Dodge Royal

MODEL YEAR: 1954-1959

NUMBER MADE: Unknown

SPECIAL REMARKS: The Royal range was only available with the V-8 "hemi" engine. In 1954 this was 3,954 cc, producing 152 bhp at 4,400 rpm. By 1959, this was 6,286 cc, delivering 345 bhp (SAE) at 5,000 rpm.

Chrysler sold 273,286 cars in 1955. A high proportion were Royal series.

Dodge Dart

MODEL YEAR: 1960-1975

The Dodge Dart was available with either a six-cylinder of V-8 engine in 1966. A convertible cost $2,700 or $2,828.

Dodge sold 63,700 Dart Customs in 1969 of which 41,600 had six-cylinder engines and 22,100 boasted a V-8 motor.

NUMBER MADE: Unknown

SPECIAL REMARKS: The Dart was a compact Dodge and was found to fill a clear demand. More than 300,000 were sold in the first year of production.

Dodge Challenger

MODEL YEAR: 1970-1974

NUMBER MADE: 186,441

The 1971 Challenger had the most powerful engine fitted up to then in a Dodge. It was 6,974 cc, producing 431 bhp (SAE) at 5,000 rpm.

SPECIAL REMARKS: The Challenger was a great success in its first year of production, when 83,032 were sold as coupé or convertible. The car was only available after 1972 as a fixed-head coupé.

Dodge Coronet

MODEL YEAR: 1965-1975

NUMBER MADE: Unknown

The Brougham was the most expensive Coronet in 1971. It was only available as a four-door sedan and cost $3,332.

SPECIAL REMARKS: The Coronet filled the gap in 1965 between the "small" Dart and huge Polara. In 1965, the car was 204 in (5,190 mm) long and ten years later 218 in (5,540 mm).

Dodge Monaco

MODEL YEAR: 1971-1975

NUMBER MADE: Unknown

SPECIAL REMARKS: The Dodge Monaco was the most luxurious and therefore most expensive version of the Polara. Customers could choose two or four-door coupé, four-door sedan, or five-door estate. The estate had room for six to nine persons.

IA 1972 Monaco two-door coupé cost $4,153 compared with $3,641 for an standard Polara with the same body.

Edsel

In the mid fifties, the American car industry could sell every car it could make. The standard of living was high and whenever possible, cheaper cars were exchanged for a more expensive model. Someone who drove a GM model might switch from an Oldsmobile to a Pontiac and a Chrysler enthusiast migrated from a Plymouth to a Dodge. Such a step was difficult with Ford because the gap between Ford's basic range and Mercury was too large. In 1955, 41 per cent of the US market consisted of these mid-range cars but Ford could not profit from this. A new model was therefore essential and it could be neither a Ford or a Mercury. The name Edsel was derived from the father of Henry Ford II.

The inexpensive Edsel Rangers and Pacers were to be slightly more expensive than the dearest Ford while the Edsel Corsair and Citation could be slightly more expensive than the Mercury.

Ford's promotional campaign was tremendous. For two years long, the trade press continually wrote about the subject. Finally the cars were launched on 4 September 1957. "Three million curious people have looked at the long awaited car," Ford wrote in its press releases. But they did not buy the cars.

The 1958 Edsel Pacer of which 6,534 coupés and 914 convertibles were sold.

Dealers who had ordered too many Edsels had financial problems. The cars were eventually sold but at a loss and they either went bankrupt or changed to a different brand of car. Masses of people were fired at Ford in Detroit and when a minor slump hit America so that people preferred to buy a cheap Volkswagen, things looked even bleaker for the Edsel. Accountants advised Ford that they needed to build 650 Edsels per day to break even yet in the first ten days after the launch the dealers had failed to sell even 409 units per day. This quickly dropped to fewer than 300 so that by the end of 1959, Ford had sold 100,000 Edsels beneath its break-even level. The entire management of the new marque was fired and then in 1959 even fewer cars were sold to complete the disaster. Ford decided on 19 November 1959 to pull the plug on Edsel, although a few thousand were built from existing parts. Ford had lost $300 million in the space of a few years, equivalent to billions today.

The Edsel was certainly not a poor car and if it had been launched two years earlier or even two years later, the outcome might have been entirely different.

The cheap Ranger and Pacer were based on the 118 in (3,000 mm) chassis of the Ford Fairlane but a special new chassis with 124 in (3,150 mm) wheelbase was developed for the Corsair and Citation. The cheaper and more expensive models were virtually identical in appearance; the difference lay under the bonnet or hood. The two cheaper cars had a 5,911 cc V-8 of 307 bhp except for export models, which had a 5,440 cc V-8 of 235 bhp.

The more expensive models were equipped with a 6,719 cc engine of 284 or 350 bhp. The more expensive models disappeared in 1959, leaving only the Ranger and Corsair. The Corsair had a slightly more powerful engine and was also available as an station wagon. Known as the Villager, this car and the Ranger could be fitted with a 3,655 cc six-cylinder engine.

The new 1960 models were introduced on 15 October 1959. To everyone's surprise, the Edsels had been given new bodies. There were now just two models: the Ranger and the Villager. These had a 145 bhp six-cylinder engine or 300 bhp V-8 motor. These new models remained just as unsaleable.

Only 275 station wagons and 2,571 Rangers were sold in 1960.

The 1958 Edsel Pacer was available with choice of three-speed manual or automatic gearbox.

Edsel cars

COUNTRY OF ORIGIN: USA

Edsel Ranger

MODEL YEAR: 1958-1960

NUMBER MADE: 50,803

SPECIAL REMARKS: The Ranger was available in four body types: two-door or four-door models, with or without hard-top.

Edsel Corsair

MODEL YEAR: 1958-1959

NUMBER MADE: 17,845

SPECIAL REMARKS: The 1958 Corsair had a 6,719 cc V-8 engine which was replaced by a 5,440 cc one in 1959. Power dropped from 284 to 228 bhp.

1960 Edsels had new bodies that were lower and wider than their forerunners.

The final Corsairs were built in 1959. Only 8,653 were sold, which was 539 fewer than in 1958.

Facel Vega

Facel built bodies for Panhard, Simca, and Ford, just outside Paris. The head of the company, Jean Daninos, decided in 1954 the company should make their own cars. These had nothing in common with the usual French saloons and sports cars. The Facel Vega, as the car was named, was of unparalleled quality. Daninos built his cars with mechanical parts from USA, in part because he saw America as an important market but also because he regarded their mechanical parts as extremely reliable. The Facel Vegas were among the best-looking and fastest cars on Europe's roads. They were not sports cars though, rather grand tourers that could cover long distances in a short time.

The cars were built on tubular frame chassis and the first had a 4.5 litre De Soto engine but Daninos quickly changed to Chrysler engines. The race for more horsepower was well under way in the USA at that time and so these French cars saw a steady increase in their power output as can be seen from this table:

1954	4,524 cc	180 bhp/4,000 rpm
1955	4,768 cc	203 bhp/4,400 rpm
	5,407 cc	250 bhp/4,600 rpm
1956	4,940 cc	253 bhp/4,600 rpm
1958	5,907 cc	360 bhp/5,200 rpm

The majority of the cars were spacious 2+2 coupés but there was also the Excellence four-door saloon. Between 1958-1963, 152 units were built of this model. The rear doors opened "the wrong way" because there was no door post between the front and rear doors, making it easy to get in and out of the car.
Unfortunately this weakened the construction and the doors quickly started to be difficult to close.

Daninos was regularly accused of creating "hybrids" because marques such as Ferrari, Jaguar, Maserati, or Aston Martin had their own engines but Facel had a cheap American power unit. This criticism troubled Daninos and in 1959 he introduced an entirely French Facel Vega in both coupé and convertible models.

In the place of the Detroit V-8 there was a four-cylinder engine developed together with the gearbox by Pont à Mousson. The engine had twin overhead camshafts and produced 115 bhp but these cars missed the reliability of the American mechanical parts. In fact the quality was so poor that claims under guarantee arrived by the bag full as soon as the cars left the factory. The Facel Vega name was ruined and although a new and better 126 bhp engine was brought in as a replacement in 1961, it could not prevent the failure of the company.

Customers had no confidence in the French engine. In its place the proven Volvo B18 engine was used, leading to the Facel III. It was all too late and even the Facelia 6 with an Austin-Healey engine could not bring the customers back to the showrooms.

Jean Daninos.

Facel Vega wanted to reach a larger market with a small car. The car was built of entirely French components which proved to be a huge mistake.

Daninos was forced to shut the factory in 1964. If he had ignored the press criticism and remained with American engines, perhaps his cars would still be made today.

Facel Vega cars

COUNTRY OF ORIGIN: France

Facel Vega FV

MODEL YEAR: 1954-1957

NUMBER MADE: 351

SPECIAL REMARKS: Only 46 were made of the FV-1, 103 of the FV-2, and even 205 of the FV-3.
In reality, they were all prototypes which varied widely from each other. The cars formed the basis for the famous HK500.

Facel Vega HK500

MODEL YEAR: 1958-1961

NUMBER MADE: 548

SPECIAL REMARKS: The HK 500 was the highest volume seller Facel Vega. The big V-8 was coupled to a Chrysler automatic gearbox but was also available with a four-speed manual

The HK500 was the best-selling Facel Vega. The finish was superb with leather, wood, and all the equipment the American automobile industry could supply.

box by Pont à Mousson. In the final two years, the cars had disc brakes and power steering.

Facel Vega Excellence

MODEL YEAR: 1958-1963

NUMBER MADE: 152

SPECIAL REMARKS: This car was supposed to compete with Rolls-Royce and Bentley. Its price was similar but the quality was unsatisfactory.

Facel II

MODEL YEAR: 1961-1964

NUMBER MADE: 184

SPECIAL REMARKS: The Facel II was the replacement for the HK 500. The body had

Competition was tough for the Facel II. At the time of its launch, cars such as the Jensen CV8, Ferrari 250 GTE, and Iso Rivolta were also on the market.

been simplified and given a more powerful engine. The 2,660 mm (104³/₄ in) chassis was the same as the HK but this car was slightly quicker at 150 mph (240 kph).

Facelia

MODEL YEAR: 1959-1962

NUMBER MADE: 1,258

SPECIAL REMARKS: The Facelia was relatively less expensive than the bigger Facel Vegas but the quality of this entirely French car was a problem. The company was inundated with guarantee claims and lost its reputation with this model.

Facel III & 6

MODEL YEAR: 1963-1964

NUMBER MADE: 402 & 42

In a final but misguided attempt at survival, Facel developed the Facel III, first with a Volvo engine then with an Austin-Healey power unit.

SPECIAL REMARKS: In a final but misguided attempt at survival, Facel installed first a Volvo engine then an Austin-Healey power unit in the small car. The cars had no more teething problems but the recovery had come too late.

Felber

The Austrian car industry dates back to early times and some Austrians insist that their

The roof could be removed in an instant to make an open roadster.

A canvas roll-back roof was ideal for taller drivers.

Siegfried Marcus built cars before Daimler and Benz. Ferdinand Porsche also built his first cars in Austria before moving to Germany. Austrian car makers include Steyr, Puch, and Felber.

Back in 1923, A. Felber & Co made sidecars for motor-cycles but in 1951 the first efforts with a three-wheeler were put in hand. The vehicle only required a motor-cycle licence and was cheap to insure.

The two-seater was built on a tubular chassis and was powered by a 398 cc two-stroke engine that produced 15 bhp. The gearbox had four forward gears and reverse. Power was fed through the single rear wheel to avoid the need for a back axle and differential. The car was sold as a Felber TL400, weighed 340 kg (748 lb), was 2,780 mm (109 in) long and 1,500 mm (59 in) wide. Its top speed was 50 mph (80 kph) and fuel con-

The Rotax engine drove the rear wheels by a double chain which was immersed in an oil bath.

Ferrari

Ferrari did not only make the sporting supercars in Maranello for which they are famous. The company has also produced 2+2 tourers which could incorporate the "family", but were far more suited to sporting use. Various specialist car body makers have also created 2+2 cars on Ferrari chassis. The first true Ferrari "family" car though was the 250 GTE. This model was launched at the Paris show in 1960. Pininfarina designed the body and with its wheelbase of 2,600 mm (102 in) and length of 4,700 mm (185 in) there was room for a small family. The V-12 engine was 2,953 cc and it produced 240 bhp at 7,000 rpm. The type designation 250 refers to the engine capacity but relates to the size of just one of the twelve cylinders! Late in 1963, a 4-litre engine was installed to create the 330 America.

This was a transition model because when just fifty had been built it was succeeded by the 330 GT. This car had an entirely new body and was powered by a 3,967 cc engine. It was launched in January 1964 at Ferrari's annual press conference. Once again, Pininfarina had designed the body, which was larger in every respect than its forerunner. The wheelbase had been increased by 50 mm (2 in) which was mainly for the benefit of the rear passengers. Striking features included the twin headlights fitted to the first batch of cars. Not everyone liked them but they were in vogue at the time. The engine capacity was 3,967 cc and power output was 300 bhp at 6,600 rpm. This could easily move the 1,380 kg (3,036 lb) car to a respectable 150 mph (240 kph). The gearbox, in common with the 250 GTE had four ratios and a temperamental electrical overdrive.

This was replaced in the second series by a five-speed box. The GT had cast aluminium wheels and single headlights. In 1967, a 330GT was introduced to replace the 365GT 2+2. This car had little relationship with a sports car. The engine had been increased to 4,390 cc with power up to 320 bhp at 6,600 rpm.

These were impressive figures but the horsepower was rarely unleashed because the car was only suitable for fast driving on motor-

sumption was 66 miles per gallon (4.5 litres per 100 km). When import restrictions on cars were lifted in 1954, the public preferred to buy a "real" car rather than settle for a Felber.

Felber cars

COUNTRY OF ORIGIN: Austria

Felber TL400 Autoroller

MODEL YEAR: 1951-1954

NUMBER MADE: Approx. 350

SPECIAL REMARKS: The Viennese firm of Felber & Co experimented with the model for two years before putting it in production in 1953. The two-stroke engine was produced by Rotax-Wels.

ways. The standard equipment included air conditioning, radio, eight-track cartridge player, power-steering, servo-assisted braking, and electrically-operated windows. The car was of great interest from a technical standpoint for it was the first Ferrari with independent suspension on all four wheels. The rear wheels had four Koni dampers, with two of them ensuring automatic levelling. A limited-slip differential ensured even power to the rear wheels.

The 356GT 2+2 continued until late 1971 but the successor did not appear until the Paris show of the following October, 1972. The new 365 GT4 2+2 had a more modern body that was longer, wider, and lower than the 365 GT 2+2. The car was also more attractive from a technical standpoint. The power now came from a 4,390 cc engine with four overhead camshafts instead of two. Ferrari chooses not to reveal the power output but the figure must lie in the region of 340 bhp. Far more important is the tremendous amount of torque the engine produces which makes its possible to pull away in third or fourth gear.

Ferrari has also made comparatively "inexpensive" cars. These were sold in 1968 as the Dino 206 GT with a 2-litre six-cylinder engine. This was subsequently uprated to 2.4 litres. When further uprating of this engine proved impossible, the first production cars with V-8 engines appeared in 1974. These cars were the 308 GT4 2+2, which had been shown at Paris for the first time in October 1973. The type designation is derived from 3 litre engine capacity (2,926 cc), eight cylinders, four overhead camshafts, and room for two with occasional room for two in the back.

There was a five-speed gearbox and the engine was mounted transversely in front of the rear axle, or immediately behind the rear seat. In spite of this arrangement, Bertone was able to design a reasonably useable 2+2. The engine was based on the V-8 that Ferrari had used in 1964 in its Formula One racing cars. The power of 250 bhp at 7,700 bhp was entirely adequate for a speed of 156 mph (250 kph).

Despite this there were negative points about this car. The biggest was that in common with the 206 and 246 GT, this was not a Ferrari but a Dino. This was the name on the front of the car, stamped on the various parts, and in the handbook. The cars were made in the Ferrari works at Marenello, so why name the car Dino instead of Ferrari? In Ferrari circles every Ferrari had a Pininfarina body and Nuccio Bertone was an unknown who had designed several special bodies for Ferrari chassis for himself some years earlier. Yet the 308 GT4 was an attractive and fine car which had leather upholstery and trim, air-conditioning, and electrically-operated windows, unlike the Pininfarina designed 246, GT.

The works placed Ferrari's prancing horse emblem on the front in 1978 and the Dino badge at the back and from then the public regarded the cars as Ferraris.

Ferrari cars

COUNTRY OF ORIGIN: Italy

Ferrari 250 GTE

MODEL YEAR: 1960-1963

NUMBER MADE: 950

SPECIAL REMARKS: Ferrari was quite happy with production volumes between 100-300 right up until the 1960s. There proved to be real interest in such a 2+2 tourer.

The 250 GTE was a thoroughbred Ferrari in every respect but had room for a small family.

The second 330 GT series had standard single headlights instead of twins, magnesium wheels, and an indestructible 5-speed gearbox.

Ferrari 330 GT

MODEL YEAR: 1964-1967

NUMBER MADE: 1,080

SPECIAL REMARKS: The first series of 330 GT had wire wheels which cost more for the second series. Power steering and air conditioning were also not available as standard equipment.

Ferrari 365 GT 2+2

MODEL YEAR: 1967-1971

NUMBER MADE: 801

SPECIAL REMARKS: The 365 GT 2+2 had a 2,650 mm (104 in) wheelbase and was 4,980 mm (196 in) overall. It was launched in 1967 at the Brussels motor show.

The Ferrari 365 2+2 incorporated such technical innovations at independent rear suspension.

The Ferrari 365 GT4 2+2 was a Daytona with a four-seater body and detuned engine.

Ferrari 365 GT4 2+2

MODEL YEAR: 1972-1976

NUMBER MADE: 470

SPECIAL REMARKS: A detuned version of the engine from the 365 GTB4 Daytona throbbed under the bonnet of this car. With its 340 bhp at 7,000 rpm, it achieved the impressive speed for those days of 125 mph (200 kph).

Ferrari 308 GT4

MODEL YEAR: 1974-1980

NUMBER MADE: 2,826

SPECIAL REMARKS: This car heralded a new era for Ferrari which is not yet closed. It was a difficult task to create a 2+2 car with a mid-positioned engine on a chassis of 2,550 mm (88 in) and marked a major achievement for Bertone.

Bertone was given the difficult task of designing a 2+2 on a short wheelbase chassis and the added difficulty of an engine transversely mounted in front of the rear axle.

Fiat

![FIAT]

The first Fiat, built in 1899, was a four-seater in which the driver sat at the back on the left and the passengers were seated next to and opposite the driver. Steering was by means of a tiller-like mechanism. In 1901, Fiat cars acquired steering wheels and had bench seats placed one behind the other. The first racing cars, such as the S76, also appeared early on, in 1911. This was powered by 28,353 cc (yes more than 28 litres) four-cylinder engine that produced 290 bhp at 1,900 rpm. But Fiat also made small cars with little engines.

These days, the racing cars are left to Ferrari and high performance cars are the preserve of Ferrari and Maserati. Both companies form part of the huge Fiat empire. Fiat has always built sporting cars for the public highway and continues to do so alongside its many other and smaller models. It is the smaller cars in particular, such as the 500 Topolino, that made the company big. This was designed in 1936 by Dr. Dante Giacosa. The car remained in production until 1955. The 500 was the first small car to be mass produced. It was intended for a couple or small family with one or more dogs. The car was inexpensive, reliable, and was the first car for many people.

The Topolino was succeeded in 1955 by the Fiat 600 which now had the engine in the back. This model was also tremendously successful and 1,000,000 were sold within five years. Two years later, the Nuova 500 made its appearance, which resembled the former 500 only in its dimensions. A rear-mounted twin-cylinder air-cooled engine had replaced the front-mounted water-cooled four-cylinder engine of its forerunner. Once again, the car was a hit with the Italians and was continuously improved, with doors that opened "the wrong way" being replaced by ones hinged at the front. The engine grew steadily in size and power. It started at 479 cc and 13 bhp and finally became 594 cc with 18 bhp. The 500 was never really quick. The final Topolino had achieved just under 60 mph (95 kph) with difficulty but its successor with 18 bhp could only manage a little over 65 mph (105 kph).

Cars tend to start small and grow as they mature. This was the case of the Fiat 850, which succeeded the 600. With its 843 cc engine and 34 bhp, it was already much more car than its forerunner. The Fiat 850 was launched in May 1964. By the time it was taken off the market in 1971, almost 1,800,000 had been sold without counting the 350,000 coupés, and 124,000 convertibles.

The final Nuova 500 had a 594 cc twin-cylinder engine which was also used in its successor, the Fiat 126. This small 2+2 from 1972 was built for more than twenty years, during which time millions of them were sold.

Fiat also built larger models than these baby cars, such as the Fiat 1100 which was launched in 1939 and re-appeared after World War II. By this time it no longer looked very up-to-date. The headlights were still on top of the wings but the central column between the doors had vanished to make it easier to get in and out of the car. The 1100B of 1949 had a slightly more powerful engine and the final 1100E model no longer had the spare wheel mounted on the back of the car but was inside the boot. There was also a Fiat 1500 with the same body but with a 45 bhp six-cylinder engine of 1,493 cc. An entirely new range was introduced in 1953. The new 1100 only shared its name with the predecessor. The bodies were now of unitary construction and were available with either bench seats front and back or two seats at the front and a bench seat at the rear.

The Fiat 1100 was constantly improved both mechanically an in appearance. In 1960, the car had a new grille. The 1,089 cc 4-cylinder engine produced 50 bhp at 5,200 rpm and top speed was 81 mph (130 kph).

The 1100TV was a quicker version with a 50 bhp engine in place of the standard 36. The Fiat 1200 Granluce had a 1,089 cc engine bored out to 1,221 cc with an identical body to the 1100 except for the grille and two-tone paint finish.

In 1961, the Fiat 1500 made its return with a four-cylinder 1,481 cc engine of 72 bhp. The body was similar to that of the 1100. When equipped with the 1,295 cc engine the car was known as a Fiat 1300.

In a higher price bracket, Fiat brought out the 1400 in 1950 and 1900 two years later. Their bodies were much larger and more spacious than those of the 1100/1200. Italian designers built some superb coupés and convertibles on the basis of these cars. The four-cylinder engines were 1,395 cc/44 bhp and 1,901 cc/60 bhp.

Italy's economy started to improve during the late fifties, increasing the demand for more expensive cars so Fiat launched their Fiat 1800 and 2100 in 1959. These models had new engines and entirely new, spacious bodies. The only difference between the two models was in the capacity of their six-cylinder engines: 1,795 cc and 2,054 cc. Two years later a larger 2,279 cc version of this latter engine appeared in the top-of-the-range Fiat 2300. This car did not make way for the greater comfort and luxury of the Fiat 130 until 1968. This prestige car was available as both four-door saloon and coupé. Both of course offered automatic transmission and electrically-operated windows as standard equipment.

From 1966, the models were given names that no longer related to the engine size. Hence there were the Fiat 124 and 125 with four-cylinder engines of 1,197 and 1,608 cc. The cars were visually identical and yet the bigger engined 125 was also slightly larger than the 124. The other difference was the rectangular headlights of the 124 compared with round ones for the 125.

The Fiat 128 was launched in March 1969 to succeed the 1100 which it resembled. The biggest difference was beneath the bonnet. The 128 was the first Fiat with a transverse-mounted engine with overhead camshaft and front-wheel drive. The 128 was available in various forms and was a great success. When production in Italy finally ceased in 1978, more than 3,000,000 had been sold.

The first post-war Topolinos were identical to those of 1940. The 500B appeared in 1948 with the same body but an overhead valve engine.

Fiat cars

COUNTRY OF ORIGIN: Italy

Fiat 500 Topolino

MODEL YEAR: 1946-1955

NUMBER MADE: 520,207

SPECIAL REMARKS: A total of 376,371 of the final 500C version were sold. This had the headlights incorporated into the wings and the spare wheel at the rear of the car.

This Fiat 500C estate appeared in 1954, known as the Belvedere.

Fiat 600

MODEL YEAR: 1955-1969

NUMBER MADE: 2,612,367

SPECIAL REMARKS: The 600 was also available as Multipla which was a forerunner of

Until 1964 the doors of the Fiat 600 opened the "wrong way" to make it easier to get in and out of the car but this was highly dangerous if they opened while driving.

The 600 Multipla was highly regarded by many. It had space for six persons and was therefore used as a taxi.

today's MPV or multi-purpose vehicles. The Fiat 600 was built in a number of countries, including Poland and Spain.

The Nuova or new 500 successor to the Topolino only appeared two years after its predecessor had disappeared from the market.

Fiat Nuova 500

MODEL YEAR: 1957-1975

NUMBER MADE: 3,427,648

SPECIAL REMARKS: Evidence that the world was waiting for the new Fiat 500 is provided by the production figures. Both the Topolino and Nuova 500 were designed by Dante Giacosa.

Fiat 850

MODEL YEAR: 1964-1971

From 1966 on the Fiat 850 was available with an automatic gearbox, which was extremely rare for a small car.

NUMBER MADE: 1,780,000

SPECIAL REMARKS: When the Fiat 600 had run its course, it was replaced by the Fiat 850. This was powered by the reliable water-cooled four-cylinder. The 850 was more suitable as a family car than the 500 which was cramped for space.

The Fiat 126 was little more than a Nuova 500 with a more modern and slightly more roomy body. The first cars had a 594 cc engine but subsequent cars were powered by a 652 cc four-cylinder engine of 24 bhp.

Fiat 126

MODEL YEAR: 1972-1987

NUMBER MADE: 1,970,000

SPECIAL REMARKS: Motoring writers throughout Europe enthused over the 126 as an ideal and thrifty small car for urban motoring.

Fiat 1100B

MODEL YEAR: 1948-1953

NUMBER MADE: Approx. 80,000

SPECIAL REMARKS: The post-war 1100 was a slightly improved version of the 1939 Fiat 1100 that had succeeded the 508 Balilla 1100. The 1948 Fiat 1100 can be recognised by the pointed radiator grille.

The Fiat 1100 and 1500 re-appeared in 1948 but looked like the pre-war models, although they now had pointed front ends and improved suspension.

Fiat launched the new Fiat 1100 at the Geneva motor show in March 1953. Fuel consumption was 36 mpg (1 litre per 12 km) and the engine produced 36 bhp at 4,400 rpm. In the autumn of 1953 the 1100TV version was introduced with a 50 bhp engine.

Fiat 1100-103

MODEL YEAR: 1953-1969

NUMBER MADE: 1,768,375

SPECIAL REMARKS: The Fiat 1100 was given a new monocoque body in 1953. This new model was also available as an estate from 1954.

Fiat 1200 Granluce

MODEL YEAR: 1957-1960

NUMBER MADE: 400,066

The Fiat 1200 appeared for the first time at the Turin motor show in 1957. It was a replacement for the 1100TV and had a 1,221 cc engine giving 55 bhp at 5,300 rpm for a top speed of 87 mph (140 kph).

SPECIAL REMARKS: The successor to the Fiat 1100TV was the Fiat 1200. The engine was the same 1,221 cc four-cylinder engine delivering 55 bhp at 5,300 rpm, which had fuel consumption of 35 miles per gallon (8.5 litres per 100 km) and a top speed of 87 mph (140 kph).

Fiat 1300/1500

MODEL YEAR: 1961-1968

NUMBER MADE: Approx. 600,000

SPECIAL REMARKS: The 1300/1500 range had to fill the gap between the 1100 and 1800 left by the 1200 Granluce when it was taken out of production.

Fiat 1400

MODEL YEAR: 1950-1958

The Fiat 1300 and 1500 appeared at the end of April 1961. These cars had the same bodies but different 1,295 and 1,481 cc engines.

The top of the line from Fiat in 1952 was the 1900 which was based on the 1400 but with a 1,901 cc 4-cylinder engine of 60 bhp at 4,300 rpm.

Fiat celebrated its fiftieth birthday with the 1400, which was launched at Geneva in 1950. It was the first Fiat with a monocoque body.

Fiat launched the 1800 and 2300 at Geneva in 1959. Once again the cars had the same bodies but different six-cylinder engines of 1,795 and 2,054 cc. There was also an estate version.

NUMBER MADE: 120,356

SPECIAL REMARKS: The Fiat 1400 was launched at the Geneva motor show of 1950. It was the first truly new post-war Fiat and had a monocoque body. There was also a diesel model for the Italian market.

Fiat 1900

MODEL YEAR: 1952-1958

NUMBER MADE: 15,759

SPECIAL REMARKS: The 1900 was the big stable-mate of the Fiat 1400.
This model was launched in Paris in 1952 and had a 1,901 cc engine that delivered 60 bhp at 4,300 rpm.

Fiat 1800/2100

MODEL YEAR: 1959-1961

NUMBER MADE: 31,174

SPECIAL REMARKS: The first post-war six-cylinder engine from Fiat was used in the 1800 and 2300. These cars were also the first to have torsion struts for the front suspension.

Fiat 2300

MODEL YEAR: 1961-1968

NUMBER MADE: Unknown

SPECIAL REMARKS: The six-cylinder engine of the 2300 produced 105 bhp at 5,300 rpm. In the 2300 S model there was 136 available at 5,600 rpm. This roomy 2+2 version of the 2300 was produced by Ghia.

Fiat introduced the 2300 in 1961. Its engine was 2,279 cc with power of 105 bhp at 5,300 rpm.

The Fiat 130 – introduced as a saloon in 1969 – was also available as a coupé from 1971. It was one of the finest looking reasonably priced Italian cars.

Fiat 130

MODEL YEAR: 1969-1977

NUMBER MADE: 19,584

SPECIAL REMARKS: The Fiat 130 was Fiat's prestige car to compete with the Mercedes 280 and BMW 2800. A total of 4,491 of the coupé version were sold.

Fiat 124

MODEL YEAR: 1966-1974

NUMBER MADE: 1,974,382

SPECIAL REMARKS: The 124 was another great success for Fiat. It was available in various body types including convertible (151,710 units), coupé (279,672 units), and estate.

Fiat 125

MODEL YEAR: 1967-1972

NUMBER MADE: 603,870

SPECIAL REMARKS: The main difference between the Fiat 124 and 125 was under the bonnet. The Fiat 125 had a four-cylinder engine that was also used in the sporting versions of the Fiat 124. This had twin overhead camshafts which is now commonplace but was quite exceptional then.

Fiat 128

MODEL YEAR: 1969-1978

NUMBER MADE: 3,106,897

SPECIAL REMARKS: The Fiat 128 introduced a new era of front-wheel drive to Fiat. The 1,116 cc engine with its overhead camshaft delivered 55 bhp at 6,600 rpm.

When the Fiat 1100 became unsaleable it was replaced in 1969 by the Fiat 128. This car had a 1,116 cc engine mounted transversely at the front and driving the front wheels. It developed 55 bhp. This is a 128 3P version with three doors.

Ford (Germany)

Ford AG or Ford of Germany was incorporated as a company on 18 August 1925. This new company was established to import Ford cars from USA but also to manufacture Ford cars under licence. By the time the first Model-T Ford left the factory on 8 April 1926, 37 people were employed there. The Model-T was succeeded by the Model-A and business was so good that the factory was too small. Its position in Berlin was also far from ideal. Henry Ford and Konrad Adenauer, who was mayor of Cologne at that time, laid the foundation stone for a new factory in 1930 and eventually the entire process was moved to Cologne.

During World War II, the Ford factory built trucks for the Germany army but this did not escape the attention of the allies who quickly destroyed the plant in bombing raids. Despite this, trucks rolled from the lines once more quickly in 1945. It was not until 1948 though that cars were again made. These were small Taunus models of the type Ford had made before the war. These two-door saloons were four-seaters with a 1,172 cc four-cylinder side-valve engine under the bonnet which produced 34 bhp at 4,250 rpm. The Taunus was not very fast but could exceed 62 mph (100 kph). The Taunus also became available as a convertible in 1949 with a bodies assembled by Deutsch Coachworks. The Taunus Spezial or "special" followed later with a different grille and power-

Two-tone paintwork was very popular in the fifties. This is a Taunus 17M as the factory built it from 1957-1960 under the works name P2.

steering and then the Deluxe in January 1951, which for the first time had a single element windscreen. Meanwhile development was under way for a successor to the "Buckel" Taunus. This made its appearance in 1952 as the Taunus 12M which had a modern monocoque body and no separate chassis yet in the base model was still powered by the old 1.2-litre side-valve engine. For those who found this too little power, there was the 15M with a 1,498 cc four-cylinder overhead valve engine delivering at first 50 and later from 1956, 55 bhp. This model had a relatively high top speed for its day of 81 mph (130 kph).

The British and German Ford factories work closely together and this was also true during the fifties when Dagenham produced the Consul and Cologne built the 17M. Although there was no external resemblance between the cars, they had much in common and shared many parts, such as engines, brakes, and suspension. The four-cylinder engine was now a 1,698 cc overhead valve engine that delivered 55 bhp at 4,250 rpm. This model was known in the factory as the P2 and was also available as an estate and convertible. The P2 was succeeded by the P3 which had less boxy lines and then by the P5, which looked much like the P3. Both the P3 and P5 were available in TS versions in which the engine was bored out to 1,758 cc to produce 70 instead of 60 bhp. The Taunus 12M was succeeded by the P4 which differed considerably in technical respects from its forerunners. There was now a V-4 engine and front-wheel drive. The P6 and P7 were improved versions of the 17M with V-4 and V-6 engines. The P7 was also available as a 20M with a 1,998 cc or 2,293 cc engine.

The "Buckel" Ford Taunus resembled a smaller version of pre-war American Ford cars.

The cars grew steadily bigger. both in dimensions and engine size. The 26M followed in 1968, which was a 17M with a 2,550 cc V-6 engine of 125 bhp at 5,300 rpm. Teamwork between Dagenham and Cologne became more intensive and both factories produced large numbers of Capri and Escort models. In 1972 Ford of Britain and Ford Germany launched a joint model as the new Ford Taunus in Germany and new Cortina in Britain in which Ford had invested over £150 million. The first Granadas were luxury versions of this model.

Ford cars (Germany)

COUNTRY OF ORIGIN: Germany

Ford Taunus

MODEL YEAR: 1948-1952

NUMBER MADE: 74,128

The first Taunus can be recognised by the divided grille with its herring-bone pattern.

SPECIAL REMARKS: In 1952, this car was also produced at the Ford Factory in The Netherlands as a Taunus 10.

Ford Taunus 12M

MODEL YEAR: 1952-1962

In 1955, the 12M was also available with 1.5-litre engine as a 15M. In addition to the other engine, this model had a different grille.

The dashboard of the 15M. The column gear-change was something new introduced from USA.

NUMBER MADE: 306,609

SPECIAL REMARKS: More than 300,000 were built of the Taunus 12M and 12M Supers, which had 1.5-litre overhead valve engines. A "mere" 134,127 rolled off the lines of the 15M. This model could be identified by its different grille.

Ford Taunus 17M

MODEL YEAR: 1957-1960

NUMBER MADE: 239,978

SPECIAL REMARKS: Ford entered the market for mid-ranged cars with the 17M. This car had a length of 4,380 mm (172 in) and a 2,600 mm (102 in) wheelbase.

Ford Taunus 17M P3

MODEL YEAR: 1960-1964

NUMBER MADE: 669,731

The 1960 17M was available with either a 1.5 or 1.7-litre engine which produced 55 or 60 bhp.

SPECIAL REMARKS: The Taunus P3 had a body with good aerodynamic properties that resulted in a CW value of 0.40.

Ford Taunus 17M P5

MODEL YEAR: 1964-1967

NUMBER MADE: 710,059

SPECIAL REMARKS: The P5 model was available in the showroom as a Taunus 20M and Taunus 20M TS with a V-4 engine of 1,699 to 1,998 cc.

Ford Taunus 1 (New Cortina)

MODEL YEAR: 1973-1975

The P5 model Ford Taunus was longer and wider than its forerunners with less rounded side panels. The convertible had space for five.

The Taunus 1 of 1973-1975 (new Cortina in UK) had a straight 4 or V engine and included luxury Ghia models.

NUMBER MADE: Unknown

SPECIAL REMARKS: The 1973 Taunus 1 (the same car was the new Cortina in Britain) resembled its predecessor but was significantly improved mechanically. The cars now had four-cylinder and V-6 engines ranging from 1,285-2,274 cc, giving 55-108 bhp.

Ford (France)

Henry Ford extended his activities in 1934 by entering the French market. He entered into co-operation with Emile Mathis who had built small cars in Strasbourg since 1898. The result was a Matford, a American style car

The 1949-1952 Vedette had a rounded rear end and two-piece windscreen.

with a V-8 engine. The relationship did not resume in 1945 after the war. Ford moved production to a second factory in Poissy on the Seine where the first saloon cars were built in 1947. The resulting Ford Vedette was very modern for its time with a streamlined "fastback" designed by Bob Gregorie in Detroit. It boasted independent front suspension at a time that Ford in Detroit still had rigid axles. The Vedette's engine was a 2,158 cc side-valve V-8 of 60 bhp, which increased after 1951 to 66 bhp. Unfortunately this engine was not reliable and former Vedette dealers may still recall that every new Vedette was supplied with important spares for the fuel system. The initial Vedettes were four-door saloons but coupés and convertibles appeared in showrooms during 1949. The Facel-Metallon company developed a sporting coupé which was sold as a Comète. The bodies for these cars were built by Facel who were later to make their own Facel Vega cars.

The drivers Trilland and Simille broke several records at the Montlhéry circuit in the summer of 1952, including that of the 10,000 kilometre race with a fastest lap of 106 mph (169.872 kph). Sales shot up as a result of this success. The Vedette was shown with a new body at the 1952 Paris motor show. The windscreen was now one unit, the rounded rear end had gone to make space for a boot which did not improve the vehicle's looks. In the spring of 1953, the V-8 engine was increased in capacity to 2,355 cc and when the compression ratio was increased from 7 to 7.4:1 the power climbed from 66 to 80 bhp. Later in the autumn of that year customers also had a 4-litre V-8 engine available of 95 bhp.

By this time the Vedette's body styling was very dated and Ford had a replacement de-

signed with a monocoque body. This did not go into production with Ford though, because in August 1954 they sold the factory complete with everything to Simca. The first of the new Vedettes that appeared were still sold as Ford cars though.

Ford cars (France)

COUNTRY OF ORIGIN: France

Vedette

MODEL YEAR: 1949-1954

NUMBER MADE: Approx. 100,000

SPECIAL REMARKS: The Vedette was designed in the North America in 1944 which explains

The second and final version of the Vedette had a new front end. It was 4,540 mm (179 in) long and had a top speed of 81 mph (130 kph).

The rounded rear end disappeared in 1952. A major facelift also incorporated boot space at the rear.

why the car had such American styling. The side-valve V-8 engine was the same as the one used in the Matford before World War II.

Ford (UK)

Henry Ford opened his first factory in Britain in 1911. Model-T and later Model-A Ford cars were built at Trafford Park, Manchester. The company moved to its present-day home beside the Thames at Dagenham in 1932. This is where the first truly British Fords were built. The first cars were small in both size and engine capacity. The Ford-Y, for instance, was powered by a side-valve 933 cc engine that could only manage 8 horsepower. Ford UK specialised in small cars but also assembled American models with V-8 engines. The pre-war Ford Anglia and Prefect re-appeared after World War II. These cars were virtually identical at first glance. The difference was under the bonnet where the Anglia had a 933 cc engine, while the Prefect had a 1,172 cc motor; both engines were side-valve affairs. The Prefect also had four doors instead of the Anglia's two and was therefore $3^1/_2$ in (90 mm) longer than the Anglia at 155 in (3,950 mm) overall. The Anglia was equipped with the Prefect's 1.2-litre engine in 1949. This engine was the power unit of countless motor sport cars that were built in small workshops throughout Britain and by do-it-your-self enthusiasts.

The Ford Pilot made its appearance in August 1947, at first with a 2.5 and subsequently 3.6-litre side-valve V-8 engine. The car had the looks of a pre-war American car. Ford introduced their first truly post-war cars at the London motor show in the autumn of 1950. The Consul and Zephyr were very popular with the masses who visited the show. The Consul had a four-cylinder engine while the Zephyr had a six-cylinder motor. Both engines in these cars now had overhead valves. Both cars had apparently the same bodies of unitary construction, although the Consul was 4 in (100 mm) shorter than the Zephyr, which had independent suspension of the front wheels. This quite revolutionary suspension for its time was an invention of Earle and MacPherson (MacPherson struts). A luxury version of the Zephyr was introduced as the Zodiac in 1953.

This model could be identified by its two-tone paintwork. In this same year, a new Anglia and new Prefect were also introduced, again with two-door and four-door bodies but now with bodies of monocoque construction. The 1.2-litre side-valve engine remained virtually unchanged. Meanwhile, the old Anglia now re-appeared as the Ford Popular. The Anglia 100E was tremendously successful but not to the same extent as its successor, the Anglia 105E of 1960. This car was powered by a four-cylinder overhead valve engine, which seems to be capable of unlimited performance enhancement. The engine was widely used in Formula Junior and small sports cars with great success. The standard Anglia engine was 997 cc (1,197 cc after 1962) and these engines produced 40 and 53 bhp respectively. The most strik-ing feature of the car was the inward-slant-ing rear window. This certainly remained clean and dry when it rained but devoured the entire space for anyone to place their hats. Some regard the feature as unattractive too.

New Consuls, Zephyrs, and Zodiacs were presented at the Geneva motor show in 1956. They had entirely new bodies and as was customary in those times, the cars had all grown larger. The engines were now 1,703 and 2,553 cc instead of 1,508 and 2,262 cc, while the cars had grown in length by $5^1/_2$-$7^1/_2$ in (140-190 mm). The gap between the Anglia and larger Consul 1700 was not filled until 1961, when the Ford Classic (also known as Consul 315 in certain markets) was introduced. It was not a success, perhaps because it shared an inward-slanting rear window with the Anglia. The Consul and Zephyr were produced for six years without major changes and were not replaced until 1962. The Consul now became the Zephyr 4 but

Not everyone liked the slanting rear window of the Anglia. The Dutch Ford organisation insisted on photographing the car so that the window was not visible.

was identical apart from its engine to the Mark 3 Zephyr and Zodiac.

One of Ford UK's great past successes was the Ford Cortina of which more than one million were sold between 1962-1970. The Cortina was the UK version of the German Ford Taunus. The model was continuously improved and customers had a choice from 1,340, 1,498, or 1,558 cc engines with power output across the range 46-106 bhp. The Mark 2 Cortina of 1967 had a choice of 1,498 or 1,599 cc engines.

The Ford Classic or Consul 315 was the basis for the Ford Corsair which could be admired in showrooms from 1964. The Corsair had a choice of straight four-cylinder or V-4 engines. The standard four was 1,498 cc, producing 58 bhp at 4,600 rpm, while the V-4 was either 1,663 or 1,996 cc with 72-88 bhp at its disposal.

Other major successes from Dagenham include the Escort and Capri, The Escort succeeded the Anglia in 1968 and was also made in Germany. There was a broad range of four-cylinder engines. The base model had a 1,098 cc of 45 bhp. There were also 1,330, 1,330 GT, 1,558 Twin-Cam, and 16 valve RS 1600 engines. The later two engines were mainly for motor sport.

The Capri was also designed in Britain and was soon also produced in Germany. This coupé had a choice from 1,298 or 1,599 cc four-cylinder engines, 1,996 cc V-4, or 2,994 cc V-6 engines.

The Zephyr and Zodiac were withdrawn in 1972 and succeeded by the Granada which was only available with V-engines. Customers could choose from a 1,996 cc V-4 of 82 bhp or from 2,495 or 2,994 cc V-6 motors of 120 or 138 bhp.

The Ford UK range in 1975 consisted of Escort, Cortina, Consul, Granada, and Capri.

Ford cars (UK)

COUNTRY OF ORIGIN: United Kingdom

Ford Anglia/Prefect

MODEL YEAR: 1939-1953

NUMBER MADE: 166,864 & 379,339

The first post-war Anglia still had a separate chassis with fixed axles and leaf springs front and back.

SPECIAL REMARKS: These small Fords were enormously popular in both Britain and Europe because they were easy to self-maintain. This model remained in production from 1953-1959 as the Ford Popular. At least 55,340 of this final version were sold.

New Ford Anglia/Prefect

MODEL YEAR: 1953-1959

NUMBER MADE: 348,841 & 100,554

SPECIAL REMARKS: These cars were also built at various Ford factories elsewhere in Europe, including the Ford works in Amsterdam, Holland, where the car was known as an Escort (of which 33,131 were made).

Ford Anglia 105E

The Anglia 105E had a body designed with the help of a wind tunnel.

MODEL YEAR: 1960-1967

NUMBER MADE: 1,083,960

SPECIAL REMARKS: The 105E Anglia was mechanically a much more modern car than its forerunner, the 100E. The rear window originated from a Lincoln Continental Mark 3.

Ford Consul/Zephyr

MODEL YEAR: 1950-1956

NUMBER MADE: 231,481 & 175,311

The style of the monocoque bodies of the Consul and Zephyr were very modern for their day.

SPECIAL REMARKS: The total number of Zephyrs includes 22,634 Zodiacs. The Zodiac was introduced in 1953 and was always finished with two-tone paintwork. It had a more generous level of equipment and trim and boasted 72 instead of 69 bhp from its six-cylinder engine.

Ford Consul/Zephyr Mk 2

MODEL YEAR: 1956-1962

NUMBER MADE: 682,400

This MK 2 Zodiac and its stable-mates the Consul and Zephyr looked like small American cars.

SPECIAL REMARKS: The Consul and Zephyr were first shown at Geneva in 1956. These cars averaged 27-33 miles per gallon (9-11 litres per 100 km) and had a top speed of 78 mph (125 kph).

Ford Granada

MODEL YEAR: 1972-1977

NUMBER MADE: Unknown

SPECIAL REMARKS: The Ford Granada replaced the German Ford Taunus 17, 20, and 26, plus the British Zephyr and Zodiac. It was built both in Germany and the UK. Customers could choose from 2.3, 2.6, and 3-litre V-6 engines.

Ford Classic/Consul 315

MODEL YEAR: 1961-1963

The 1961 Ford Classic or Consul 315 was a larger version of the Anglia. At 171 in (4,340 mm) it was 13 in (440 mm) longer than the Anglia.

NUMBER MADE: 111,225

SPECIAL REMARKS: This car, which had different names in various markets, was an enlarged version of the Ford Anglia, complete with awkward slanting rear window. The car had disc brakes on the front wheels. The engine was initially 1,340 then from 1963 1,498 cc.

Ford Cortina

MODEL YEAR: 1962-1970

NUMBER MADE: 1,107,650

SPECIAL REMARKS: The Cortina was a tremendous success. There were also 7,333 Lotus Cortinas sold with cylinder heads with twin overhead camshafts. Some 4,032 Mk 2 Lotus Cortinas were sold.

A 1965 Ford Cortina Estate which had room for the entire family.

The Cortina GT was introduced in 1963, with the engine from the Classic/Consul 315. This four-cylinder unit was equipped with a Weber carburettor and produced 84 bhp.

The Ford Corsair filled the gap between the Cortina and the Zephyr.

Ford Corsair

MODEL YEAR: 1964-1970

NUMBER MADE: 294,591

SPECIAL REMARKS: The Corsair succeeded the Classic/Consul 315. It was launched at the Paris motor show in 1963. Its 1,498 cc straight four-cylinder engine was replaced in 1965 with a 1,663 cc V-4 engine.

Ford Zephyr/Zodiac Mk 4

MODEL YEAR: 1969-1972

NUMBER MADE: Approx. 150,000

SPECIAL REMARKS: The Mark 4 Zephyr was available with 1,996 cc V-4 or 2,495 cc V-6 engines. The Zodiac had a 128 bhp V-6 engine of 2,994 cc. This engine was also available in the Zephyr from 1967 on.

The Mark 4 Zephyr was 185 in (4,700 mm) long. The Zodiac and subsequent V-6 Zephyr were 3/4 in (20mm) longer. This is a Zodiac.

Ford USA

Ford Escort Mk 1

MODEL YEAR: 1968-1974

NUMBER MADE: Unknown

SPECIAL REMARKS: The basic model of this replacement for the Anglia was initially equipped with drum brakes but disc brakes were available as an optional extra on the front wheels.

Ford Capri Mk 1

MODEL YEAR: 1969-1977

NUMBER MADE: More than 1,000,000

SPECIAL REMARKS: Like the Escort, the Capri was a Ford UK design and both cars were also produced in Germany. The Capri was a smaller version of the Ford Mustang and it was also popular in motor sport.

Enthusiasts for the Mk 1 Ford Capri 2+2 had a wide choice of engines. These ranged from 1,300 to 2,600 cc.

The upholstery and trim of the 1950 Ford Custom convertible was leather. An overdrive was available as an optional extra.

World War II began for the USA when the Japanese attacked Pearl Harbour on 7 December 1941. Ford had launched its 1942 models three months earlier but was only able to supply a small number of these. The plant had to switch over to production of Jeeps, trucks, and aircraft.

The first post-war cars left the factory on 2 June 1945 but these were hand-built examples and full production did not get going until October 1945. Customers were offered a choice from ten models even at this early stage. There was a choice of 3.7-litre six-cylinder or 3.9-litre V-8 engines. The demand for cars was enormous but this was not necessarily good news for Ford. The US government had determined that prices should not be more than 9 per cent higher than in 1942 which meant a loss of $300 per car for Ford and cumulative losses for the company of $10 million per month. The government policy changed in June 1946 and prices shot up. When the accounts were published for 1946, the company had made a net profit of just $2,000.

Ford introduced its first new post-war car on 18 June 1948. This was an entirely modern concept with development having cost $118 million but the effort was worth it. The wheelbase was unchanged at 114 in (2,900 mm) but the car was ³/₄ in (20 mm) longer than its predecessors and at least 8¹/₄ in (210 mm) lower, with a height of 62¹/₂ in (1,590 mm). The waiting lists remained long, even though 1,118,762 cars were delivered by the end of 1949. The cars suffered from many faults though. Doors flew open in bends because the engine was placed too far forwards. Driving on ice and snow was dangerous and when it rained, water got into the cars. The problems were not fully solved until 1950. In 1952, Ford changed all the model names to create the Mainline, Customline, and Crestline. There were other changes in addition to the names: the elderly six-cylinder side-valve engines made way for modern overhead valves motors which were more powerful and used less fuel. There were new bodies too, designed by George Walker. The range comprised eleven different models and these were available in eighty different colour combinations.

Ford's side-valve V-8 had been continuously improved from 1932 on but 1954 finally saw the introduction of the long awaited overhead valve version. Cylinder capacity was 3.9 litres with power of 130 bhp at 4,200 rpm. For those who wanted more, there was a 4.1-litre engine of 160 bhp available. Customers flooded back and Ford sold more cars for the first time in November 1954 than its competitor Chevrolet (GM).

Ford has always set the pace with estates in America. The famous designer Gordon Miller Buehrig, who had worked for Cord and Auburn for a long time, designed the Range Wagon with an entirely steel body, of which 93,000 were sold in 1954. The cars been ever more popular and in 1958, Ford sold 184,613 of these estates.

Ford's response to the ever increasing flood of imported cars was the Falcon, launched in 1960. It was the first American car with a monocoque body and no separate chassis. The Falcon was a tremendous success with at least 417,00 units being sold in its first year.

A new record was achieved by Detroit in 1963, with almost eight million cars being made. Of these, 61 per cent had a V-8 engine and every eighth car was an estate. Ford was able to sell 1,500,000 cars that year with a substantial proportion being the small Falcons, of which Ford had sold almost 1,500,000 between 1960 and 1963. The Falcon gradually grew bigger and was 184 in (4,680 mm) in 1969, when Ford introduced a new "small" Ford that was "only" 179 in (4,560 mm) long. This was the Maverick which was termed a "sub-compact" in the USA.

The Maverick was powered by 2.8 and 3.3-litre six-cylinder engines so that it was not in reality a small car. When the demand for a

The Ford Fairlane Crown Victoria hardtop coupé of 1956 had a brought chrome strip across the roof which was a continuation of the door-post.

The Victoria Hardtop version of the Ford Crestline was Ford's most expensive car in 1952.

Ford's cars in 1946–1948 were still the 1942 model, although the Super Deluxe Convertible Sports Coupé illustrated was an entirely new one.

genuine small car increased, Ford introduced the Pinto in late 1970. This was finally a car of European proportions: the wheelbase was 94 in (2,390 mm), length was 163 in (4,140 mm), width was 69 in (1,760 mm) and height 50 in (1,270 mm). For comparison the relevant dimension for a VW Beetle are 94 in (2,400 mm), 158 in (4,030 mm), 61 in (1,550 mm), and 59 in (1,500 mm). The rear wheels were driven by a 1,599 or 1,998 cc engine for power of 55 or 87 bhp. Since the car weighed less than 2,200 lb (1,000 kg) its top speed was from 87 mph-100 mph (140-160 kph). But unfortunately the Pinto too was not allowed to remain small and in 1975 its four cylinder engine was increased to 2,301 cc and a six-cylinder 2,793 cc motor added to the options. The car had also grown by 6 in 150 mm.

Ford dealers had a broad range in 1975 consisting of: Pinto, Mustang, Maverick, Granada, Torino, Elite, LTD, Thunderbird, and Station Wagon(estate).

Ford USA sports cars

COUNTRY OF ORIGIN: USA

Ford Deluxe

MODEL YEAR: 1946

NUMBER MADE: 94,870

SPECIAL REMARKS: Customers could choose in 1946 between the Deluxe and Super Deluxe. This model was offered with a straight six-cylinder engine or a V-8. The more expensive version had chromium-plated window frames and two sun visors.

Ford Custom Deluxe

MODEL YEAR: 1950

NUMBER MADE: 818,371

SPECIAL REMARKS: There were 50,299 sold of the six-seater convertible version of the Custom Deluxe. Only second and third gears of the three-speed gearbox had synchromesh.

Ford Fairlane Skyliner

MODEL YEAR: 1957

NUMBER MADE: 20,766

The Ford Fairlane Skyliner Retractable was built between 1957-1959.

This is how the steel roof of the Retractable was stowed in the trunk or boot. This is a 1958 example.

The Ford Galaxy was introduced in 1959. Its body originated from the Fairlane 500, except the roof, from a Thunderbird.

A 1957 Fairlane 500 Club Victoria Hardtop Coupé.

Although the Falcon was not that good looking it sold well. It was the first US car in 1960 with a wholly monocoque body.

SPECIAL REMARKS: The roof could be stowed in the boot (or trunk) by automatic operation with the Skyliner. This took 40 seconds with the aid of seven electric motors, eighteen relays, thirteen switches, and 600 ft (183 m) of cable.

Ford Fairlane 500

MODEL YEAR: 1957

NUMBER MADE: 637,161

SPECIAL REMARKS: Only the Station Wagons were more expensive in 1957 than the Fairlane 500. The car cost about three times as much as a VW Beetle in Europe.

Ford Galaxy

MODEL YEAR: 1959

NUMBER MADE: 464,336

SPECIAL REMARKS: Ford introduced the

Galaxy in 1959 as their top of the range car. Customers could choose from a 3,655 cc/147 bhp six-cylinder engine or from three V-8 power units of 185, 235, or 300 bhp.

Ford Falcon

MODEL YEAR: 1960

NUMBER MADE: 435,676

SPECIAL REMARKS: When introduced in 1960, the Falcon was a "mere" 181 in (4,600 mm), making it 29$\frac{1}{2}$ in (750 mm) shorter than most US cars. Beneath the bonnet or hood was either a 2,365 cc/91 bhp or 2,781 cc/102 bhp engine.

Ford Galaxy Sunliner

MODEL YEAR: 1962

NUMBER MADE: 55,829

SPECIAL REMARKS: The Galaxy Sunliner was

The powerful engine of the 1962 Galaxy Sunliner took it to a top speed of more than 125 mph (200 kph).

A mere 11,832 Galaxy 500 convertibles were sold in 1968 compared with 117,877 sedans.

Ford's only convertible in 1962. It had a 6,638 cc V-8 engine of either 390 or 411 bhp at 5,800 rpm.

Ford Galaxy 500

MODEL YEAR: 1968

NUMBER MADE: 339,262

SPECIAL REMARKS: The Galaxy customer of 1968 could choose from a 3,929 cc/152 bhp six-cylinder engine or from five V-8 units of 4.9-7 litres.

Ford Maverick

MODEL YEAR: 1969

NUMBER MADE: 127,833

SPECIAL REMARKS: The Maverick appeared in the middle of 1969 so that only a relatively small number were sold that year. It was based on the Falcon running gear and was

The Ford Maverick appeared in June 1969 to take on Volkswagen.

Ford sold 291,675 Mavericks in 1973. The best-seller was the two-door sedan with a total of 148,943. The Grabber model shown was aimed at enthusiasts and sold 32,350.

only available as a two-door sedan with six-cylinder engine.

Ford Pinto

The small Pinto was intended to stem the European and Japanese invasion of imported cars. The motor was developed in Britain for the Ford Cortina.

The carburettors of the first Pintos sometimes burst into flames when the car was started after standing in the sun. The first 220,000 Pintos had to be recalled in March 1971 for remedial action.

MODEL YEAR: 1971

NUMBER MADE: 352,402

SPECIAL REMARKS: The Ford Pinto was introduced in 1971. The car was the size of al European car and had a choice of two four-cylinder engines under the bonnet. These were 1.6 litres/54 bhp and 2 litres/86 bhp. The bigger engine had an overhead camshaft and twin carburettor.

Fuldamobil

The Carnival procession wend its way in March 1950 through the German town of Fulda and there was much laughter as usual. There was no laughter though when Norbert Stevenson drove by in his new three-wheeler car for this was a serious matter. Many of the onlookers wanted a car. The prototype was the first of 1,500 cars of the type that were built. It had a strong tubular chassis and was powered by a 198 cc single-cylinder motor-cycle engine which drove the rear wheels.

The car weighed a mere 310 kg (682 lb) and had a top speed of 40 mph (65 kph). There was a huge demand at that time in Germany for such cars but production did not get under way until February 1951. The production model had a 247 cc two-stroke engine developed for use in chain saws. The engine produced 8.5 bhp at 4,200 rpm.

To save weight and costs, the body was made of plywood covered with leather. Since no-one was entirely happy with the Fuldamobil N-1, Stevenson designed a new N-2 model in the summer of 1951 which had a body of beaten aluminium, for which paint was unnecessary. The N-2's single-cylinder 359 cc engine was by Fichtel & Sachs and it produced 9.5 bhp. The N-2 was supplied until 1952. Fuldamobil only sold 380 which seems rather few compared to the 700 sold by NWF (Nordwestdeutscher Fahrzeugbau) who built the N-2 under licence.

A four-seater S-2 was introduced in 1954 and the S-7 first appeared at the Paris motor show in 1957. The S-7 had a polyester body shell, more elegant lines, and twin wheels, close together, at the back. This enabled the car to be treated as a three-wheeler by the German law so that it could be driven by someone with a motorcycle licence. In Britain, the S-7 was sold as a kit car under the name Nobel 200 and the model was also built in Greece, India, and Chile under licence.

Once the economic miracle of post-war Germany worked its way through to the common man, interest in the Fuldamobil declined rapidly.

Fuldamobil cars

COUNTRY OF ORIGIN: Germany

A single-cylinder two-stroke engine was rear mounted in the cars, such as this N-2.

The Fuldamobil got an aluminium body in 1952, which did not need painting.

Fuldamobil N-2

MODEL YEAR: 1952-1955

NUMBER MADE: 380

SPECIAL REMARKS: The first N-1 Fuldamobils had plywood bodies covered with leather. From the N-2 on, the bodies were aluminium.

Fuldamobil S-7

MODEL YEAR: 1957-1965

NUMBER MADE: 440

SPECIAL REMARKS: The S-7 was the best-selling Fuldamobil. Its 191 cc engine was tuned up to give 10 bhp at 5,250 rpm. The S-7 did 64 mpg (4.7 litres per 100 km and had a top speed of 50 mph (80 kph).

The Fuldamobil S-7 was sold in Britain by York Nobel under his own name. His Nobel 200 was available as a kit car.

Nobel 200

MODEL YEAR: 1958-1961

NUMBER MADE: 260

SPECIAL REMARKS: The British version of the Fuldamobil had a polyester body shell. It was built in Britain for York Nobel by Lea Francis.

Ghia

Ghia is better known for car bodies than its cars. The company was founded in Turin by Giacinto Ghia in 1915. Ghia built special bodies on the chassis and running gear of Fiat, Lancia, and Alfa-Romeo. The company gained world fame after World War II by creating the "dream" concept cars for Chrysler but the Italian company wanted higher things by building cars bearing the Ghia name. This resulted in the Ghia L.6.4 in 1960. This five-seater coupé was mainly built using Chrysler parts, including the running gear and all mechanical parts. The car had a 6.4-litre V-8 engine that produced 340 bhp at 4,600 rpm. The Ghia L.6.4 therefore seemed ideally suited for the US market but only a few examples were sold, despite Frank Sinatra being one of their first customers. Ghia were more successful with their 1500 GT, which was a 2+2 coupé based on the Fiat 1500. This car was comparable with the Karmann Ghia of Volkswagen: it looked fast and sporting but in reality was not. The 1500 GT had a monocoque body.

Ghia cars

COUNTRY OF ORIGIN: Italy

Ghia L.6.4

MODEL YEAR: 1960-1962

NUMBER MADE: 26

SPECIAL REMARKS: This car was 5,330 mm (210 in) long and weighed 1,800 kg (3,960 lb). The American customers included Frank Sinatra and Dean Martin.

Ghia 1500 GT

MODEL YEAR: 1962-1967

NUMBER MADE: Approx. 920

SPECIAL REMARKS: The Ghia 1500 GT was a fairly small car at 4,170 mm (164 in). 1500 chassis with the wheelbase reduced from 99 in (242 cm) to 92½ in (235 cm). The converted 1,481 cc Fiat four cylinder engine provided 84 bhp at 5,200 rpm.

The Ghia 1500 GT was intended for the European market. This example is seen cornering at Zandvoort circuit.

Glas

Hans Glas was a manufacturer of agricultural machinery. In 1951 he started to make scooters together with his son Andreas and Karl Dompert, who was an out-of-work aeronautical engineer. In the early years, business was very good but as more Germans switched over from two wheels to small cars, Glas decided in 1955 to switch to making small cars. The famous Goggomobil's name was derived from his grandson's nickname of Goggo.

Help in designing the 2+2 car with a twin-cylinder two-stroke engine sited behind the rear seat came from Schorsch Meier, a famous pre- and post-war driver, who was an acquaintance of Glas. The first Goggomobil was introduced in the spring of 1955. The initial 5,000 Goggomobils were more rudimentary in their construction than subsequent cars. Because the company did not have the money at first for the necessary presses, the early wings were screwed on to the body. Subsequently they were formed as one unit with the body. The small car was a staggering success and ten months after the launch the ten thousandth car was delivered. The first cars were of the T 250 type. This four-seater was powered by a 247 cc twin-cylinder engine mounted in the rear that produced 13.5 bhp at 5,400 rpm. For those who wanted more power, the T 300 was developed with a 296 cc engine for 15 bhp. The T 400 was introduced in 1957 with a 395 cc engine for 20 bhp at 5,000 rpm.

The cars were promoted as four-seaters and it was conceivable for two small passengers to be transported for short distances in the back. The space was adequate of course for two children and this was one of the Goggomobils strong selling points. Few other makers of comparable cars dared advertise them as four seaters.
There was also a sports coupé Goggomobil but the space in the rear was only suitable for

After BMW took over Hans Glas GmbH the final GT models were renamed as BMW 1300 and 1700 GT.

really small children. This sports 2+2 was an attractive looking car but since the engine was the same as the saloon models, performance was nothing special. The TS 250 could just about struggle to reach 52.5 mph (84 kph) with a following wind, the TS 300's limit was 56 mph (90 kph) but the factory claimed the TS 400 could break the magical 100 kph barrier (62.5 mph).

History shows that small cars have a tendency to get bigger. Not only do engines get bigger and more powerful, the dimensions expand too. It is not surprising then that Hans Glas introduced a larger Goggomobil T 600 at the Frankfurt motor show in 1957. The newcomer had a wheelbase 200 mm (8 in) longer than its predecessors at 2,000 mm (78^3/$_4$ in). The overall length at 3,430 mm (135 in) was 530 mm (21 in) longer than the previous model. There was still a two-stroke engine sputtering away at the back but this was now 586 cc, delivering 20 bhp at 4,900 rpm. Once more there was also a more powerful version available, the T 700, with a 688 cc engine of 30 bhp that was capable of 68.75 mph (110 kph). There were estate versions available of both these models which were denoted by K (Kombi) as K 600 and K 700.
The cars sold well in neighbouring countries such as The Netherlands, even though prices did not compare favourably with a VW Beetle or Renault 4CV.

In 1959, Glas introduced his "big" Goggomobils under the names of Glas-Isar 600 and 700. It seems as though Glas was still not content with his Glas-Isars and wanted to scale greater heights. Consequently, he introduced the Glas 1004 in 1961 at Frankfurt. The Glas 1004 was a medium-sized car with a four-stroke engine and not just any four-stroke: for the first time ever, the engine had an overhead camshaft driven by a toothed belt. The engine's capacity was 992 cc but power was initially 42 and later 64 bhp. The maximum torque was 7m/kg (10.44 ft-lb) at 2,500 rpm, which caused driver's to have to change gear a lot. When many customers found this a disadvantage, Glas introduced the 1204 in 1963, powered by a 1,189 cc engine of 53 bhp and maximum torque of 9.15 mkg (13.64 ft-lb) at 2,000 rpm. The Glas 1204 and 1004 had identical bodies. The subsequent Glas 1304 series had 1,290 cc engines delivering 60-85 bhp. The most powerful engine was incorporated in the Glas 1300 GT. The body of this attractive sports cars was designed by Pietro Frua in Italy.

Glas built his first and last true sports car in 1965. It was the 1700 GT with a 1,682 cc engine of 105 bhp.
This engine was also available in 1964 in a saloon. Glas intended to take on the likes of BMW and Mercedes. For these markets he got Frua to design a Glas car for a V-8 engine. This engine was created by joining cylinder blocks from two 1,300 cc engines. The 2,580 cc engine produced 150 bhp, which was sufficient for 125 mph (200 kph).

The Glas company was always successful with small cars and hundreds of thousands of them were sold but when Glas's ambitions took him into new territory business went downhill. In 1966 Hans Glas was forced to sell his company to BMW for 10,000,000 Deutschmarks. BMW continued to make the 1700 GT and the V-8 until 1968 except with BMW engines. Hans Glas died aged 79 on 14 December 1969.

Glas cars

COUNTRY OF ORIGIN: Germany

Goggomobil 250

MODEL YEAR: 1954-1969

NUMBER MADE: 214,198

The Goggomobil was one of the few baby cars that was mass produced.

The Goggomobil Coupé looked very sporting but the grille was mere decoration for the engine was rear mounted.

SPECIAL REMARKS: The two-stroke engine of the Goggomobil ran on a mixture of 25 to 1 and emitted stinking blue smoke from the exhaust.

Glas Isar 600/700

MODEL YEAR: 1958-1965

NUMBER MADE: 87,585

SPECIAL REMARKS: The Isar had an entirely new opposed twin-cylinder engine of 584 or 688 cc to give 20 or 30 bhp at 4,900 rpm. The engines were powerful enough for speeds in excess of 62 mph (100 kph).

Glas 1004

MODEL YEAR: 1961-1967

NUMBER MADE: 9,346

SPECIAL REMARKS: Glas attempted to enter the market for medium-sized cars with the 1004. The 1004 was also available as the 1004 TS with a 64 bhp engine instead of the standard 42.

The Glas 1204 was a 1004 with a bigger 1.2-litre engine and improved torque which reduced excessive gear-changing.

The Glas 1700 was introduced in the autumn of 1964 with mechanical parts from the 1700 GT and a body designed by the Italian firm of Frua.

Glas 1300 GT/1700GT

MODEL YEAR: 1964-1967

NUMBER MADE: 3,760 and 1,802

SPECIAL REMARKS: The Glas 1300 GT was available as a coupé or convertible. The 1.3 litre engine delivered 85 bhp but more power was provided for those who wanted it with the 1.7 litre 105 bhp engine of the 1700 GT (available from 1965-1967). Only 364 GT models were sold as convertibles.

Glas V-8

MODEL YEAR: 1966-1968

NUMBER MADE: 371

SPECIAL REMARKS: Of the 371 V-8 cars built, 71 were supplied as a BMW 3000. These cars had a 3-litre BMW V-8 engine which produced 10 bhp more at 160 bhp than the Glas engine.

Pietro Frua designed the Glas V-8 which became the BMW 3000. The car had room for 5 persons.

Healey

The name Healey is automatically associated with the Austin-Healey but enthusiasts may also recall the Jensen-Healey and true experts may consider the only true Healey were those Donald Healey built in the immediate post World War II years. Donald Healey was born in 1898 in Cornwall and later worked for the Sopwith Aviation Company until he became a pilot in World War I. Following a crash in 1917 Healey's war ended and he started a small garage, went racing, and won many rallies such as the Monte Carlo. In 1934 he was engineering director at Triumph and he worked for Humber during the war on the development of tanks. He established his own Donald Healey Motor Company in March 1945 with the intention of specialis-

The doors opened "the wrong way" but this made it easier to get in and out.

Donald Healey (1898-1988)

ing in sporting cars. The first car left the factory in 1946. Initially these were a coupé and convertible known as the Healey Elliot and Healey Westland. Both models had a Riley 2.4-litre six-cylinder engine. The body was largely formed of timber struts covered with aluminium sheet. The Elliot was the fastest British car of its age and the Westland was capable of 106 mph (170 kph). A number of

The Silverstone was a great success. Between September 1949 and March 1950, 105 of these were sold.

other models followed, such as the Duncan, Sportsmobile, and Tickford, which was introduced in January 1950. This final coupé sold 224 units. The open version of this was known as the Abbott and 77 of these were built. These were the final road cars from the Donald Healey Motor Company. Subsequent cars such as the Healey Silverstone, Nash-Healey, and of course the Austin-Healey were outright sports cars or motor sport cars.

Healey developed the Riley engine to produce 105 bhp. The six-cylinder had two high-positioned (but not overhead) camshafts.

Healey cars

COUNTRY OF ORIGIN: United Kingdom

Healey Elliot

MODEL YEAR: 1946-1950

NUMBER MADE: 101

SPECIAL REMARKS: The side windows were made of Perspex to reduce weight and the body was made of aluminium because steel sheet was still unavailable.

Healey Westland

Most Healeys were exported, often as a rolling chassis. The car illustrated was given its body in 1949 by the Swiss builder, Beutler.

MODEL YEAR: 1946-1949

NUMBER MADE: 64

SPECIAL REMARKS: The Westland was technically identical to the Elliot with its independently-suspended front wheels and 105 bhp Riley engine.

Healey Tickford

MODEL YEAR: 1950-1954

NUMBER MADE: 224

SPECIAL REMARKS: The open version of the Tickford was known as Abbott Drophead Coupé (of which 77 were built). The cars derived their names from the body company that built them. Both were powered by a Riley 2.4-litre engine.

Heinkel

Ernst Heinkel, in common with Willi Messerschmitt, was a famous German aircraft constructor. Before and during World War II he was responsible for producing 10,000 bombers, fighters, and the Volksjäger jet fighter for the young men of Germany to take on the Allies.

After the war, Heinkel switched to making scooters and soon managed to sell more than 100,000 of them. The Heinkel company built its first car in 1956, which closely resembled the Isetta of BMW but they were powered by a single-cylinder engine that Heinkel had developed for their scooters. With the cars weighing only 245 kg (539 lb) these cars could reach 53 mph (85 kph). There were two models: the Kabine 175 and 200, with the figures related to the engine capacity. These four-stroke engines produced 9.3 and 10 bhp at 5,500 rpm but were extremely noisy at full throttle. The gearbox had four forward speeds plus reverse and there was independent suspension at the front with rubber rings and at the rear with coil springs. The brakes were hydraulic but only operated on the front wheels, while the hand brake operated all wheels. If the car had four wheels, the rear wheels were as close together as possible so that they could be counted as one by the law.

In contrast with the BMW Isetta which had a hinged steering column, the Heinkel's was fixed, which made getting in and out more difficult. BMW had patented its system and was not prepared to allow Heinkel to profit from it.

There was room in the back for two small children but they had to climb over the back of the front seats. This acrobatic manoeuvre was also necessary to check the oil level of the engine via a gap in the rear window sill. If the car had four wheels, no spare wheel was provided, since the fourth wheel could be used as a spare for any of the other three as the car could be driven on three wheels.

The demand for midget cars in Germany fell off in 1958 but Heinkel was unable to invest in creating bigger cars. He was also too old and too ill to do develop his business. He died on 30 January 1958, aged 71. His death brought an end to the German bubble cars but Trojan in Britain purchased the rights and introduced the Trojan 200 three-wheeler in 1966.

Heinkel cars

COUNTRY OF ORIGIN: Germany

Heinkel Kabinen-Roller

MODEL YEAR: 1956-1958

NUMBER MADE: Approx. 12,000

SPECIAL REMARKS: Professor Ernst Heinkel was the spiritual father of the scooter. He was less successful with the Kabinen-Roller bubble car which was powered by a scooter motor.

The Heinkel had a fixed steering column. With the BMW Isetta the column moved aside to make it easier to enter.

The Heinkel was a true midget car: its wheelbase was 1,760 mm (69 in) and overall it was 2,550 mm (100 in).

The shape of the Heinkel was similar to the BMW Isetta. It too only had one door.

Hillman

The Hillman name disappeared in 1976 which was a pity considering that the company had built relatively inexpensive cars of good quality since 1907. Racing driver William Hillman built his first racing car together with Louis Coatalen, who was already a recognised constructor. When Coatalen departed for Sunbeam, Hillman concentrated on larger saloon cars but the company made too little from them so that Hillman had to add smaller models to his range. But these were not too successful either and in 1928 the Rootes brothers, William and Reginald bought the business. Several years later, they introduced the famous Hillman Minx. This instantly made Hillman world famous. A modernised version of the Minx was put on the market in 1945 with a new front end. Beneath the bonnet was a 1,184 cc side-valve engine that delivered 36 bhp at 4,100 rpm. This car still had rigid axles front and back but the body was virtually of unitary construction, which helped with the weight of the car.

The 1948 Minx had headlamps incorporated in the wings, a gearbox with column change, and hydraulic brakes. The gearbox was fairly modern with syncromesh on all but first gear. The Minx had a new body in 1949 that was quite different from its predecessor. The model was regularly improved. New versions were added, such as the California hardtop coupé in 1953 that was developed for the US market and the Husky estate which had a shorter 85 in (2,160 mm) wheelbase than the 93 in (2,360 mm) of the Minx. The engine was also pepped up to 35 bhp. The Hillman

Minx finally got an overhead valve engine in 1954. The Minx Mk VIII had a 1,390 cc engine of 43 bhp at 4,400 rpm.

The first cars with an entirely monocoque body left the factory in May 1956. This new Minx was instantly recognisable by its panoramic rear window. The car had also grown in size with a wheelbase of 96 in (2,440 mm). Most of the extra $3^1/_4$ in (80 mm) was for the benefit of rear seat passengers. There were also mechanical improvements to the car. The new Minx had the front wheel suspension from the Sunbeam Rapier.

Automatic gearboxes were generally put in bigger cars but from 1960 it was possible to order a Hillman Minx with one, which was reason enough for many to switch to a Minx. The London motor show in October 1961 had an entirely new Hillman Super Minx which was longer, wider, and lower than its forerunners.

The headlamps were now in the grille, giving the car an identity of its own. There was a 1.6-litre four-cylinder engine of 67 bhp (SAE) under the bonnet. About six months later the Super Minx Estate was introduced with a fifth door at the rear which opened in two halves: the top opening upwards and the bottom section dropped down.

Meanwhile Austin and Morris had become famous for their Mini. Rootes wanted to share in this success and built a new factory at Linwood in Scotland to produce a new small car. The first example left the line in 1963 bearing the name Imp. With its overall length of 139 in (3,530 mm) the car was considerably shorter than its stable-mates. The motor was of considerable interest. In contrast to the Mini, the Imp's engine was rear mounted, driving the rear wheels. The engine was specially developed for Hillman

The first overhead valve engine appeared in a Hillman Minx in 1954. The 1,390 cc motor gave 43 bhp.

by Coventry Climax. The 875 cc four-cylinder had an overhead camshaft and delivered 47 bhp (SAE). Its compression ratio of 10:1 was unusually high but the engine was capable of being tweaked for higher performance. The aluminium gearbox was fully-synchronised with a floor-located gear-lever.

The larger Minx was not forgotten of course. It had another new body in 1963 to become the Minx Series V. The Super Minx was added in 1964 with an entirely new body. Rootes sold the business to Chrysler in 1964 and at first this had no adverse effect on Hillman. On the contrary, the car was further improved and additional models were introduced.

The Super Minx GT followed in 1965 with a 1,725 cc engine which was also added to other cars within a few months. Yet another new Minx appeared in 1967 with a 1.5-litre engine. The little Imp could also be ordered as an estate from 1968 and a Minx Deluxe appeared with the 1.7-litre engine, plus a new GT with 79 bhp from this four-cylinder motor. The final two models were the Hillman Hunter and the Avenger but these were in reality Sunbeams. Only the grille was different.

The Hillman name was dropped in 1977 on the seventieth anniversary of the marque's foundation.

Hillman cars

Country of origin:
United Kingdom

Hillman Minx

Model year: 1945-1947

Number made: Unknown

The 1955 Minx was the first with an overhead valve engine.

The 1958 Minx had a new body which remained in production until 1963. This is a 1961 Minx with fashionable small fins on the rear wings.

Special remarks: The first post-war Minx closely resembled the pre-war model. The headlamps were still mounted on the mudguards but a sunroof was standard.

Hillman Super Minx

Model year: 1961-1966

A Hillman Super Minx with the headlights in the grille and side-lights and indicators above.

Unlike many other British makers, Hillman usually had a convertible in its range.

NUMBER MADE: Approx. 135,000

SPECIAL REMARKS: The first Super Minx had a 1,592 cc engine of 67 bhp at 4,800 rpm. This was uprated in 1965 to 84 bhp. In the final year of production, this model was given a 1,725 cc engine of 91 bhp.

Hillman Imp

MODEL YEAR: 1963-1976

NUMBER MADE: 440,032

SPECIAL REMARKS: The Imp's engine was up-to-date in every respect. It had an overhead camshaft and aluminium cylinder head. The engine block and gearbox housing were also of aluminium.

The Imp was available as a saloon, California coupé, and Husky estate.

Hillman Hunter

MODEL YEAR: 1970-1977

NUMBER MADE: Unknown

SPECIAL REMARKS: The Hillman Hunter was intended for the UK market while Sunbeam Hunters were exported. The car was powered by a 1,725 cc engine of 88 bhp at 5,200 rpm.

Hillman Avenger

MODEL YEAR: 1970-1981

NUMBER MADE: Unknown

SPECIAL REMARKS: This car was also intended for the UK market. After the Hillman marque disappeared, the car was first sold as a Chrysler and then as a Talbot. The Chrysler had a 1,248 cc engine but the Talbot's was 1,498 cc.

Holden

The Holden company began building bodies for Morris cars in the 1920s but was taken over by General Motors before World War II. From then on, Holden built General Motors models under licence.

The first Holdens were produced in 1948 and ten years later in 1958, more than 100,000 cars per year were being sold. Although the models were designed in USA or Britain, they had their own specific national characteristics.

Holden cars

COUNTRY OF ORIGIN: Australia

Holden 48/215

MODEL YEAR: 1948-1953

NUMBER MADE: 120,402

SPECIAL REMARKS: This car was designed before World War II but did not leave the factory until 1948. The six-cylinder overhead valve engine was 2,170 cc, producing 61 bhp at 3,800 rpm.

The Holden 48/215 was the first truly Australian car. It had a monocoque body, space for five people and a top speed of 75 mph (120 kph).

Although the Holden FJ resembled the 1948 Buick, it was sold as an Australian design.

Holden FJ

MODEL YEAR: 1953-1956

NUMBER MADE: 169,969

The coupé version of the Holden Torana closely resembles the Opel Manta.

SPECIAL REMARKS: The 2.1-litre six-cylinder engine in the FJ produced 65 bhp and had a top speed of 75 mph (120 kph). The FJ was 175 in (4,440 mm) long with a 103 in (2,620 mm) wheelbase.

Holden Torana

MODEL YEAR: 1967-1976

NUMBER MADE: Unknown

SPECIAL REMARKS: The Torana was available with three different engines: a 1,159 cc four-

It was also possible to get a 5-litre V-8 engine for the Torana that produced more than 200 bhp.

The Torana coupé could also be easily converted to form a camper. The necessary equipment was available from Holden.

cylinder, 2,261 cc six-cylinder and 1.2-litre engine tuned by Jack Brabham to produce 80 bhp at 5,600 rpm.

Honda

Soichiro Honda was born in Japan in 1906. He founded the Honda Motor Company in September 1948 and the company delivered its first motorcycle in August 1949. This 98 cc single-cylinder two-stroke motor was the basis on which the Honda empire was founded.

Honda became motorcycle world champions and grew to become the world's biggest manufacturer of motorcycles in the 1950s. The company wanted other things though and the first Honda cars appeared in 1962. These first models were midget cars. To take advantage of the Japanese tax categories, the engine was a mere 360 cc divided between four cylinders of 90 cc each. This engine had four carburettors and twin overhead camshafts. The compression ratio of 9.5:1 and a crankshaft that turned at 9,000 rpm produced 33 bhp from this tiny engine.

A bigger engine soon followed of 492 cc that produced 40 bhp at 8,000 rpm. This was mainly used in sports cars. All four wheels of the cars had independent suspension and customers could choose between four-speed and five-speed gearboxes.

In order to improve his cars, Honda decided to get involved in Formula One racing and built a car with a superb engine. This V-12 engine with four valves per cylinder was located transversely in front of the rear axle. The Honda Formula One car made its first circuit appearance in 1964 and Richie Ginther won the Mexican Grand Prix in 1965 in the car.

The Honda S600 and S800 sports cars suited smaller persons who wanted a nippy car and these were followed by the N360 and N600 which had enough space for small people. The N360 with its 354 cc engine was intended for the Japanese market while the N600

The 81 mph (130 kph) N600 was 100 mm (4 in) longer than the N360 but both cars had the same wheelbase of 2,000 mm (78³/₄ in).

was intended to conquer the world. This did not happen because the car was really too advanced. It had a twin-cylinder air-cooled engine that gave 42 bhp at 6,600 rpm. The 3,100 mm (122 in) long car could reach the frighteningly quick speed of 81 mph (130 kph) and was also available with an automatic gearbox.

The first true Honda was introduced at the Tokyo motor show in late 1968. Although the car was a prototype, it was clear Honda intended to move into the medium-sized car market. The Honda 1300 looked a totally conventional car but had an interesting engine that drove the front wheels. This motor was air-cooled and had an overhead camshaft and a compression ration of 9:1. The cylinder capacity was 1,298 cc and power was at least 100 bhp at 7,200 rpm. There was also a sporting version of this engine with four carburettors and power of 110 bhp at 7,500 rpm.

These new cars were initially only sold in Japan with exports not yet under way. This soon changed. An example of this is the

The Honda Z 2+2 was a dangerously fast car which needed its front wheel disc brakes.

Honda Civic which first appeared in July 1962 and was a huge success throughout the world.

Honda cars

COUNTRY OF ORIGIN: Japan

Honda N360

MODEL YEAR: 1967-1975

NUMBER MADE: Unknown

The first Honda cars, such as the N360, were built for the smaller Japanese drivers and were too small for most western people.

SPECIAL REMARKS: The final N360 was built in 1971 and then became the Honda N III and subsequently Honda Z. The N360 was available with Hondamatic automatic transmission from its very first year.

Honda N1300

MODEL YEAR: 1968-1972

NUMBER MADE: Unknown

SPECIAL REMARKS: Honda won a place for itself in the medium-sized car market with the N1300. The air-cooled engine drove the front wheels. The unitary body was 3,890 mm (153 in) long.

The indestructible Civic appeared first in 1972. It was an export hit and is still made in a different form.

Honda Civic

MODEL YEAR: 1972-present day

NUMBER MADE: Unknown

SPECIAL REMARKS: The Honda Civic replaced the N1300. It was 480 mm (19 in) shorter than its predecessor and the 1,169 cc engine "only" produced 60 bhp (SAE) at 5,500 rpm.

Hotchkiss

The American Benjamin Berkely Hotchkis established a workshop in the French town of St Denis in 1867 where he built guns. When the demand for weapons was reduced in 1903, he decided to build vehicles. Hotchkiss specialised in big and heavy cars with engines that could be and were used in trucks. Production never ran at high volume. In 1939, a mere 2,751 cars were built.

After World War II Hotchkiss struggled to get going again. There was little demand for big vehicles and in 1946 the factory sold 117 of the pre-war 686 model. These had a 3,485 cc six-cylinder engine with overhead valves that produced 100 bhp at 4,000 rpm. The 686 Grand Sport which appeared in 1947 even had 125 bhp at its disposal. Cars of this type won their first two Monte Carlo rallies in 1949 and 1950. Most Hotchkiss cars were equipped with a Cotal electro-magnetic automatic gearbox but a four-speed manual box could be fitted on request. A smaller car, the 864 S 49 was added in 1949 with a 2,312 cc four-cylinder engine. It was the first Hotchkiss to have independent front suspension.

Immediately before the war Hotchkiss became the owner of the factory of Joseph Lamy and Emil Akar in St Denis where small sports cars had been built since 1921. When the business got into financial difficulties in 1939, Hotchkiss took the firm over. Nothing was done with the business during the war but afterwards the famous French constructor and proponent of front-wheel drive J.A. Grégroire convinced Hotchkiss to build a new car he had designed. The resulting Hotchkiss-Grégroire was revealed to the world at the Paris motor show in 1950. Beneath its aluminium streamlined body it had a great deal of innovation, such as independent suspension of all four wheels, adjustable shockbreakers, front-wheel drive, and a water-cooled four-cylinder boxer engine with an aluminium cylinder head. The engine was located immediately before the front axle and it was initially 1,998 and later 2,188 cc for 60 and then 70 bhp at 4,000 rpm. Through the wide use of aluminium, the car was economical with the expensive French petrol. It was fast enough at 94 mph (150 kph) to be a perfect touring car but the public judged otherwise. Only 250 of them were ever sold.

Unfortunately things were little better with the more conventional models. In addition to the Grégroire, another new model, the Anjou, was shown at Paris that year.

The headlights were now within the wings and the car was available with either a four-cylinder or six-cylinder engine. These were a 2,312 cc 74 bhp motor and a 3,485 cc 100 bhp power unit.

These were also fine cars with just one problem: they did not sell. Delahaye and Delage who also made pres-tige cars were confronted with the same problem. The three companies decided to work together in making trucks and military vehicles.

Hotchkiss cars

COUNTRY OF ORIGIN: France

Hotchkiss 686

MODEL YEAR: 1946-1950

NUMBER MADE: Unknown

SPECIAL REMARKS: The first examples closely resembled the cars of 1939. The body was modernised in 1949 to create the 686 S 49 with a six-cylinder engine and the 486 S 49 with a 2,312 motor.

The Hotchkiss convertibles were from the hand of Henri Chapron. This is a 1952 Anjou.

The 686 was the first post-war Hotchkiss. Its externally-mounted headlights made it look pre-war.

The Hotchkiss-Grégroire was a superb car but unfortunately it did not sell.

A 1950 Anjou with the headlights now incorporated in the wings. Note the gun motif on the radiator grille.

Hotchkiss-Grégroire

MODEL YEAR: 1950-1954

NUMBER MADE: 250

SPECIAL REMARKS: The Hotchkiss-Grégroire was a superb car from a technical point of view. Much of the chassis was moulded from aluminium. The car had a 2,500 mm (98 in) wheelbase and was 4,500 mm (177 in) long.

The shape of the Hotchkiss-Grégroire was designed by J.A. Grégoire. It had some of the appearance of the post-war American bodies.

Hotchkiss Anjou

MODEL YEAR: 1950-1954

NUMBER MADE: 3,687

SPECIAL REMARKS: This car was also available with either a four or six-cylinder engine. Most of the cars were equipped with a Cotal automatic gearbox while the first and second gears of the manual box did not have synchromesh.

Hudson

The history of Hudson goes back to 1909 when Roy D. Chapin (1880-1936) built his first car which he named after his financier Joseph L. Hudson. The Hudson Motor Car Company was an immediate success and sold 4,000 cars in its first year. Hudson always had a modest level of output in comparison to the "big three". In 1941 that was 80,000. A new model for 1942 was introduced in August 1941 with a new body and significant technical improvements. These included a "Drive-Master" pre-selector semi-automatic gear box. Only 46,661 of the 1942 model were sold because the factory had to switch on 5 February 1942 to war production. Three-and-a-half years later on 1 October 1945 new Hudson cars were once more with the dealers. Hudson had stolen a March of a couple of months on its rivals.

The 1946 models were known as the Super and Commodore. These were available with either six or eight-cylinders in-line side-valve engines of 3,472 and 4,165 cc and power of 102 or 128 bhp. The cars were still built on heavy chassis but had independent front suspension and hydraulic brakes. The braking system was termed "Duo-Automatic" because if the hydraulic system failed they could also be operated mechanically. Only second and third gear were synchronised in the three-speed gearbox. The gear-change lever was mounted on the steering column. The clutch was faced with cork and had an oil bath in the same manner as the 1911 Hudson!

The designers at Hudson also worked on providing a new model of course and this was introduced in November 1947 after an investment of $16,000,000. The low roof line of the monocoque body was quite striking. Until now it had been the norm to fit the body on to the chassis but Hudson's designers had incorporated the load-bearing elements into the design of the body. This resulted in a car just $62^1/_4$ in (1,580 mm) high which was very low when compared with Ford, Chevrolet, and Chrysler which were 71 in (1,800 mm), 67 in (1,700 mm), and $67^1/_4$ in (1,710 mm) respectively. The Hudson was popular with the public and 118,621 of them were sold in the 1948 model year and the following year 142,454 were built for a record net profit of $13,225,923, which was never surpassed by Hudson.

Hudson introduced a new model, the Hornet, in 1951. This was in reality a Commodore with a more highly tuned engine but not all body styles were available. Customers could only choose from a Sedan, Club Sedan, or a Convertible. The car was also only available with a 4,930 cc engine outputting power of 146 bhp at 3,800 rpm. This was the American car industry's biggest six-cylinder engine and the final motor with side-valves, In addition to 161,000 cars, Hudson also made parts for B47 bombers for the Korean war. Hudson had earned good money fulfilling government orders during World War II but at the end of the 1951 financial year they were shown to have made a loss of more than

$1,000,000. Something had to change and it was decided to give the 1952 cars new names. The Super Six became Wasp and only the Commodore was available with an eight-cylinder engine. The 1952 models only came onto the market in January 1952 because so many 1951 cars stood idle gathering rust.

To create new market segments, Hudson built the Jet in 1952. This was a small car in American terms that looked more like an Opel Olympia than a Hudson. Unfortunately the car was too expensive to sell and only a little over 21,000 of them were sold in 1953. The following year this was a mere 14,000 which caused losses of tens of millions of dollars.

The president of Nash, George Mason, had already been in touch with Abraham E. Barit, who ran Hudson, back in 1946. He suggested the companies merge to better withstand competition from the "big three". In 1946 Barit had no interest because Hudson was successful. Now Barit approached Nash with the same plan. The American Motors Corporation was formed in January 1954. Hudson though had nothing but debt to offer the new company. Because things at Nash were slightly better, Mason became the overall head of the new company with Barit one of the directors.

Hudson cars were fitted with Nash bodies and were sold as Hudson Rambler, Wasp, and Hornet. There was a new model though built for Hudson by Touring of Milan. It was an attractive car but only a few were ever sold and when Mason realised the car was too expensive to make at a profit he scrapped

Hudson astonished the world with its "Step-Down" design in 1949. Other cars seemed old-fashioned compared to them.

the project. Hudson continued to lose money and eventually Mason decided to let the marque disappear.

The final true Hudson was made on 31 October 1954 at the Jefferson Avenue factory in Detroit. The factory was closed and the work force laid off. To keep the Hudson dealers sweet, Nash still built Ramblers with Hudson badges on the radiator grille but the Hudson had vanished.
After forty-five years the Nash name also vanished from the scene.

Hudson cars

COUNTRY OF ORIGIN: USA

Hudson Super Six

MODEL YEAR: 1946-1947

NUMBER MADE: 61,787

Hudson offered the Super with five doors and Commodore with three in 1946-1947.

SPECIAL REMARKS: Apart from a new grille, the body of this model was the same as in 1942. The wheelbase was 121 in (3,070 mm) with overall length of 206 in (5,250 mm).

Hudson Super Eight

MODEL YEAR: 1946-1947

NUMBER MADE: 3,961

SPECIAL REMARKS: The Super Eight was available as a sedan or coupé. There was a eight-cylinder in line engine with side valves and an old-fashioned 6.00 x 16 in tyre size.

Hudson Commodore Eight

MODEL YEAR: 1948-1952

NUMBER MADE: 98,092

The Hudson no longer looked like a pre-war car.

SPECIAL REMARKS: Hudson introduced its famous "Step-Down" body in 1948. In contrast with other cars, the car's floor was now lower than the "chassis" members instead of above them. This feature gave the body its name.

Hudson Hornet

MODEL YEAR: 1951-1956

NUMBER MADE: 141,561

SPECIAL REMARKS: Until 1953 the 5,047 cc six-cylinder engine provided 146 bhp at 3,800 rpm. After this the power was raised to 172 bhp at 4,000 rpm from the same cylinder capacity. Customers in 1955 could also

The Hudson Hornet was just a Commodore with a more powerful engine. Some important races were won with these cars.

A 1952 Hornet. The back-end looked just as attractive as the front.

choose a V-8 (from Packard) of 5,237 or 5,773 cc. These engines remained in production until 1957.

Hudson Jet

MODEL YEAR: 1953-1954

NUMBER MADE: 35,367

SPECIAL REMARKS: The Jet had no family resemblance whatever with a Hudson. This relatively small car had a 104 in (2,650 mm) wheelbase and was 180³/₄ in (4,590 mm) long. The 3,310 cc engine gave 105 bhp in the Jet and 115 bhp in the Super Jet.

Hudson Wasp

MODEL YEAR: 1955-1956

NUMBER MADE: 21,313

SPECIAL REMARKS: The 3,320 cc six-cylinder engine of the Wasp produced 112 bhp at

Only 26 examples were built of the Hudson Italia. It was created just as Hudson was taken over by Nash which did not rate the new car.

4,000 rpm initially, increased in 1956 to 132 bhp to provide a top speed of 94 mph (150 kph).

Hudson Italia

MODEL YEAR: 1954

NUMBER MADE: 26

SPECIAL REMARKS: The Italia sports car was based on the underframe of the Jet. It was designed by Hudson's designer Frank Spring. The car was introduced on 14 January 1954 but this was the same day that Hudson signed a co-operative merger agreement with Nash.

Humber

Thomas Humber established a factory in Coventry to make cycles in 1868 where he later also built cars. He built tri-cars and small tri-cars, known as Voiturettes. Later on the company's exploits took it into full-blown cars.

Although the pre-war Humbers were very conservative in appearance they were quite advanced mechanically. The six-cylinder models had front-wheel independent suspension in 1936 and most Humbers already had hydraulic brakes in 1939. This was the year the Humber Super Snipe made its appearance and this was built throughout the war

In 1952 the Humber Super Snipe got a new overhead valve engine. This is a 1956 example.

In 1958 the Super Snipe got the Humber Hawk's body but could be discerned by the mass of chrome at the front.

for the armed services. They were introduced to the market as a limousine, spacious convertible, and wooden estate car. One loyal user of Humber was Field-Marshal Montgomery who took his "Old Faithful" with him from North Africa to Germany. The "Old Faithful" was an open-topped Humber with a special body by Thrupp & Maberly. Humber's war time speciality though was in building 4 x 4 all-terrain vehicles with the 4-litre Super Snipe engine.
The Super Snipe re-appeared after the war, together with the Hawk which had a 1.9-litre engine derived from the 1939 Hillman 14.

Post-war Humbers were of the same excellent quality as the older examples. There was also a large limousine known as Pullman that was intended for use by those with a chauffeur. But even the ordinary models were full of luxury. For instance from 1947 a six valve radio with pre-heating by His Master's Voice could be fitted. The first major improvements were made in 1948 when both the Hawk and Super Snipe got entirely new bodies. Over-

head valves were all the talk of the car magazines in 1952 and this mechanical innovation was to be found in the Super Snipe's new engine which was 4,139 cc with power of 114 bhp. Additionally, first gear had synchromesh too for the first time, which made changing down much easier. The Hawk had to wait until 1954 for its overhead valve engine. Once this happened, power rose from 59 to 71 bhp from the same 2,267 cc four-cylinder capacity.

Many luxury cars had to wait an age before they saw the end of separate chassis. It took until 1957 for the Humber Hawk to appear with a simpler and lighter construction. The body did not resemble its predecessors and now had panoramic front and rear windscreens, room for six people and their luggage, and also had a lower roof line to give it a more sporting appearance. This Hawk could also be ordered with a glass partition between front and rear seats. Although the engine remained at 2,267 cc, power was now 74 bhp at 4,400 rpm. The car, which weighed 3,139 lb (1,427 kg) had a top speed of at least 90 mph (145 kph). A new Super Snipe with the same body as the Hawk was introduced at the London motor show in 1958. The Snipe had masses of chrome on its grille and a different engine. The six-cylinder engine was now 2,651 cc but power remained at 114 bhp at 5,000 rpm. Customers had a choice of three gearboxes: a three-speed manual, three-speed manual plus overdrive, or an automatic gearbox. This Super Snipe remained no lightweight at 3,234 lb (1,470 kg) and the estate car weighed 3,342 lb (1,519 kg).

Humber could not stop tinkering with the Super Snipe and when a prospective buyer saw one at the 1959 London motor show it

A 1960 Humber Super Snipe with space for six and a very large boot for their luggage.

then had a 2,965 cc six-cylinder engine of 131 bhp. A year later the car had acquired the fashionable twin headlights of the era.

February 1963 saw a cheaper Humber launched on the market in the form of the Sceptre. Rootes not only built the top of the range Humber but also Hillman, Singer, and Sunbeam. The new Sceptre was in reality a Hillman Super Minx with twin headlights and the grill of the Sunbeam Rapier. In common with the Hillman, the four-cylinder engine was 1,592 cc but with twin carburettors and a higher compression ratio power was increased from 62 to 87 bhp. For those who ordered the manual gearbox it now had four speeds plus an electrically-operated overdrive. There were disc brakes on the front wheels.

Humber brought out yet another luxury car in 1965. It was named Imperial and shared its body with the Hawk and Super Snipe. This car was only available with a saloon body but had a choice of partition glass for those with a chauffeur.

After Chrysler took over the Rootes Group times were hard for Humber. Exports disap-peared so that cars were only built with right-hand steering but when the British too lost interest in the big car they disappeared from the range. Only the Sceptre was allowed to continue until 1967 when Chrysler decided to close the Humber factory so that from then on the only Humbers to be bought were second-hand ones.

Humber cars

COUNTRY OF ORIGIN: United Kingdom

Humber Hawk

MODEL YEAR: 1945-1948

NUMBER MADE: Unknown

SPECIAL REMARKS: Rootes shared bodies be-tween models even before World War II so

One of the final Humber Super Snipes. This is a 1965 model with fashionable twin headlights.

Humber introduced new bodies in 1948. This is a Super Snipe Pullman on its long wheelbase chassis.

that the Humber Hawk had the same body as the Hillman 14.

Humber Super Snipe

MODEL YEAR: 1945-1948

NUMBER MADE: Unknown

SPECIAL REMARKS: The standard Super Snipe had the same 113³/₄ in (2,890 mm) wheelbase and 180 in (4,570 mm) length as the Hawk. The Pullman version had a longer 127¹/₂ in (3,240 mm) wheelbase and was 198 in (5,030 mm) overall.

Humber Sceptre

MODEL YEAR: 1963-1967

NUMBER MADE: Unknown

SPECIAL REMARKS: The Humber Sceptre was a more luxurious version of the Hillman Super Minx. When the big Humbers proved impossible to sell only the Sceptre remained.

The Humber Sceptre had power-assisted disc brakes on the front wheels, an electrically-operated overdrive for the manual gearbox, and twin headlights. A 1966 example is illustrated.

IFA

Most of the Auto-Union factories were within the Russian zone after World War II and this was also true of DKW (see DKW). The debris and rubble was piled so high in Zwickau where Audi and DKW had been built before 1940 that it took until 1948 before anyone could think about producing cars but they did return. These were no longer Audis or a DKW but IFA for Industrieverband Fahrzeugbau (industrial union for vehicle construction). An early type F9 could be admired at the Leipzig trade fair in 1948. In contrast to the pre-war and immediate post-war DKW cars, the F9 had a three-cylinder engine which had been under development by Auto-Union in 1939. Engines of this type did not appear in western-built DKW cars until 1953. This two-stroke engine was 900 cc and produced 28 bhp at 3,600 rpm. Its price of 13,200 Ostmark was outside the ordinary person's reach and the F8, which was a fairly faithful copy of a pre-war DKW with two-stroke engine, was also very expensive at 8,415 Ostmark. At least these prices were too high for those living in East Germany but in the West these cars were among the cheapest on the market. The first F9 cars were built at the former Audi factory in Zwickau but from 1953 production was moved to the former BMW factory in Eisenach.

The IFA F9 was virtually identical to the DKW built in Düsseldorf. Only the grille was different.

The body of the F8 was largely made from plywood but this quickly rotting material was no longer used for the F9. IFA cars remained in production until they were replaced by the famous or perhaps infamous Trabant.

IFA cars

COUNTRY OF ORIGIN: East Germany (German Democratic Republic)

IFA F8

MODEL YEAR: 1948-1955

NUMBER MADE: 26,254

SPECIAL REMARKS: The F8 was produced in East Germany as a saloon, convertible, estate, and van. A 684 cc engine sputtered away to produce 20 bhp at 3,500 rpm.

A dream for every East German: a row of IFA cars from which to choose one. This remained a dream because there was usually a waiting time of at least two years.

Until the spring of 1951 the IFA F9 had a two-piece windscreen. Later this became a single sheet of glass.

IFA F9

MODEL YEAR: 1950-1956

NUMBER MADE: 40,663

SPECIAL REMARKS: Because the East Germans had both the drawings and several prototypes of the new three-cylinder engine, they were able to produce it earlier than DKW.

Iso Rivolta

Commendatore Renzo Rivolta built a variety of different cars. He started with the Isetta bubble car (see BMW), which was the forerunner of mini-cars and finished up making very fast supercars that were powered by huge American V-8 engines. When Renzo died in 1966, aged 55, his 26-year-old son Piero took over the business. The first thing he did was the design a four-door car which was shown in Frankfurt in 1967 as the Iso S4-Fidia. The body had been designed by the then still young Giorgetto Giugiaro and the car was built by his boss's company of Ghia in Turin. This was a large car with a 2,850 mm (112 in) wheelbase.

The length from bumper to bumper was 4,970 mm (195 in). At first known as the S4 – the S4-Fidia name did not come into use until 1969 – was available in two models with a choice of two engines, although initially only with a Chevrolet Corvette 327 engine of 5,354 cc; the Ford V-8 engine came later. The S4-300 model's engine produced 304 bhp(SAE) at 5,000 rpm while in the S4-350 the same unit supplied 355 bhp (SAE) at 5,800 rpm. Piero Rivolta claimed that his Fidia was the fastest production saloon in the world. The top speed was between 137 and 144 mph (220-230 kph) so he certainly did not have many cars that could keep up with it. Such performance was certainly remarkable for a car that weighed 1,620 kg (3,564 lb)

Iso Rivolta cars

COUNTRY OF ORIGIN: Italy

Iso Rivolta S4-Fidia

MODEL YEAR: 1968-1974

NUMBER MADE: 192

The Iso Fidia was an expensive car. It cost more than a 4-door Maserati and was more than twice the price of a Jaguar XJ6 with 4.2-litre engine.

SPECIAL REMARKS: The 1973 and 1974 cars had 5,768 cc Ford V-8 engines of 330 bhp (SAE) at 5,800 rpm. With this powerful unit under the bonnet the factory guaranteed a top speed of 150 mph (240 kph).

Isuzu

Isuzu had established a reputation before World War II as a truck builder and since the biggest demand in post-war years was for trucks Isuzu Motors of Tokyo concentrated mainly on making them and did not branch out into cars until 1953.

The first cars to be produced were Hillman Super Minx, built under licence and then the range was expanded in 1961 with a design of their own, the Bellel. This car was powered by a 1,491 cc or 1,991 cc engine. This was

134

followed two years later by the Bellett, which was the first Japanese car to be sold in Europe.

Unfortunately the car was designed for the smaller Japanese and did not sell well but things were more successful when Isuzu conformed to European norms. The new designs were produced by specialists such as Giugiaro.

Isuzu cars

COUNTRY OF ORIGIN: Japan

Bellett

MODEL YEAR: 1963-present day

NUMBER MADE: Unknown

Giugiaro designed the Bellett in 1964 for Isuzu. The car shown had right-hand steering because it was intended for the Japanese market.

SPECIAL REMARKS: The Bellett was made with at least eight different engines. The smallest was a 1.3 litre with the biggest petrol engine being a 1.6 litre unit. There was also a 1.8-litre diesel engine in the range.

Jaguar

William Lyons and William Walmsley founded Swallow Sidecars in 1922 to make sidecars for motorcycles. The business expanded

in 1927 into making special car bodies for Austin Sevens, the small Morris, and Standard. When the Blackpool factory became too small the business moved to Coventry which was then the centre of the British car industry. It was in Coventry that the first car of his own design was introduced in 1931. It was a two-door car using parts from the Standard Motor Company and was known as SS 1. The car was a great success because it was not expensive but looked as though it was. The letters represented Swallow Sidecars but after the war Lyons did not want to use the Swallow name anymore and he named his cars after one of his pre-war models – the Jaguar. The Swallow Sidecars firm was sold and continued to build sidecars and in 1954 also brought out its own sports car under its new owners, known as a Swallow Doretti.

The first Jaguars in 1945 were pre-war models of course. They were big cars chiefly aimed at the export market in the USA. There were three models with which only the engines differed. Customers could choose from a 1,776 cc four-cylinder motor of 66 bhp or from two six-cylinder units of 2,664 or 3,486 cc. The engines had overhead valves but the front and back axles of the cars were still rigid and there were huge chromium-plated headlights attached to the front wings. The headlights were incorporated in the wings from 1949 onwards, giving rise to the Jaguar Mk V. The front wheels now had independent suspension, the braking system was hydraulically operated, and four-cylinder engines were no longer fitted. Apart from the headlights, the Mk V closely resembled pre-war models. This did not change until 1950 when the Mk VII Jaguar was introduced. Jaguar never made a Mk VI because of the Bentley of this name. There was a superb engine in the Mk VII which was also used in the XK120 sports car. This engine had twin overhead camshafts and was 3,442 cc in cylinder capacity. The car had a top speed of 106 mph (170 kph) even though it weighed 3,685 lb (1,675 kg). This made it one of the fastest cars of its era. The front wind-screen of the Mk VII still consisted of two pieces of glass but this was changed to a single piece windscreen in 1956 when the car became the Mk VIII. To accentuate the change, the MK VIII also had a wider grille and two-tone paintwork. It was entirely predictable that Jaguar too would grow in size. The first car in 1945 would fit in a garage 173 in long (4,400 mm) but when the Mk IX was introduced in 1958 it was 196 in (4,990 mm) long and weighed 3,894 lb (1,770 kg). This new car closely resembled its forerunner but there were big differences under the bonnet. This new car had all-round disc brakes and was powered by a new 3,781 cc engine of 223 bhp at 5,500 rpm. Almost all the cars were sold with an automatic gearbox and power-steering. As had become customary for Jaguar, the finish inside the new car was superb with an unbelievable level of luxury: walnut, leather, thick carpets on the floor, folding tables, back support for the front seats and an extensively equipped dashboard are just a few examples. But customers wanted even more.

The last name in luxury without doubt was the 1961 Mk X which had a length of 202 in (5,130 mm) and weighed in at just under two tons. The car was now powered by a more powerful six-cylinder engine bored out to 3,781 cc and in 1967 for the 420G to 4,235 cc. Power was in the region of 270 bhp. For the first time with a Jaguar the rear wheels also had independent suspension.

Jaguar's first car with a monocoque body was made in 1955. This relatively small car for a Jaguar was first sold as a Jaguar 2.4 litre but later became known as the Mk I. The actual engine capacity was 2,483 cc and the motor

Jaguar moved into a new and successful era with the Mk I and Mk II. This is a 1963 Mk II with 3.8-litre engine.

produced 114 bhp at 5,750 rpm. The body had four doors but this did not prevent people from using the car for motor sport. The car was also available in 1957 with a 3,442 cc engine that delivered 213 bhp. Since the top speed of this car was in the region of 119 mph (190 kph) Jaguar sold it as a "sports saloon" in some markets. The successor Mk II in 1959 was even more successful in motor-sport.

This model was available with both 2.4 and 3.4 litre engines and it was possible to order a 3.8-litre unit until 1968. This 3,781 cc engine produced 223 bhp at 5,500 rpm and took the car to almost 125 mph (200 kph). The Mk II was replaced by the Jaguar 240 and 340 which differed little from their predecessors except they were simpler and therefore cheaper. In addition to the Mk II there was also a larger Jaguar S with the same shape as the MK II which was available from 1963-1968. It was both larger and more mechanically advanced than the Mk II, with the independent rear suspension from the Mk X, and it also had more boot space and leg room. For those who found the 420G too big and the S too small Jaguar brought out the 420 in 1966. This car had a 4,235 cc engine and was also available as a Daimler Sovereign.

The 1968 London motor show exhorted the public to "Buy British" and many did just then when they saw the new Jaguar XJ6. Everything about the car was new and it only compared with previous Jaguars in terms of its sound mechanical engineering. This newcomer in 1968 set the tone for future Jaguars for some time to come and modern day Jaguars can still be readily traced back to their thirty-year-old predecessor.

Jaguar achieved high production volumes with the XJ6. The British enthusiasts were not put out that the XJ6 had been revealed first to the public a few weeks earlier at the Paris motor show, for this was the car for which they had eagerly waited. Sir William Lyons, who had started building sidecars, designed most Jaguars himself and if he was not behind the drawing board himself, Sir William let his staff know precisely what he wanted. The XJ6 was one of his creations but was unfortunately his last. Sir William retired from Jaguar in 1972, aged 70 and the legendary motor engineer died on 8 February 1985.

The initial XJ6, which became known as the Series I, had a choice of two six-cylinder motors: a 2,792 cc that produced 149 bhp and a 4,235 cc, giving 186 bhp at 5,200 rpm. There was also a Daimler model with a grille covered in chrome. The Series II XJ6 was also launched elsewhere than London: this time Jaguar chose Frankfurt in 1973. The car was a disappointment since the only immediately noticeable difference was the lower front grille.
Further scrutiny revealed that the instrument panel was now directly in front of the driver instead of being spread across the entire wooden dashboard. The car had a choice of 2.8, 3.4, and 4.2-litre engines but the short-stroke 2.8 was unreliable and not up to its task and few were delivered.

In July 1972 Jaguar and Daimler launched the new XJ12 super car with a V-12 engine. This superb but thirsty engine had a cylinder capacity of 5,343 cc and an output of 253 bhp at 6,000 rpm. The top speed of the XJ12 was 147 mph (235 kph). The second series XJ12 appeared barely a year later in September 1973 with significant mechanical improvements.
Jaguar brought out two further models that were aimed at those who wanted a performance car but had small children. These were the XJ6 and XK12C 2+2 coupés with 4.2-litre V-6 or 5.3-litre V-12 engines.

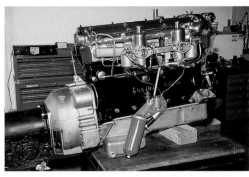
Even a big 3.8-litre engine does not go on for ever. This engine has been fully restored.

The cars were identical externally with the saloon models except for the lack of a rear door in the sporting model. The following model in the Jaguar family was a genuine sporting coupé but this meant less leg room in the back of the5.5-litre XJS.

Jaguar cars

COUNTRY OF ORIGIN:
United Kingdom

Jaguar 1.5, 2.5, & 3.5 litre

MODEL YEAR: 1945-1948

NUMBER MADE: 11,952

SPECIAL REMARKS: The numbers given include 664 convertibles. These were the final cars with Standard engines which were also fitted pre-war.
Subsequent engines were all designed and built by Jaguar.

Jaguar Mk V 2.5 & 3.5 litre

MODEL YEAR: 1949-1951

NUMBER MADE: 1,675 & 8,791

SPECIAL REMARKS: The engines of these models did have overhead valves but were the final Jaguar engines without overhead

The traditional shape is still recognisable but the headlights are now incorporated in the wings. The Mk V illustrated is as built from 1949-1951.

camshafts. Subsequent engines had twin camshafts.

Jaguar Mk VII/VIII

MODEL YEAR: 1950-1954

NUMBER MADE: 20,908

The Mk VII M was a fast version of the Mk VII with 190 instead of 160 bhp. This is an 1954 example.

The MK VIII was a MK VII with a two-tone body, and single unit windscreen.

SPECIAL REMARKS: The Mk VII M (10,061 sold) was the faster version of the Mk VII. It had an uprated 190 bhp engine instead of the usual 160. The 6,212 Mk VIII sold were all given a two-tone paint finish.

Jaguar Mk IX

MODEL YEAR: 1958-1961

NUMBER MADE: 10,009

Externally the Mk IX was little changed and differed only mechanically from the Mk VII and VIII.

SPECIAL REMARKS: By increasing the bore of the cylinders of the 3.4-litre engine from 83 to 87 mm Jaguar created a 3.8-litre motor for the Mk IX.

Jaguar Mk X

MODEL YEAR: 1961-1966

NUMBER MADE: 18,358

SPECIAL REMARKS: The model lived on beyond 1966 as the Jaguar 420G of which 6,554

The Mk X was a keen competitor with the big cars of Detroit with its 202 in (5,130 mm) overall length. Most of these cars were exported to the USA.

were sold. The 3.8-litre engine now had triple SU carburettors to produce 46 bhp more then the Mk IX for a total of 269 bhp at 5,500 rpm.

Jaguar 2.4 & 3.4 (Mk I)

MODEL YEAR: 1955-1959 & 1957-1959

NUMBER MADE: 19,992 & 17,405

SPECIAL REMARKS: The Jaguar 2.4 was the first Jaguar with a monocoque body. The net weight of the vehicle was 2,860 lb (1,300 kg). The car heralded a new era with excellent sales for Jaguar.

Jaguar Mk II

MODEL YEAR: 1959-1969

NUMBER MADE: 91,222

SPECIAL REMARKS: Of the 91,222 Mk II cars sold, 7,242 were of the "cheap" 240 and 340 versions. The Mk II was available with choice of three engines giving 112, 213, and 223 bhp.

A Series I XJ6. Older Jaguars were still echoed in the XJ6 that was introduced in 1977.

S Type

MODEL YEAR: 1963-1968

NUMBER MADE: 25,171

SPECIAL REMARKS: The road-holding of the S-Type was considerably improved thanks to its independent rear suspension. The S-Type was really a luxury version of the Mk II.

Jaguar XJ6

MODEL YEAR: 1968-1979

The Jaguar S had the front-end of a Mk II and large rear and boot of the Mk X. The S was a luxury version of the Mk II.

NUMBER MADE: 156,104

SPECIAL REMARKS: Only 26,202 were sold with the 2,792 cc engine. This six-cylinder with its 149 bhp lacked sufficient power for this heavy car.
There were a lot of problems with the engine and it was quickly replaced by a 4,235 cc unit of 186 bhp at 5,200 rpm.

Jaguar XJ12

MODEL YEAR: 1972-1979

NUMBER MADE: 19,238

SPECIAL REMARKS: Only 754 of the first series of XJ12 had a long wheelbase which became standard in the second series (1973-1979). The V-12 in the later series produced 285 instead of 253 bhp.

Jaguar XJ6 C/ XJ12 C

MODEL YEAR: 1975-1978

NUMBER MADE: 6,487 & 1,855

SPECIAL REMARKS: The engines of these coupés had the same power output as the

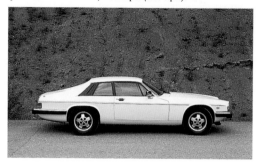

The wheelbase of the XJS was a mere 102 in (2,590 mm) yet it was 191³/₄ in (4,870 mm) long. The official top speed was in excess of 150 mph (240 kph).

saloons. The coupés could only be told apart from the saloons by viewing from the side.

Jaguar XJS 5.3

MODEL YEAR: 1975-1993

NUMBER MADE: 79,447

SPECIAL REMARKS: There was far less room in the XJS than an XJ coupé. The power unit was the same V-12 engine driving the wheels in the standard version through an automatic gearbox although a manual five-speed box was available as an option.

The XJ coupé was really a saloon with two doors instead of four. This is an XJ12C with twelve cylinders. Both the wheelbase (109 in/2,770 mm) and length (191 in/4,850 mm) were reduced by 4 in (100 mm) by comparison with the saloon.

Kaiser-Frazer

Virtually every independent car maker succumbed to the might of the big three in Detroit. Kaiser-Frazer are certainly no exception to this and were forced to close in 1954 after eight years in which losses of $100,000,000 were made for each year of operation. And yet matters had begun so promisingly.

Henry J. Kaiser was born the son of a German immigrant in 1882 at Sprout Brooks, New York. By 1904 he had a photographic shop and by 1914 he had switched to building bridges, dams, and highways. Kaiser worked both in the USA and Cuba. He had also always been interested in ship-building and became famous during the war for being able to build Liberty ships within one week. The record was 4 days 15 hours 26 minutes! He built at least 1,490 Liberty ships and also fifty aircraft carriers.

His foray into the automobile industry came after World War II when he decided to build cars with Joseph Washington Frazer. Kaiser was new to the industry but Frazer had easily won his spurs. He had worked for all the major automobile manufacturers, ending up as President of Graham Paige.

The pair revealed their first prototypes at the Waldorf Astoria hotel in New York on 20 January 1946. Three months later there were 266,849 people on the waiting list for one of the new cars. The 100,000th car was supplied in September 1947. The range consisted of four models: the Kaiser Special, Kaiser Custom, Frazer Standard, and Frazer Manhattan. All four cars shared the same body and differed from each other only in detail. A great deal of money was lost in the first year but after a while things were going well. The company made $10,000,000 in 1948 but this was entirely re-invested in new models. These were lower, longer, and wider than their forerunners and had much more chrome. For the first time convertibles were also available. The Kaiser Vagabond was an entirely new sedan with a rear window which could be lowered to form a fifth door.

The firm brought out a small car in 1951 named the Henry J but when Kaiser-Frazer described it as "The car every American family can afford" no-one wanted to buy one. The car was sold by the famous Sears Roebuck department store as an Allstate but this too back-fired on the good name of Kaiser-Frazer. The car was inexpensive and not bad in the slightest but what American cared to admit he could not afford a "decent" car?

The cars were regularly given facelifts and a new name but they remained unsaleable. The other factories were now also in a position to deliver and names such as Ford and Chevrolet gave the buyers more confidence. Kaiser also built cars in Europe between 1949-1954 at a factory in Rotterdam. The Dutch factory switched over in 1954 to producing the

The Kaiser (illustrated) and the Frazer had the same body and could only be told apart by their grilles and bumpers.

The 1953 Kaiser Manhattan was the deluxe version of the Deluxe. It was characterised by broad chrome trim, large nave plates, and broad bumpers.

A 1951 Kaiser Deluxe which was available with a General Motors Hydra-Matic automatic gearbox.

Kaiser-Frazer cars

COUNTRY OF ORIGIN: USA

The numbers built:

	Kaiser	Frazer	Henry J	Allstate	Darrin
1947	70,480	68,775			
1948	91,851	48,071			
1949/50	95,175	24,923			
1951	145,013	10,214	84,905		
1952	32,131	–	23,568	1,566	
11953	32,004	–	17,505	2,363	62
1954	6,101	–	1,125	–	435
1955	270				

Willys Jeep, Simca, and Hillman. The Kaiser Motor Corporation bought Willys Overland in 1953 and moved to Toledo. The Frazer name had now disappeared. It was in Toledo that the Kaiser Darrin sports car was developed but this too did not produce the necessary profits. The car was interesting for its polyester body shell and sliding doors in the front wings.

Things went from bad to worse for Kaiser. No-one was interested in big cars that were still powered by old-fashioned six-cylinder side-valve engines. Other makers offered V-8 overhead valve engines for the same price. The final Kaiser rolled off the line in 1955 and was exported to South America. The company now concentrated on the Willys Jeep.

When production in the USA closed down it was moved to Argentina where Kaisers were built for a time as Kaiser Carabela with a Willys engine.

Kaiser departed in 1955, aged 73, for Hawaii, where he built an hotel, cement works, radio station, and hospital. When a journalist interviewed him on his eighty-fifth birthday he said: "If people remember be it will be for my hospitals. They give people what they most need – good health."

Kaiser Special

MODEL YEAR: 1947-1948

NUMBER MADE: Unknown

SPECIAL REMARKS: The famous designer "Dutch" Darrin designed the bodies for the Kaiser and Frazer.
The low-slung bodies were very modern for their time. The cars were produced in the enormous Willow Run works where Ford had built B-24 bombers.

Kaiser Henry J

MODEL YEAR: 1951-1954

NUMBER MADE: See table

A rare sight: of the 71,568 1951 Kaiser Deluxe sold, only 8,888 had two-door bodies.

SPECIAL REMARKS: The Henry was only 9 in (230 mm) longer than a VW Beetle with its 174 in (4,430 mm) from bumper to bumper. The model had a choice of two engines: four-cylinder 2,199 cc of 69 bhp or six-cylinder 2,638 cc and 81 bhp.

Kaiser-Darrin

MODEL YEAR: 1953-1954

NUMBER MADE: See table

SPECIAL REMARKS: This car was based on the Henry J running gear with a six-cylinder side-valve engine. When Kaiser ceased its production, "Dutch" Darrin took making the car until 1958 but with a Cadillac engine.

Kleinschnittger

The demand for means of transport were greater in post-war Germany than ever before. Cars had been left behind on the eastern front, motorcycles had been taken as booty and the trains did not run because of widespread bomb damage. It is little wonder then that do-it-yourself efforts at building small cars were undertaken. The engineer Paul Kleinschnittger was on of these hobbyists. His "motorcycle with a fairing" made its first test run in 1947. The "car" was powered by a 98 cc DKW RT motorcycle engine. Even though the car was not fully enclosed there were still people standing in line to buy one. Kleinschnittger found himself in 1949 both a

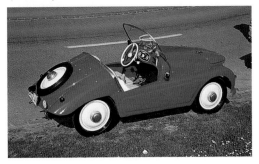

The Kleinschnittger looked very sportive from behind and must once have been much coveted by the youth of Germany.

financier and an assembly shop, where he could finally get to work. His F125 now had a 123 cc Ilo motor which produced 5.5 bhp power for the front wheels. The gearbox was from a motorcycle and therefore had no reverse, meaning that the 130 kg (286 lb) car had to be pushed back if necessary. The single cylinder engine was placed in front of the front axle to leave space under the bonnet for the driver's and passenger's legs. There were no doors and also no side windows. Since the canvas hood did little to keep out the elements, most people left it at home.

History shows that cars constantly grew in size and the same is true of the Kleinschnittger. Its creator of the same name designed a larger car with 250 cc engine which was due to go into production in 1957 but this never happened. The time for midget cars was over and Kleinschnittger became bankrupt when the financiers turned off the money supply.

The Kleinschnittger had no starter motor or battery. The engine was started using a rope on a recoil starter as with lawn mowers and outboard motors.

Kleinschnittger cars

COUNTRY OF ORIGIN: Germany

Kleinschnittger F125

MODEL YEAR: 1949-1957

NUMBER MADE: 2,980

SPECIAL REMARKS: The Kleinschnittger F125 was a midget among midget cars. Its engine produced 5.5 bhp at 5,00 rpm that was barely able to take it to 40 mph (65 kph).

Lagonda

Wilbur Gun was born in America where he worked for a time as sewing machine repairer for Singer, and sang for pleasure in operas. In 1897 Gun came to Britain where he built his first car in 1900. He chose the name Lagonda after the river at the back of the house in Springfield, Ohio, where he was born. At first the Lagonda Motor Company made small racing cars and large prestigious vehicles for wealthy customers. Tsar Nicholas II was a Lagonda owner. In 1935, Lagonda won the Le Mans 24 hour race, making the company world famous. The famous W.O. Bentley joined the firm in 1939 to design superb engines including a V-12 and six-cylinder with twin overhead camshafts. This subsequent engine was built for many years after the war.

Lagonda was one of the few factories which made nothing out of the war and times were hard for them in 1945, leading to the company being sold in 1947. The new owner, David Brown, managed to breathe new life into the business and when the Lagonda 2.6 litre

(with Bentley's engine) was introduced in 1948 it was an immediate success. This car was one of the few with both front and rear independent suspension and certainly the first English car with such construction. To reduce the load on the suspension, the rear brakes were placed next to the differential. This was a technique that had only been used for racing cars until then. The engine, which was also used in the Aston Martin, was 2,580 cc capacity and produced 106 bhp at 5,000 rpm. Gear change was by means of either a four-speed manual box or Cotal semi-automatic.

Aston Martin and Lagonda worked closely together which is understandable given their same owner and when Aston Martin had a new 3-litre engine, Lagonda had access to it in 1953. The engine produced 142 bhp at 5,000 rpm in the Lagonda, giving the family car a top speed of over 100 mph (160 kph). The Lagonda 3 litre was 8 in (200 mm) longer than its forerunner with an overall length of 196 in (4,980 mm). The wheelbase remained the same at 113 in (2,880 mm). At first this model was only offered as a coupé but after a few months a convertible and saloon were also available. Only the four-door saloon was sold after 1957 and David Brown decided in 1958 to temporarily remove Lagonda from the market. Three years later in 1961 a new Lagonda was exhibited. This Lagonda Rapide had a modern monocoque body designed by Touring of Milan. It still had the six-cylinder engine under the bonnet that Bentley had designed before the war but the cylinder capacity was now 3,995 cc and power output was 236 bhp at 5,000 rpm. The car was expensive; too expensive it proved, for only 55 of them were sold. Lagonda stopped making the Rapide in 1964 and then in 1969 the company built a four-door Lagonda prototype on an extended underframe from an Aston Martin DBS. This model went into production in 1976.

A 1952 2.5 litre four-door saloon with lots of leather and wood and space for five persons.

Lagonda cars

Country of origin: United Kingdom

Lagonda 2.6 litre

Model year: 1947-1953

Although virtually all Lagonda cars were exported, the factory continued to produce them in the 1940s and 50s with right-hand steering. This is a 1949 2.6 litre.

NUMBER MADE: 550 (all models)

SPECIAL REMARKS: The Lagonda was not a sports car but a sporting grand tourer. The top speed of 94 mph (150 km/hour) was quite outstanding in 1947. It might seem commonplace today but it was quite sensational then.

Lagonda 3 litre

MODEL YEAR: 1953-1957

NUMBER MADE: 430

SPECIAL REMARKS: By increasing the capacity of each cylinder the 2.5 litre engine from 78 to 83 cc, a new six-cylinder engine of 2,922 cc was created. The car weighed more than 1.6 tons but still managed 97 mph (155 kph).

Lagonda cars were never mass produced. Only 55 3 litre convertibles were made between 1953-1957.

Lagonda Rapide

MODEL YEAR: 1961-1964

NUMBER MADE: 55

SPECIAL REMARKS: The Rapide was in reality an Aston Martin DB5 with a longer chassis and four-door body. Four disc brakes and a complicated De Dion rear axle made the car exceptionally expensive.

Lamborghini

Lamborghini is famous for its sports and super cars such as the Miura and Countach but Ferruccio Lamborghini has also built saloon cars. Not just 2+2 with room only for small children but a comfortable four-seater. The Espada was the sole and last saloon built by Lamborghini. The car was designed by the Bertone firm which has been responsible for designing and building all but two or three Lamborghini bodies. Bertone tried to persuade Ferruccio Lamborghini for some time to build a four-seater and a functioning prototype was made. This was named Marzal and its design came from Marcello Gandini. It was a four-seater with two winged doors which hinged back from the roof to make it easy to get in and out. A six-cylinder engine was mounted transversely in the rear. This was half a V-12 Miura engine. The new six-cylinder motor produced 175 bhp. The Marzal was shown in Geneva for the first time where it attracted a lot of attention but the public reaction was such that Lamborghini did not consider putting the car into production.

A second effort by Gandini and Bertone was more successful. The Espada had the Marzal's shape but with normal doors. The car also had a standard 4-litre engine that was also used in other models. The public found this powerful V-12 much more worthwhile. The engine was entirely cast in aluminium and was 3,929 cc with power of 350 bhp at 7,500 rpm. The valves were operated by four overhead camshafts and the pistons derived their mixture from six twin Weber carburettors. The Espada was shown at Geneva in March 1968.

Once the order book continued to grow both Bertone and Lamborghini were convinced to go ahead. With its top speed of 156 mph (250 kph) the Espada was the world's fastest saloon car at that time. And it was a truly comfortable saloon car in which four adults could travel in comfort. No luxury touches were ignored of course. The upholstery was leather, as was customary for Lamborghini at that time, and with power-steering and air-conditioning, it was as pleasant a ride as a Mercedes or Jaguar.

The Espada was much faster though. If necessary, it could accelerate from 0-100 kph in 6.9 seconds (0-62.5mph). Lamborghini hoped to sell the car in the USA, which is why an automatic gearbox was also available. The Espada was built for ten years and became one of the best selling Lamborghinis.

Carrozzeria Bertone created a stir with the Marzal. It always drew a crowd at every show.

Ferruccio Lamborghini (1916-1974).

Lamborghini cars

COUNTRY OF ORIGIN: Italy

Lamborghini Espada

MODEL YEAR: 1968-1978

NUMBER MADE: 1,217

SPECIAL REMARKS: The Espada shared its V-12 engine with the Islero and Jarama but unlike these 2+2 cars, the Espada was a true

The Espada was a big car at 4,740 mm (186 in) long.

Fastest saloon in the world? The Espada.

Carrozzeria Frua even built a four-door Espada but this remained a prototype.

four-seater. Rear seat passengers suffered no back problems after long journeys.

Lancia

Vincenzo Lancia was a sociable man who enjoyed a glass of his Piedmont wine in his favourite restaurant Gobatto on Turin's Via Superga. He might spend the entire night in discussion with friends such as Pinin Farina or Count Biscaretti. He loved the music of Wagner and people such as Arturo Toscanini, Erich Maria Remarque, and Ernest Hemingway were his personal customers. Vincenzo Lancia did much for his personal customers and also for his employees. He financed an opera house, built inexpensive homes, and was the first manufacturer to have a recreational villa built beside the Mediterranean for his employees. Lancia was born on 24 August 1881 in the village of Fobello at the foot of the Monte-Rosa massif. He went to Turin aged 17 where he was employed a book-keeper by Giovanni Ceirano, a car manufacturer. Two years later he became a test driver for Fiat and then a racing driver and quickly became one of the best drivers in the world. He established Lancia & Co Fabricca Automobili with a friend in 1906 and their first prototype car was being driven through the streets of Turin. Lancia achieved a great deal. In 1919 he was granted a patent for a monocoque construction body and his 1922 Lancia Lambda not only had such a body, it also incorporated brakes on all four wheels and a V-4 engine with an overhead camshaft. Lancia died in 1937, aged 56, of a heart attack and was succeeded by his son Gianni.

After World War II Lancia introduced the Aprillia and smaller Ardea which both had monocoque bodies, independent front suspension, and a V-4 engine. The Aprillia also had independent rear suspension. This car had a 1,486 cc engine producing power of 48 bhp at 4,300 rpm. The smaller Ardea had a 903 cc V-4 that gave 29 bhp at 4,600 rpm. The cars had been developed before the war

Vincenzo Lancia (1881-1937).

and the Aprillia was the last car to be created under Vincenzo Lancia's leadership. Both cars seemed modern though in 1946 with their streamlined bodies with no pillars between the doors.

The Aurelia appeared with a 1,754 cc V-6 engine in 1950 and its engine grew in size up to 1991, to first 2,266, then 2,451 cc and power increased from 58 to 118 bhp. The mechanical aspects of the Aurelia were designed by automobile engineer Vittorio Jano who was renowned for his racing cars, so it is not surprising that the small Aurelia was powered by a motor with overhead camshaft and had the gearbox incorporated with the differential of the De Dion rear axle. A number of fine cars arose out of the Aurelia: both big ones seating up to seven and small two-seaters which won races.

Another famous car from the marque was the Flaminia which was launched with a 2,458 cc V-6 engine from the start that produced power of 140 bhp. Lancia did not only build cars though for the "upper ten per cent" of society. On the contrary, there were inexpensive small cars such as the 1,090 cc V-4 engine powered Appia and the Flavia, which was Lancia's first front-wheel drive car with a aluminium four-cylinder boxer engine. This engine produced 78 bhp at 5,200 rpm from the 1,500 cc unit in 1960 but this increased in 1974 to 126 bhp at 5,600 rpm.

The Fulvia was an extremely forward-looking and modern car for its time when it was launched in 1963. It had four disc brakes and was powered by a tilted V-4 engine. A further world-famous design was the Beta which was produced in a diverse range of versions, including the HPE or High Performance

The Lancia Beta HPE was a cross between a sports cars and an estate with the speed of the first and the space of the latter.

Executive which was a sort of sporting estate car, plus the Monte-Carlo, a sports coupé that was like a small Ferrari Berlinetta Boxer. Both cars were designed by Pininfarina.

Lancia had been part of the Fiat empire by this stage for many years but the name lives on as a separate and distinctive marque. We must hope that another piece of automobile history will not be lost.

Lancia cars

COUNTRY OF ORIGIN: Italy

Lancia Aprillia

MODEL YEAR: 1946-1949

NUMBER MADE: 27,642 (from 1939)

The Aprillia had a monocoque body before the war.

SPECIAL REMARKS: The Aprillia was a compact car with space for four adults with a wheelbase of 2,750 mm (108 in) and 3,960 mm (156 in) from bumper-to-bumper.

Lancia Ardea

MODEL YEAR: 1946-1949

NUMBER MADE: Unknown

SPECIAL REMARKS: The Ardea was powered by the smallest engine ever produced in series by Lancia. This overhead valves were sited behind each other instead of next to one another.

The Ardea was the "common man's" Aprillia with a 900 cc engine instead of the 1,486 cc unit.

The Flaminia was one of the most expensive Italia cars and was therefore much favoured by politicians and film stars.

Lancia Aurelia

MODEL YEAR: 1950-1957

NUMBER MADE: 12,786

The Aurelias were exceptionally good-looking cars. The coupé and convertible versions were built by Pininfarina.

SPECIAL REMARKS: The total includes 3,871 Aurelia GT and Spider models. All the bodies were designed and built by Pininfarina.

Lancia Flaminia

MODEL YEAR: 1957-1970

NUMBER MADE: 3,943

SPECIAL REMARKS: The Flaminia was specially-developed as a six-seater for wealthy persons.
The Pope was driven in a Flaminia. The coupé version was even more expensive but sold well in spite of its high price.

A rear view of the Flaminia coupé by Pininfarina.

Lancia Appia

MODEL YEAR: 1953-1963

NUMBER MADE: 98,995

SPECIAL REMARKS: The 1,090 cc engine of the first 42,429 cars produced 38 bhp at 4,800 rpm. The second series had the same size

An Appia from the third and final series which was first show at Geneva in 1959.

The door pillars were missing from this Lancia too, which made it easier to get into and out of.

The Lancia Fulvia had twin headlights and a body shape that could have been a Fiat.

engine but this now produced a higher power output of 48 bhp.

Lancia Flavia

MODEL YEAR: 1960-1974

NUMBER MADE: 106,476

The most attractive and rarest Flavia had bodies by Zagato. Only 628 were built.

SPECIAL REMARKS: The Flavia was produced in several versions with the four-door saloon being the most common, with 79,764 being built. There were also two coupés: one by Zagato (628 built) and another by Pinanfarina (26,084 built).

Lancia Fulvia

MODEL YEAR: 1963-1972

NUMBER MADE: 339,653

SPECIAL REMARKS: The Fulvia too was also available as four-door saloon and as a coupé,

both of which had four doors. The total of saloons was 192,097. Both types had a choice of 1,091, 1,216, or 1,298 cc engines but the coupés were also available with a 1,584 cc motor.

Lancia Beta

MODEL YEAR: 1972-1981

NUMBER MADE: 394,970

SPECIAL REMARKS: The Beta was powered by a four-cylinder engine that was mounted transversely and slightly tilted forwards under the bonnet. The engines ranged from 1,297-1,995 cc and had double overhead camshafts.

Lea Francis

Richard Lea and Gordon Francis started building cycles in 1895 and they built their

The first post-war cars still had stand-alone headlights.

first car in 1903. This was interesting from a technical standpoint because of its three-cylinder engine with overhead camshaft but few were built.

The company started building motorcycles in 1905 and did not return to cars until 1920. Before World War II they built both smaller cars, including sports cars and bigger cars with 2.5-litre engines. The first post-war models were the Twelve and Fourteen, which were respectively powered by 1,496 and 1,767 cc engines.

The company did not manage to sell them in large volume with only 326 cars being built in 1946. This had risen in 1948 to 551. Although demand rose steadily, with the best result being achieved in 1950 with more than 700 cars being sold, it remained too few to keep the company going. The low volume was largely due to the hand-made method of construction instead of mass production techniques.

When only 170 cars were sold in 1952 production had to stop. The company lost

£74,000 in 1959. A final effort was made to save the company in 1960 with the launch of a new sports car. This used parts from the Ford Zephyr, no longer built but with an adequate supply of parts, but the project never got beyond the prototype stage.

A new company under the name Lea-Francis Cars Ltd was founded in 1980 to breathe life into the old name, with the intention of bringing out a sports car based on Jaguar parts. Six years later in 1986 they issued a press statement that the car would be built in small numbers but the first model has yet to be seen.

A further bulletin in 1991 said production would start in 1992 with the intention to build 12 to 20 cars to be sold for £67,000 each. Since then there has been no further news.

Lea Francis cars

COUNTRY OF ORIGIN: United Kingdom

Lea Francis 14 hp

MODEL YEAR: 1946-1954

NUMBER MADE: 3,360

SPECIAL REMARKS: The Lea-Francis Fourteen was a pre-war design with fixed axles front

Lea-Francis built many of its cars as estates. Of the 551 cars sold in 1948, at least 243 were wooden-backed estates.

This 1947 Lea-Francis could be a Twelve or a Fourteen. Seen here prepared for a Concours d'Elegance.

and back and mechanical brakes. Wilson pre-selector semi-automatic transmission could be fitted as an option. From 1949 this model had independent front suspension.

Lea Francis 12 hp

MODEL YEAR: 1946-1948

NUMBER MADE: 13

SPECIAL REMARKS: The Twelve was virtually identical to the Fourteen except for the 1,496 cc engine.
The car proved not to be popular with only 13 sold between 1946-1947. The engine produced 55 bhp at 4,700 rpm.

Lea Francis Sports

MODEL YEAR: 1950-1954

NUMBER MADE: 77

SPECIAL REMARKS: Lea-Francis attempted to

The Lea-Francis Sports was more of a 2+2 tourer than sporting-car.

The instrument panel of a 1951 Lea-Francis Sports.

reach a bigger market with its sports car but unfortunately this failed. The 2,496 cc four-cylinder initially produced 106 then 125 bhp at 5,200 rpm.

Lincoln

A Chrysler Imperial, Rolls-Royce, and Lincoln have one thing in common: these are the cars bought by queens, emperors, and wealthy people. Lincoln cars are solely made to order and are therefore much rarer than Cadillacs, which are the most numerous cars among the wealthy.
Lincoln's history starts in 1901 with Henry M. Leland, who built his first Oldsmobile in that year. He then founded Cadillac in 1903 but left General Motors in 1917 and with his son started again with his own company in 1921. The result was Lincoln but father and son had difficulty with the tough competition. There were more than one hundred car makers in the USA alone at that time. One third of these directed their efforts to the higher segments of the market. The Lelands tried to break into the upper sector with their V-8 engines. Their major opponents were Cadillac, Packard, and Franklin. Despite financial help from Leland's friend Henry Ford, the company got into difficulties and only a take-over by Ford could save the company. At that time Ford sold more than one million cars each year so he could afford to take the risk. With injection of funds from Ford things went better for Lincoln. The cars were of exceptionally high quality so that soon several hundred were being sold each

The last aesthetically pleasing model was the Continental Mark II which was very expensive at $10,000. A total of 3,000 were sold between October 1955 and May 1957.

year but it did not remain at this level. The Dutch specialist Johan Tjaarda van Sterkenburg, known more simply in Detroit as John Tjaarda, designed a new model, the Lincoln Zephyr in 1936. This was a superb car with a streamlined body and front-mounted V-12 engine. Lincoln had sold fewer than 4,000 cars in 1935 but in 1936 they sold 22,000 of which 15,000 were Zephyrs. The Lincoln Continental made its appearance in 1940. This car was the foundation of the post-war models. In common with other car makers, Lincoln worked for the army during the war, making 145,000 Jeep bodies, 25,332 tank engines, and 24,929 engine mounts for B-24 bombers. There was no time during the war for the development of new car models so the Lincolns that rolled off the line on 10 January 1946 were almost the same as those of 1940.

Only the bumpers, wheel nave plates and chrome trim on the bonnet or hood were different. The cheapest model was just known as a Lincoln and had a 5-litre V-12 with power output of 130 bhp at 3,600 rpm. The standard equipment for this car included electro-hydraulically operated windows. Previously this had been an optional extra. In addition to the "cheaper" Lincolns, there were also the more expensive Continental models in coupé and convertible versions. The Continental cost three times as much as a Ford

coupé or convertible of those days. Of the 13,496 cars Lincoln sold in 1946, there were 466 Continentals (265 coupés and 201 convertibles). The cars remained virtually unchanged the following year until the 1949 models were introduced on 22 April 1948. The range now consisted of the Lincoln and Lincoln Cosmopolitan. These cars looked similar and had the same mechanical parts but the standard Lincoln had a 121 in (3,080 mm) wheelbase compared with the 125 in (3,180 mm) of its bigger stablemate. The V-12 engine had now been replaced by a more modern V-8 of 5,520 cc and 152 bhp and there was independent suspension at the front.

The North Koreans invaded South Korea on 25 June 1950 and once the US decided to get involved the sales of cars shot up. Everyone remembered World War II when no new cars were built for several years. Lincoln launched two new hard-top models several weeks later: the Lido and Capri. The Capri became a separate model in the Lincoln family in 1952.

Lincoln's V-8 engines were still old-fashioned side-valve units at a time when their competitors offered modern overhead valve motors. Lincoln dealers were pleased to be able to offer a modern engine from 1952.

All Lincolns were equipped as standard with power-assisted brakes and steering from 1960 plus a heater and believe it not, a clock! The model illustrated is a Premiere.

It was a 5,203 cc V-8 that produced 162 bhp at 3,900 rpm. It was considered thrifty with its consumption of "only" 15 miles per gallon (20 litres per 100 km). Of interest to the hobbyist was that this engine proved to have almost endless possibilities for improving its performance. The works participated in the Carrera Pan-America and carried off first prize in 1953 and 1954.

Lincoln appeared with a new Lincoln Continental Mk II at the Paris motor show in the autumn of 1955. The car cost $10,000, which was a great deal of money at that time but for this sum the buyer got an entirely hand-built two-door coupé. The Mk II followed in 1958 with a monocoque body. The days of the practical and delightful Lincolns were now over. The cars got steadily bigger and their engines more powerful so that in 1970 they were 225 in (5,720 mm) long with a 7,536 cc engine that produced 370 bhp at 4,600 rpm.

What of today? Today's Lincolns only share their high prices with their predecessors. There are four models: Lincoln Continental, the Town Car, the Mark VIII, and the Navigator, which is an off-road vehicle with a 5.8-litre V-8 engine of 232 bhp. The other models have a 4.6-litre V-8 unit of (in order) 264, 284, or 294 bhp. Except for the 4x4, all the other cars have front-wheel drive. The motors have double twin overhead camshafts with four valves per cylinder.

Lincoln cars

COUNTRY OF ORIGIN: USA

Lincoln Continental

MODEL YEAR: 1946-1948

NUMBER MADE: 3,334

Lincoln brought out this Continental in 1946. Apart from its heavier bumper and altered grille it was the same as the 1942 model.

SPECIAL REMARKS: The Continental was a superb hand-made car which was only available as a coupé or convertible. It was about 25 per cent more expensive than the "ordinary" Lincoln.

Lincoln Cosmopolitan

MODEL YEAR: 1949

NUMBER MADE: 35,123

SPECIAL REMARKS: This model replaced the Continental in 1949. The 5,520 cc V-8 engine had power of 154 bhp at 3,600 rpm.

Lincoln Premiere

MODEL YEAR: 1956

NUMBER MADE: 41,531

SPECIAL REMARKS: The Premiere was a new model that was positioned in 1956 between the cheaper Capri and more expensive new Continental Mk II. The V-8 engine was now 6,031 cc and produced 304 bhp.

Lincoln Continental Mk III

MODEL YEAR: 1971

NUMBER MADE: 27,901

SPECIAL REMARKS: The final Lincoln Continental Convertible was supplied in 1967. The

The Continental Mk III of 1958 was an ugly monster by comparison with its predecessor. It had strange headlights and inward-slanting rear window.

Both the Continental and Continental Mk III were available in 1971. The former could be purchased as coupé or four-door saloon but the Mk III was only available as a coupé.

Mk III was also only available as a six-seater coupé. The 7.5-litre V-8 motor produced 370 bhp in 1971 giving a capability of 134 mph (215 kph).

Lotus

In common with Ferrari, Lamborghini, and Maserati, the Lotus name is linked to sports cars. But like its Italian competitors, Lotus also built 2+2 cars and we do mean 2+2 and not four-seaters for the rear of these cars were really only suitable for small children. This meant that the children could travel with their parents in the sports car, for the Elan+2 and Elite S1 certainly were sports cars. The Elan sports car had a 84 in (2,130 mm) wheelbase but the + 2 version had a 96$^1/_2$ in (2,450 mm) wheelbase and its 169 in (4,290 mm) long body was 23$^1/_2$ in (600 mm) longer than the basic sports car. This model was launched at

Colin Chapman (1928-1982).

the London motor show in September 1967. It was instantly clear that a true sports car lurked within the polyester body shell. The Elan had disc brakes all-round and was powered by a 1,558 cc four-cylinder engine that developed 119 bhp at 6,250 rpm. The car accelerated from 0-60 in 7.6 seconds (0-100 kph in 7.9 seconds and had a top speed according to factory information of 120 mph (193 kph).

The Elan+2 ceased production in 1974 and was followed by the Elite S1. The Elan+2 looked precisely like the sports car of the similar name but the Elite S1 had no resemblance whatever with the super sports car that was so far ahead of its rivals between 1958 and 1963. This new car looked more of an estate car than a sporting coupé. The body was polyester once more of course and there was a 1,973 cc Jensen-Healey engine under the bonnet. The cylinder head had twin overhead camshafts and four valves per cylinder to deliver 155 bhp at 6,500 rpm. The model remained in production for six years but did not sell well.

Lotus cars

COUNTRY OF ORIGIN: United Kingdom

Lotus Elan +2

MODEL YEAR: 1969-1974

NUMBER MADE: 3,300

SPECIAL REMARKS: The Elan +2 was regularly improved. A luxury S version appeared in 1970 with a 126 bhp engine. The cars were available with either four-speed or five-speed gearboxes.

Lotus Elite S1

MODEL YEAR: 1974-1980

NUMBER MADE: 2,398

SPECIAL REMARKS: The rear window of the Elite S1 acted as a "third door" which made the car look like an estate. It was fast though: the top speed was 131 mph (210 kph). The Elite S1 accelerated from 0-60 mph in 6.7 seconds (0-100 kph in 7 seconds).

The Lotus Elite S1 had a 97¹/₂ in (2,480 mm) wheelbase and an overall length of 175¹/₂ in (4,460 mm).
The American version had bigger bumpers to make it 4 in (100 mm) longer but it did not improve its looks.

The Elan +2 was slightly longer than the standard Elan but otherwise the bodies were identical.

Maserati

The Italians celebrated in 1994: Sophia Loren celebrated her sixtieth birthday and Marcello Mastroianni his seventieth, while Maserati celebrated eighty years in business. Brothers Alfieri, Ettore, Bindo, and Ernesto Maserati set themselves up on 14 December 1914 as Officina Alfieri Maserati SpA. They ran a garage and were dealers for Isotta Fraschini cars which they prepared for motor sport. During World War I the brothers also produced sparking plugs. They brought out their first sports car under the Maserati name in 1926 with which the famous driver Alfieri won his class in the Targa Florio on 25 April 1926. The famous Neptune's trident emblem was painted on the car by the sixth brother Mario.

Maserati remain interested in motor racing and cars bearing the trident emblem won the Indianapolis 500 in 1939 and 1940. Fangio drove to the Formula One World Championship in a Maserati in 1954 and 1957. Maserati also won the 500 and 1,000 kilometre races at the Nürburgring in 1955, 1956, 1960, and 1961. They have also won a number of other long distance races.

Maserati was one of the few constructors that also sold racing cars to private individuals but this did not provide enough profit to keep the business going. and it was taken over in 1937 by the industrialist Commendatore Adolfo Orsi. The contract of the sale stipulated that the brothers must work for Orsi for a further ten years. It was not until 1947 then that the brothers returned to Bologna, where they started a new company, naming their new marque Osca. When the Maserati brothers left the Modena works they were succeeded in the business by

Omer, the young son of Orsi who offered Ferrari engineers Massiminio and Bellantani money to join him. Some thirty people were employed by Officina Alfieri Maserati at that time. Just as before the war the company mainly built racing and sports cars and heavy additional financing was needed once more. The company then made the wise decision to produce a grand tourer or Gran Turismo for a wider public.

The 1,000 cc engine from the 6 CM racing car was bored out to1,500 cc for the first "family" car. The car was the A6 1500 2+2 coupé, for which the body was designed and built by Pinin Farina, still written at that time as two words. It was launched at the Geneva motor show in 1947. The engine capacity grew in 1951 to 2 litres but there was still only a single overhead camshaft. This changed when Gioacchino Colombo got his hands on the engine in 1952 and gave it twin camshafts and three carburettors instead of one of each. This engine was capable of winning races but it was also ideal for normal road-going cars. It was installed in the A6G2000 in 1954.

The car was sold in small quantity up to 1957. In that year Maserati launched its 3500 GT which formed the basis for all the future six-cylinder engines. This car was very successful and was sold for some years.

When the accounts were done in 1957 it showed that 140 road cars had been built since 1947. Sale of ten cars per year was clearly not profitable so the new technical director Giulio Alfieri was given orders to develop a new car. The A6G2000 engine was bored out to 3,485 cc to provide power of 226 bhp at 5,500 rpm. To save money, the gearbox came from ZF in Germany and back axle from Salisbury in the United Kingdom. The clutch was from Borg & Beck, brakes

Bindo, Ernesto, and Ettore Maserati.

from Girling, and the suspension from Alford & Alder. The aluminium body was produced by Touring of Milan and when the car was shown at Geneva in 1957, the orders flooded in. It was even necessary to build a new factory for the car! Alfieri continued to develop the engine and power climbed steadily with the sales figures. The 3500 GT, as the car was known, got a five-speed gearbox in 1961 and fuel injection.

Besides sports cars, Maserati has also made 2+2 cars and "saloons". The 3500 GT was followed by the Sebring with a 100 mm (4 in) shorter chassis, that was only available with an injected engine. Almost all the 3500 GT cars had an aluminium body by Touring but

the Sebrings were built in steel by Vignale. The Sebring customer could choose initially from two engines and after 1965 from three: of 3,485, 3,694, and 4,014 cc. The power ranged from 235-255 bhp.

One of the finest Italian cars of the 1950s was the Maserati 5000 GT, the first of which was built specially for the Shah of Persia. The Shah was a motoring enthusiast who loved to drive fast. He ordered the 5000 GT with a V-8 engine based on the 450 S racing car. The engine was increased in capacity to 4,935 cc and retained its quadruple overhead camshafts and twin-spark ignition. Depending on the level of tune, the engine produced between 310 and 370 bhp which could comfortably take the 2+2 to 172 mph (275 kph)! Maserati introduced its first Quattroporte or four-door saloon in 1964. It was the fastest "family" car there was.

The Quattroporte was supplied with either a 4,136 or 4,719 cc V-8 engine with quad overhead camshafts that produced 260 or 300 bhp to give top speeds of 137 (220) or 150 mph (240 kph). Maserati did not restrict itself to one body specialist and this car was designed and built by Pietro Frua. The smaller 2+2 version, the Mexico, was a very luxurious car with air conditioning as standard equipment.

The Maserati Indy followed in 1969 as a spacious 2+2 with monocoque body by Vignale. The Indy was supplied with one of three V-8 engine with the customary four camshafts of

All 60 of the A6 1500 cars had Pinin Farina bodies. This is a 1949 example.

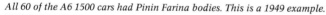

4,136 cc/260 bhp, 4,719 cc/290 bhp, or 4,930 cc/320 bhp.

Citroën took over Maserati in 1968 and this resulted in the Citroën SM or Citroën-Maserati (see Citroën) and the Maserati Merak. The subsequent owner was the Argentinean De Tomaso, followed by Fiat who decided in 1997 to merge Maserati with Ferrari. Through its changes of ownership, the long and rich history of the Maserati marque has remained distinctive.

Maserati cars

COUNTRY OF ORIGIN: Italy

Maserati A6 1500/2000

MODEL YEAR: 1946-1957

NUMBER MADE: 135

SPECIAL REMARKS: This car had a single overhead camshaft but the final 59 of the succeeding A6 2000 cars had twin camshafts. The works would never turn out a car again with fewer than two camshafts.

Maserati 3500 GT/GTI

MODEL YEAR: 1958-1964

NUMBER MADE: 2,223

SPECIAL REMARKS: The final 242 of these cars had Lucas fuel injection.
The earlier cars had triple twin-choke Weber carburettors.

The 3500 GT and GTI. were the first mass-produced Maseratis. This is a 1964 3500 GTI.

Maserati Sebring

MODEL YEAR: 1962-1966

NUMBER MADE: 444

SPECIAL REMARKS: The Sebring appeared smaller than its predecessors but offered at least as much room. The Sebring was a much more modern car than those that had gone before.

Maserati 5000 GT

MODEL YEAR: 1959-1965

NUMBER MADE: 32

Touring built a total of four bodies for the 5000 GT. The first car was supplied to the Shah of Persia in October 1959.

SPECIAL REMARKS: The 5000 GT was one of the most expensive Maseratis and was only made to order. Most customers ordered a body from Allemano.

The Shah of Persia's 2+2 had little room in the back.

The Quattroporte had a 90 mm (3¹/₂ in) longer wheelbase at 2,750 mm (108 in) than the Mexico to make it a true four-seater.

Maserati Quattroporte

MODEL YEAR: 1964-1971

NUMBER MADE: 759

SPECIAL REMARKS: These spacious and luxurious cars were fitted with complicated De Dion rear axles until 1967. The V-8 engine always had four overhead camshafts.

Maserati Mexico

MODEL YEAR: 1966-1972

NUMBER MADE: 250

SPECIAL REMARKS: The high cost of the Maserati Mexico made it equal to buying 14 Fiat Nuova 500s. Consequently few of these 2+2 cars were sold. An automatic gearbox was available as an option.

With its 4,670 mm (184 in) length, the Mexico had room in the back for two small passengers.

In spite of its attractive low lines, the Indy was big enough for four people.

Maserati Indy

MODEL YEAR: 1969-1974

NUMBER MADE: 1,136

SPECIAL REMARKS: For a long time, the Maserati Indy was the best-selling Maserati. Only the Ghibli from that era with 1,274 units sold better. Four people could travel in comfort for hours at speeds up to 137 mph (220 kph).

Mercedes-Benz

The French celebrated the centenary of the motor car in 1984 because Edouard Delamare-Deboutteville built his first car in 1884. Austrians have long insisted that their Siegfried Marcus built the first ever car but although his work was important for the development of cars, there is finally agreement that the first car was built by Gottlieb Daimler and Karl Benz. The two did not know each other with Daimler living and working in Cannstadt while Benz was in Mannheim. But they achieved their common objective in 1886. They merged their individual companies in 1926 to form Daimler-Benz AG, which is commonly known as Mercedes-Benz. Mercedes-Benz always made fine cars with outstanding pre-war examples including

The 180 and 190 were the first Mercedes-Benz cars with monocoque bodies. About half of them were sold with diesel engines.

huge sporting and touring cars with big turbocharged engines. The company has also built cars for the "common man" and restarted after World War II with relatively small cars in 1946 to a market screaming out for cars. Post-war production started with the 170 V, which was also built between 1936-1942. The first vehicles to roll off the line were equipped as delivery vans because of the tremendous demand for them. Private cars followed off the productions lines once more in 1947. These still had headlights that were separate from the body and an externally carried spare wheel at the back. The doors also opened dangerously "the wrong way". The engine was nothing special either: a 1,697 cc four-cylinder side-valve unit with a modest 38 bhp at 3,600 rpm. But that was just the beginning. Two years later in 1949 the car could be ordered as a cabriolet or convertible. The 170 series could be divided

into two: the 170 V and 170 S. The "S" types appeared in 1949 with a slightly larger body. It resembled the 170 V. Both types were available with a diesel engine. The first six-cylinder overhead valve and camshaft engined Mercedes appeared in 1951. Mercedes was back to its former position and was able to supply more expensive cars again, such as the Mercedes 300 which was sold as four-seater saloon and convertible to wealthy persons. There were also three-seater drophead or hardtop coupés and a sporting version, the SL, with gull-wing doors. These sporting cars fall outside the compass of this book but are worth mentioning in passing.

The "cheap" 170 was replaced in 1953 by the 180. There was little mechanical difference between the two. The engines were slightly bigger but still used the old cylinder-head with side valves. The stablemate, the 190, was the first four-cylinder engined Mercedes-Benz to have overhead valves and an overhead camshaft. This 190 was also available as a three-seater convertible. Unfortunately the 190 got itself a bad name in Germany as the car favoured by prostitutes.

In common with other makers, Mercedes-Benz engines steadily increased in size and power. The 190 led to the 220 that was powered by a six-cylinder engine. The 220 could be ordered as saloon, coupé, or convertible. They were expensive, superbly made cars. The 300 series was also consistently improved. The 300 SE had pneumatic suspension and disc brakes in 1961. The coupé

The 220 SE launched in 1962 looked good and had space for five persons.

Mercedes 200 and 230 had the same bodies. The 1,988 cc four-cylinder engine of the 200 produced 95 bhp in 1965 while the 2,281 cc six-cylinder unit gave 120 bhp.

and convertible models were outside the reach of most people. The real top of the tree though was the Mercedes 600, that appeared in 1964. This car was entirely hand built in various body types: with four or six doors. With the Pullman Landaulet version the canvas roof could be opened behind the rear seat while the rest of the car remained closed. The Mercedes 600 had every last word in luxury so that it was difficult to find an accessory that was not included as standard equipment. The 600's engine was a 6,332 cc aluminium V-8 with power of 250 bhp at 4,000 rpm. The car was built until 1981 with 2,677 being sold in total, including 487 Pullman bodies of which 59 had Landaulet soft-tops. Mercedes also built 44 of them with armour-plating at a cost of more than 500,000 Deutschmarks.

The top speed of 75 mph (120 kph) made the 170 S convertible a sporty car but not a sports car.

Mercedes-Benz cars

COUNTRY OF ORIGIN: Germany

Mercedes-Benz 170

The 170 S was a slightly larger version of the 170 V but had the same 2,850 mm (112 in) wheelbase. The car was 170 mm (6³/₄ in) longer than its forerunner.

MODEL YEAR: 1947-1955

NUMBER MADE: 155,958

SPECIAL REMARKS: This total includes 83,290 of the 170 V series. The model was designed before the war by Hans Nibel.

Mercedes-Benz 220

MODEL YEAR: 1951-1955

NUMBER MADE: 17,236

The 220 S coupé was shown at the Frankfurt motor show in 1955 but the first cars were not delivered until 1956. The first 220 SE (with fuel injection as shown) was added to the range in 1958.

A 220 SE convertible. This example was built in 1960.

SPECIAL REMARKS: The 220 had a modern body with headlights incorporated within the body. The six-cylinder overhead-valve engine with overhead camshaft had a capacity of 2,195 cc and power of 80 bhp at 4,850 rpm.

Mercedes-Benz 300

MODEL YEAR: 1951-1958

NUMBER MADE: 9,148

The 300 also grew in size. The 1961 300 D shown got a 100 mm (4 in) longer wheelbase at 3,150 mm (204 in) and an overall length of 5,190 mm (124 in).

SPECIAL REMARKS: The Mercedes 300 is one of the most expensive cars in the world. The 300 S in particular cost ten times as much as a Fiat 600.

Mercedes-Benz 280 SEL

MODEL YEAR: 1968-1970

NUMBER MADE: 8,250

SPECIAL REMARKS: The 280 SEL had the same

The finest of the fine: a 300 SEL with 6.3-litre V-8 engine from the 600. Its 250 bhp gave a top speed of 140 mph (225 kph).

The S types made their appearance in 1972. They were first shown at Frankfurt motor show. The 280 SE had a 2,746 cc six-cylinder engine with twin overhead camshafts to deliver 185 bhp at 6,000 rpm.

body as the 300 SEL. Customers could choose from four engines of 2,778, 2,996, 3,499, or 6,332 cc with power of 160-250 bhp.

Mercedes-Benz 600

MODEL YEAR: 1964-1981

NUMBER MADE: 2,677

SPECIAL REMARKS: The Mercedes 600 was the top-of-the-range for a long time, capable of competing with Rolls-Royce. The 6,332 cc V-8 engine produced 250 bhp at 4,000 rpm to give a top speed of 125 mph (200 kph).

The Mercedes-Benz 600 was a truly big car. The Pullman illustrated was 6,240 mm (245$^{1}/_{2}$ in) making it 2,170 mm (85$^{1}/_{2}$ in) longer than a VW Beetle.

Mercury

Mercury

During the later 1930s Henry Ford noted how some of his former customers switched to a competitor's model. The reason was that the most expensive Ford cost $947 while the cheapest Lincoln Zephyr was $1,399. Ford had nothing to offer for the gap between these two, so that customers who traded up bought a Dodge, Pontiac, or Studebaker Commander. It was only after Edsel Ford had convinced his stubborn and slightly senile father that a medium-priced range was needed that its new Mercury marque was introduced to Ford dealers in October 1938. The Mercury looked good and was technically up-to-date. Finally, three years after Chevrolet and even eleven years after Plymouth, Mercury cars had hydraulic brakes. Mercury models were offered between $946 and $1,212 to close the gap between a Ford and a Lincoln.

The US government took control of the Mercury's supply of parts on 2 February 1942 for military use. It was almost precisely four years later on 8 February 1946 that Mercury re-appeared, now in the showrooms of Lincoln dealers. Externally the cars had hardly changed but there was an entirely new V-8 engine under the hood or bonnet. This engine was 3,916 cc and produced 100 bhp at 3,800 rpm. This side-valve unit was bored out to 4,185 cc in 1949 to increase power

Ford sold its 40 millionth car in September 1953. It was this Mercury Monterey Special Custom Convertible, which was built at the Wayne Assembly Plant.

Although the 1968 Cyclone looked attractive it was not a practical car. The almost horizontal rear window made it almost impossible to sit in the back and there was precious little room in the trunk or boot.

to 127 bhp. This was a big improvement of course but the real breakthrough came in 1954 when the engine got overhead valves. Although the engine was almost the same capacity at 4,195 cc, power had shot up to 163 bhp. Once Chrysler started the horsepower wars Mercury had to join in. The technical experts reconsidered the engine afresh, bored it out, fitted different carburettors, new heads with larger valves and they were proud of the results. The 4,785 cc engine in 1955 produced 201 bhp. The following year the engine's capacity and power further increased. In 1956, 5,112 cc produced 228 bhp and the following year 6,031 cc developed 294 bhp, then 7,045 cc gave more than 400 bhp in 1958. This record remained until 1965 when a 7,015 cc produced 431 bhp.

Meanwhile the Mercury resembled a Lincoln more than a Ford and the public approved. The one millionth Mercury was produced in 1950. That same year a Mercury won the Indianapolis 500, which produced valuable publicity.

The Mercury was an expensive car in Europe. When the supply of unsold cars got too big at Ford in The Netherlands, they sent this post card out to dealers.

A 1970 Mercury Marquis with 4-door hardtop sedan body cost $3,910.

No Comets were built in 1970 but this model returned in 1971 with a new body.

The news of the year in 19512 was the "Merc-O-Matic" automatic transmission and the following year the cars were given completely new bodies. Then there were two basic models of Mercury: the Custom and slightly more expensive Monterey. Both cars had a 118 in (3,000 mm) wheelbase and were 202 in (5,140 mm) long. The cars looked modern but still had a side-valve V-8 engine. A new Mercury Montclair was added in 1955 as the top of the range. This was only available with automatic gearbox and its engine was tuned to deliver 195 bhp. The bottom of the range was extended in 1956 with a cheaper Medalist which was only produced for the US market. The Medalist did not survive long and had disappeared by 1957. The older Custom model was by then also no longer available, leaving customers to choose between a Monterey, Montclair, of Turnpike Cruiser. This latter model was a dream car

for many in those days. When the Turnpike Cruiser won the 1957 Indianapolis 500 the factory produced 1,265 replicas of the Indy car.

The Turnpike Cruiser was powered by a 6-litre Lincoln V-8 engine that had 290 bhp power available. The Cruiser was taken off the market in 1958 to be replaced by the cheaper Medalist. A new top-of-the-range Park Lane was launched as hardtop coupé or convertible. Its 7,047 cc V-8 produced almost 400 bhp.

Mercury celebrated its twentieth year in 1959 and customers shared the festive spirit with even bigger cars. The 222 in (5,650 mm) Park Lane would no longer fit in most garages. Mercury sold 150,000 cars that year:

Monterey	89,277
Montclair	23,602
Park Lane	12,523
Station Wagon	24,598

Increasing numbers of Americans switched to smaller and cheaper European or Japanese cars in the late 1950s. When the "big three" in Detroit ran into difficulties as a result, they started to build "compacts". Lincoln/Mercury dealers got a new "small" car called Comet on 17 March 1960. The interest in the car was staggering. That first year 116,331 of them were sold. In European terms the 195 in (4,950 mm) car was not small. The Comet was still 500 mm (19³/₄ in) longer than a Mer-

The 1975 Grand Marquis was an imposing car. As 4-door hardtop it weighed 4,895 lb (2,225 kg). Its 7,536 cc V-8 engine produced 221 bhp at 4,000 rpm to give a top speed of 125 mph (200 kph).

The most expensive Cougar in 1975 was also the best-seller. A total of 22,353 "standard" Cougars and 38,275 XR-7 models were sold.

cedes-Benz 180. Under its hood or bonnet was a 2,364 cc six-cylinder unit of 91 bhp. This engine quickly grew in size. In 1961 it was 2,781 cc and by 1962 then 3,620 cc. The car was available in 1963 with a 4,267 cc V-8 engine so that there was no question of economic, low-consumption, cheap, "small" American cars.

All Mercury cars got new bodies in 1965 which the public approved of. They sold 181,699 of the larger models and 165,032 of the "smaller" ones. When the cars got another set of new names in 1966, these were Comet, Capri, Caliente, and Cyclone, with Comet being the smallest and Cyclone the largest.

Meanwhile, Ford had enjoyed great success with the Mustang sports coupé. Chevrolet had developed their Camaro and the Mercury dealer got the Cougar in 1967 which sold 150,893 in the first year alone. Such figures were never to be repeated.

The Mercury Monarch was introduced in July 1974. This 200 in (5,080 mm) car was termed a "compact" in the USA.

Mercury remains a popular car in America that sells well. The cars get regular facelifts to prompt owners to buy new ones so that they are not seen in the old models. The range has grown in scope. In 1974 it consisted of the Comet, Comet GT, Cougar, Montego, Marquis, and Colony Park station wagon.

Mercury cars

COUNTRY OF ORIGIN: USA

Mercury Custom

MODEL YEAR: 1952

NUMBER MADE: Unknown

SPECIAL REMARKS: Mercury models got new bodies in 1952 with a one-piece windscreen and panoramic rear window. The V-8 engine still had side-valves. The 4,185 cc engine produced 127 bhp at 3,700 rpm.

Mercury Monterey

MODEL YEAR: 1955

NUMBER MADE: 151,453

When Mercury launched the Montclair in June 1955 Motor Trend magazine awarded it "best-looking American of the year".

SPECIAL REMARKS: The Monterey's wheelbase was 119 in (3,020 mm) and in four-door sedan body was 206 in (5,240 mm) long. It was also available as two-door hardtop coupé (69,093) and station wagon (11,968).

Mercury Turnpike Cruiser

MODEL YEAR: 1957

NUMBER MADE: 16,861

The 1957 Turnpike Cruiser was a direct descendant of a 1956 concept car taken to motor shows.

SPECIAL REMARKS: The Turnpike Cruiser was sold as a two-door hardtop coupé and convertible.
Both had a 6,031 cc V-8 engine of 294 bhp at 4,600 rpm and Merc-O-Matic automatic transmission.

Mercury Park Lane

MODEL YEAR : 1958

NUMBER MADE: 9,252

The 1958 Park Lane had Merc-O-Matic automatic transmission, together with power-steering and power-assisted brakes as standard equipment.

SPECIAL REMARKS: The Park Lane had to compete with Buick's Roadmaster. The engine was a massive 7,045 cc to deliver 365 bhp at 4,600 rpm. The Merc-O-Matic automatic gear-change was done by means of a push-button on the dashboard.

Mercury Comet (1960)

MODEL YEAR: 1960

NUMBER MADE: 116,331

The Comet 2-door sedan was the best-seller of 1962 with 73,800 being delivered.

SPECIAL REMARKS: The Comet was launched in March 1960. The car was the first Mercury with a monocoque body and also first with a six-cylinder engine. The car reached 84 mph (135 kph). It was available as two or four-door sedan and as a station wagon.

Mercury Capri

MODEL YEAR: 1966

NUMBER MADE: 30,066

SPECIAL REMARKS: In 1966 98.2 per of all Mercury cars had an automatic gearbox, 97 per cent had power-steering, while 65.6 per cent had power-assisted brakes.

Mercury Cougar

MODEL YEAR: 1967

NUMBER MADE: 150,893

SPECIAL REMARKS: The 1967 Cougar had much in common with Ford's Mustang.

Of the 20,542 Cougar XR-7 cars sold by Mercury in 1970, 1,977 were convertibles. Only 51,801 "ordinary" Cougars were sold.

Customers could choose from two V-8 engines of 4,728 cc/228 bhp or 6,384 cc/324 bhp.

Mercury Comet (1971)

MODEL YEAR: 1971

NUMBER MADE: 83,000

SPECIAL REMARKS: The new Comet was based on the Ford Maverick. It had 2,796 cc six-cylinder engine for 101 bhp or 3,272 cc/117 bhp six-cylinder unit. For the real enthusiast there was also a 4,945 V-8 to produce 213 bhp at 4,600 rpm.

Messerschmitt

Messerschmitt fighters were famous in Germany during World War II and feared by the Allies. Messerschmitt rocket-propelled fighters were brought into service right at the end of the war. If this had happened earlier, Allied air personnel might have experienced greater difficulties.

Things looked much more bleak for the company after the war. Germany was forbidden to build aircraft and Prof. Willy Messerschmitt kept his people together by giving them all manner of jobs. They were joined in 1952 by an engineer called Fritz Fend who had been building single-seater midget cars for several years and he managed to persuade Messer-

schmitt to put the car into production. One car for one person appeared not to sell well and so Messerschmitt introduced a two-seater at Geneva in 1953. The passenger sat behind the driver under a plastic bubble canopy which had to be opened to get in and out of the car.

Instead of a steering wheel there was a mini set of handlebars. The Kabinenroller KR 175, as the factory named it, was powered by a 175 cc two-stroke engine by Fichtel & Sachs. Because the engine produced 9 bhp but the car only weighed 220 kg (484 lb) the top speed was of the order of 50 mph (80 kph). A total of 10,666 Messerschmitts were sold. These were followed in 1955 by a 200 cc model which was also very successful. Sales shot up to 41,190. Meanwhile Germany had been given permission to build aircraft once more so Messerschmitt sold the factory in 1957 to Fritz Fend who continued to build them as FMR (Fahrzeug-und Maschinenbau Regensburg). It was under Fend's leadership that the "Messerschmitt" Tg 500 Tiger came into existence. The car was largely similar to the earlier models but instead had four wheels. The

Two Messerschmitt KR 200s next to each other. It could get very hot under the canopy, so many were equipped with a soft-top.

A KR 200 with radio and luggage rack (because there was no boot).

engine was twin-cylinder unit of 493 cc engine that delivered 19.5 bhp at 5,000 rpm. It was fairly heavy for a bubble car at 390 kg (858 lb) but still had a top speed of 78 mph (125 kph) which was extremely fast when sitting low to the ground between the wheels.

The Tiger was really aimed at young people but they found it too expensive and it was launched just when the boom in midget cars had waned. This car was reintroduced to the market as a replica in 1990 for 36,500 Deutschmarks, which means the owner can take to the road in an eye-catching vehicle for ten times the original price.

Messerschmitt cars

COUNTRY OF ORIGIN: Germany

Messerschmitt KR 175

MODEL YEAR: 1953-1955

NUMBER MADE: 19,666

SPECIAL REMARKS: Fend's single seater was probably originally intended for war disabled persons.
The Messerschmitt was principally for the person who did not want to ride a motorcycle. When a 200 cc engine was installed, the KR 200 was created of which 46,190 were sold.

The Tiger as seen from the front. It looked quite impressive.

FMR Tg 500

MODEL YEAR: 1958-1961

NUMBER MADE: 950

SPECIAL REMARKS: The Tiger was powered by a 500 cc twin-cylinder engine that produced 19.5 bhp. In common with the previous Messerschmitts, the engine was installed at the rear.

Metropolitan

In contrast to the "big three", Nash always built smaller cars. During the 1950s there was their Rambler which was "only" 185 in (4,710 mm) long. They also built bigger cars of course but they tended to specialise in smaller "compact" cars that were more economical with fuel. Nash and Hudson merged together in 1954 to form the American Motors Corporation and a new model that

The Tiger was dangerously fast with its top speed of 78 mph (125 kph).

A simple dashboard and three-speed gearbox with column change.

The Metropolitan was a small car. It was only 149 in (3,790 mm) long, making it 11 in (280 mm) shorter than a VW Beetle.

was developed that was to create a new marque, the Metropolitan. Nash had started developing this model back in 1950. This was an exceptionally small car in American terms. The bodies were built by Pininfarina and the cars were assembled by Austin in the United Kingdom using mechanical parts from the Austin A40. The engine was a 1,200 cc overhead valve unit that produced 43 bhp. When the British Motor Corporation, of which Austin was part, brought out a 1,500 cc engine, this was also available for the Metropolitan.

The three-seater car could be ordered as fixed-head coupé or convertible. The external appearance remained virtually unchanged during the years the car was built, though the models that left the Longbridge works after 1959 could be recognised by the boot lid or lid to the trunk. Earlier versions had no way in for luggage except via the back seat. The small car was never a tremendous success since it was far too unusual for its time and the average American preferred a "real" car.

Metropolitan cars

COUNTRY OF ORIGIN: United Kingdom

Metropolitan

MODEL YEAR: 1954-1962

NUMBER MADE: 104,368

SPECIAL REMARKS: The first cars were sold as Nash Metropolitans. In keeping with the

This 1958 model has no boot lid (or access to the trunk). The way in was through the back seat.

A small American Nash – but to smaller scale. A Metropolitan convertible.

fashion of the time, most cars were painted in a two-tone finish with pastel colours being especially popular.

MG

The MG marque is best known for its sports cars but before World War II, MG also built sportive four-seaters. Cecil Kimber (1888-1944) had developed a new car by late 1939 which should have gone into production in 1940. The war prevented this and so the plan lay dormant until 1947.

This type YA had two new advances: front wheel independent suspension by Alec (later Sir Alec) Issigonis who designed the Mini and rack and pinion steering. Otherwise the car was built out of parts from Wolseley cars and the Morris Ten. The body was from the Morris Eight, while the engine was from the MG TC sports car. The power output was brought back though to 46 bhp, which was far too low, for the YA weighed more than a

The most reliable instrument on an MG was the water temperature gauge which was screwed into the top of the radiator.

An MG for the entire family with four doors, two leather front seats and a leather bench seat in the back.

ton which kept top speed to little more than 62 mph (100 kph). To accelerate from 0-50 mph (0-80 kph) took the YA 18.2 seconds and 28.36 seconds to reach 60 mph (0-100 kph in 29.3 seconds). This was more of a luxury car than a sports saloon and it included all manner of features such as steel sunroof, leather upholstery, a curtain for the rear window, lots of walnut trim, and a windscreen that could be tilted forwards.

An open version of the YA was introduced in 1948, known as the YT, with a body produced by Morris Bodies. This four-seater had the same 54 bhp engine with twin SU-carburettors of the TC but it was not a great success and only 877 were sold.

The YB followed the YA in 1951 at a time when the competition offered the Jaguar XK120 and the Standard Vanguard. The 1949 Morris Minor also looked much more modern than the pre-war MG Y and so the sales dropped further.

A replacement for the elderly Y type was launched at the London motor show in 1953 but the public was not enthusiastic this time either. The main reason was that Abingdon's designers had named the new model the Magnette but this new car with streamlined monocoque body had nothing whatever to do with the famous Magnette sports car of the 1930s. It had a Wolseley 4/44 body with a different grille and a BMC four-cylinder engine of 1,489 cc. Despite twin SU carburettors, this overhead valve unit only produced 60 bhp. Since the four-door saloon tipped the scales at 2,464 lb (1,120 kg) it struggled to reach 78 mph (125 kph). But it was an attractive car with a body designed by Gerald Palmer who had also designed the Jowett Javelin. Palmer later became really famous for his Riley Pathfinder design.

In August 1956 the ZB was created from the ZA with the same body as its predecessor but a more powerful 68 bhp engine. A review at the time of the ZB Magnette found both engine and mechanics of the car extremely quiet and acceleration quite lively for a 1.5-litre touring saloon. The only complaint was the "sporting" sound of the exhaust which also caused a drone at speeds over 62 mph (100 kph). Otherwise the reviewer was pleased with the car in which he achieved a top speed of slightly over 90 mph (145 kph) in with average fuel consumption of 28$^1/_2$ miles per gallon (1 litre to 9.5 km). The ZB Magnette was the last saloon car to come out of the original MG works at Abingdon. Sub

A 1957 MG ZB Magnette shows her pretty lines.

sequent cars had less of an MG input. Wolseley brought out a new 15-60 model in December 1958 and this was followed a few months later by the Magnette Mk III. Once again the cars shared a body, which was designed by Pininfarina in Turin. The four-cylinder engine of the ZB Magnette was also used in the new car but the inlet and exhaust manifolds had been changed. The two SU carburettors were now type HD 4 instead of H2.

The successor Mk IV was shown in London in October 1961 with a body that was virtually unchanged. The reasons for a new model had to be searched for among the technical specification. The bore of the cylinders had been enlarged from 73 to 76 mm to produce a 1,622 cc unit instead of 1,489 cc. Furthermore, the Mk IV was optionally available with an automatic gearbox. The wheelbase had been lengthened to 100 in (2,540 mm) with a wider track. In common with other MG cars the interior of this new Magnette left omitted little anyone could desire. There were seats like two easy chairs at the front and although the rear bench seat was intended for two, there was room for three. The car had leather and wood in abundance and thick carpet on the floor.

The Magnette Mk IV brought a chapter to an end for MG. It was the last big car with the famous octagon on its radiator. A new era was opening up with the invention of the Mini, undoubtedly the most successful car ever to come out of Great Britain. The Mini was an example of modern small cars but it had one disadvantage. It was small. British Leyland had a solution for that too. In the summer of 1962 they brought out a larger version of the Mini, the Morris 1100. The 1100 body was designed by Pininfarina and several months later the same car could be seen on the MG stand in London. The Morris and MG looked identical but there was a difference between the two-door and four-door version of £90. A Morris cost £623 while the MG was £713. For this difference the purchaser got a bit more than an MG badge on the front of the car. The seats of the MG were of better quality and the MG engine was more powerful with 55 bhp instead of 48.

Both Morris and MG introduced their 1300 Mk II in October 1967. This car was really the same as the 1100 except with a 1,275 cc engine which produced 61 bhp in the Morris but 71 bhp at 6,000 rpm for the MG driver. The Morris factory at Longbridge, where the MG was also built, promised a top speed of 94 mph (150 kph) but with the wind behind it the MG could easily top 100 mph (160 kph).

MG cars

COUNTRY OF ORIGIN: United Kingdom

MG YA

MODEL YEAR: 1947-1951

NUMBER MADE: 6,158

SPECIAL REMARKS: Between 1951 and 1953, 1,301 YB cars were built from Morris and Wolseley parts.

MG YT

MODEL YEAR: 1951-1953

NUMBER MADE: 877

The MG YC appeared faster than it was but sold well in the USA.

SPECIAL REMARKS: When the YT chassis was shortened, the MG TD sports car was created. The sporty YT had a 54 bhp engine from the MG TC but it was not successful.

MG ZA Magnette

MODEL YEAR: 1953-1956

NUMBER MADE: 12,754

The body of the MG ZA Magnette was designed by Gerald Palmer. The car was certainly pretty but too lazy for an MG.

The MG ZA Magnette differentiated itself from the Wolseley 4/44 among other ways by its grille.

An MG ZA dashboard of 1954 with plenty of wood and an optimistic speedometer with a top speed of 100 mph (160 kph).

SPECIAL REMARKS: The ZA had the Wolseley 4/44 body and the same 1,489 cc overhead valve engine which only produced 60 bhp. Of the ZB, 23,846 were sold.

MG 1100

MODEL YEAR: 1962-1967

NUMBER MADE: 116,827

The MG 1300 was slightly faster than the Morris 1100 with its top speed of 94 mph (150 kph). This is a 1970 example.

SPECIAL REMARKS: Between 1967-1971 26,240 MG 1300 cars ere sold. The MG 1300 was in reality an enlarged Mini which many people found too small.

Mini

The Mini truly is a milestone in automobile history. This car started a new era in car

design. Virtually all makes which produced small cars imitated the concept. The Mini's engine, which formed one unit with the gearbox, was mounted transversely at the front of the car and drove the front wheels.

Alec Issigonis (later Sir Alec) had designed the Morris Minor immediately after World War II but he became truly world famous through the Mini which first appeared as either an Austin Seven or Morris Mini Minor 850. The Mini was a spacious four-seater with surprisingly small external dimensions. The wheelbase was 86³/₄ in (2,203 mm) and the cars was only 120 in (3,050 mm) long

Sir Alec Issigonis (1906-1988).

Almost every country in Europe has a Mini club to keep enthusiasts busy during the summer months.

The Mini has given rise to some weird and wonderful creations.

This mini-Mini convertible was on show at the 1993 Essen motor show.

Mini cars

COUNTRY OF ORIGIN: United Kingdom

Mini 850

MODEL YEAR: 1959-present day

NUMBER MADE: Unknown

SPECIAL REMARKS: The Mini was in a class of its own in the early days as a rally car and virtually invincible but the rest of the automobile industry also learned from its example.

A 1964 1,275 cc Mini Cooper at Zandvoort circuit.

compared with 94$\frac{1}{2}$ in (2,400 mm) and 160 in (4,070 mm) for the same dimensions of a VW Beetle. The engine was a straightforward 848 cc four-cylinder unit of 34 bhp but the four wheels had independent suspension with rubber dampers.

The car was launched to the press on 18 August 1959 and they quickly grasped that the Mini was more than just a family car. Minis could compete in rallies and races and win. A good friend of Issigonis was the racing and sports car constructor John Cooper, (his cars won the Formula One World Championship in 1959 and 1960), and he went to work on the Mini. The result was the Mini Cooper with the engine increased to 997 cc, twin SU carburettors, and a high compression ratio to produce 56 bhp. Pat Moss, sister of Stirling Moss won a succession of rallies in the car and Paddy Hopkirk won the Monte Carlo rally in it. The engine's power climbed steadily, as did the production figures. The factory stopped making the Cooper in 1971 when 150,000 had been sold but the car returned to the market in 1990 since when it had been available as standard Mini, Mini Cooper, or Mini Cabriolet.

Morris

The cycle-maker William Morris, who later became Lord Nuffield, started building cars in 1912 and was extremely successful in the terms of those days. He had already supplied his one thousandth car by 1914. In order to be better able to compete with European manufacturers, Morris, MG, Riley, and Wolseley joined together to form the Nuffield group which was collectively responsible for about half of all Britain's output of cars immediately before World War II.

Although Morris made both big and small cars they were most successful with the cheaper end of the market. Hence the reason why they introduced their Morris Eight and Ten just before the war.

When the motor show opened its doors in London to the public in late October 1948, visitors to the Morris stand could admire three entirely new models: the Minor, the slightly larger Oxford, and the Six. The cars were designed by the famous designer Alec Issigonis (later Sir Alec) and they looked extremely modern for their time although technically they were otherwise. Although the cars had independent front suspension both the Minor and Oxford were powered by old fashioned side-valve engines. The Six

had a six-cylinder engine with overhead camshaft. The Nuffield Group merged with Austin and Austin-Healey in 1952 to form the British Motor Corporation, which was then the largest car manufacturer in Europe. There was considerable interchange of engines and other parts between marques and complete bodies were badge engineered (given another marque's badge and different grille).

The BMC wrote an important episode in automobile history with the Mini (see Mini). Most of the marques in the group had their own version of the Mini. When there was seen to be demand for a slightly larger car BMC brought out the 1100/1300 series. Both cars were designed by Pininfarina. There were mechanical differences under the bonnet but the various marques were mainly characterised by different levels of trim and equipment.

Morris cars

COUNTRY OF ORIGIN: United Kingdom

Morris Eight

MODEL YEAR: 1946-1948

The Morris Minor was one of the most popular cars in its class and not just in Britain.

NUMBER MADE: 120,434

SPECIAL REMARKS: The Eight was introduced in 1939 and in 1946 was one of the cheapest cars made in Britain. The side-valve engine had a capacity of 918 cc and power output of 30 bhp at 4,400 rpm.

Morris Minor

MODEL YEAR: 1949-1971

NUMBER MADE: 1,293,327

Between 1948-1969 at least 74,969 Morris Minor Tourers or convertibles were sold.

The Morris Minor Traveller or estate was the most expensive Minor in the range.

SPECIAL REMARKS: The Morris Minor was built for more than twenty years during which the basic design remained unchanged but the car saw significant technical improvements. The engine grew from 918 to 1,098 cc and power output increased from 28 to 48 bhp.

The body of the Morris Oxford was designed by Pininfarina in Turin. This is a 1962 Mk IV.

Morris Oxford

MODEL YEAR: 1949-1971

NUMBER MADE: 305,418

SPECIAL REMARKS: Up to 1959 the Oxford was an enlarged version of the Minor being at $165^3/_4$ in (4,210 mm) $18^1/_2$ in (470 mm) longer than its famous sibling. The Oxford got a new, more modern body in 1959 that was shared with the Austin Cambridge, MG Magnette, and Wolseley 15/60.

Morris Six

MODEL YEAR: 1949-1954

NUMBER MADE: 12,464

SPECIAL REMARKS: The Six was a very expensive car for its time which kept its sales figures low. The 2,215 cc six-cylinder engine had an overhead camshaft that produced 66 bhp.

Morris 1100

MODEL YEAR: 1962-1971

NUMBER MADE: 801,996

SPECIAL REMARKS: Because of their similarities, the 1100 and 1300 were often considered as one model. The Morris 1300 was sold from 1967-1973. Both had much in common with the Mini but had hydro-elastic suspension.

Muntz

Frank Kurtis developed a good reputation for building competitive motor sport cars. His cars had won the Indianapolis 500 among other successes. In 1950 he also turned his hand to road-going cars. His car had a polyester body and was a two-door two-seater roadster. When Kurtis had built 36 of them he sold the factory, complete with tooling and parts, to Earl "Madman" Muntz who had made a great deal of money out of selling television sets.

He could therefore afford a certain amount of risk. Unfortunately the cars did not sell as well as Muntz hoped. Muntz extended the wheelbase by $31^1/_2$ in (80 mm) so that he could offer a four-seater and he replaced the polyester body with one of aluminium.
Although customers could choose whichever V-8 engine they preferred, the cars were supplied as standard with a Cadillac V-8 unit.

The few cars built by "Madman" Muntz are cared for in museums.

One of the final Muntz Jets. The convertible grew to become a spacious five-seater that was also available as hardtop.

Muntz moved his works from California to Evanston Illinois in the winter of 1950-1951, where 366 cars were built that all had steel bodies and a Lincoln engine.

Muntz cars

COUNTRY OF ORIGIN: USA

Muntz Jet

MODEL YEAR: 1950-1954

NUMBER MADE: 394

SPECIAL REMARKS: Externally, little was changed to the Muntz cars but the wheelbase was twice extended by $31^1/_2$ in (80 mm) which would mainly be appreciated by back-seat passengers.

The Kurtis cars has polyester bodies. This was changed in Muntz's Californian works to aluminium and then finally at Evanston to steel.

Nash

Charles W. Nash (1864-1948) was President of General Motors from 1912 to 1916 before he decided to start his own business. He bought out Thomas B. Jeffery who had built cars in Kenosha, Wisconsin, since 1897. From 1917 Nash sold cars bearing his own name and they sold well but the business could not deal with the big three of Detroit. After World War II, Nash returned with the 600 model that had been launched in 1942. It was still

C.W. Nash (1864-1948).

Nash introduced the Golden Airflytes in 1952. Little was changed mechanically but the bodies were new and the rear window was panoramic.

a modern car with monocoque body and independent front suspension. The engine was a 2,830 cc six-cylinder side-valve unit that produced 83 bhp. The larger stable mate of the 600 was the Ambassador that had a $8^3/_4$ in (220 mm) longer wheelbase and was 9 in (230 mm) longer overall. Its motor had cylinder capacity of 3,855 cc, overhead valves, and power output of 114 bhp. The first new models with bodies by Pininfarina followed in 1949. These streamlined models were termed the "Airflyte series". Both the front and rear wheels were partially hidden inside the wings and the cars had one piece windscreens. They also featured front seats that could be collapsed backwards to form a double bed. The cars sold like hot cakes and Nash beat all its own records that year with at least 142,592 cars sold. This increased further in 1950 to 191,865 but this was unfortunately that last year of reasonable fortune for the company. It was in 1950 that Nash introduced a car that was later to be termed "compact". The Nash Rambler was "only" 176 in (4,480 mm) long, making it $24^3/_4$ in (630 mm) shorter than the Statesman, which had been Nash's smallest car until then.

In 1951 the Nash-Healey came into being. It was a two-seater sports car built in Britain by Healey. The first bodies were also produced in Britain for Nash but the second series had an improved body designed and built in Turin by Pininfarina. The Nash cars always looked good and were of excellent quality but the sales continued to fall off.

1951:   161,140
1952:   152,141
1953:   135,394

When results were even worse in 1954 with only 62,911 cars sold, Nash decided to merge with Hudson, but things did not get any better. The new company was known as the American Motors Corporation. The big Nash and Hudson models did not change but the best-selling Rambler model was supplied as both a Nash and a Hudson. The Rambler was sold as a marque of its own from 1956. That was also the year that AMC first had its own V-8 engine which brought many former customers back to the fold.

Despite this success, Hudson and Nash could not compete with the "big three". Sales continued to slide and losses rose dramatically. The final Hudson left the factory on 27 June 1957 and the larger Nash models were dropped. In 1957, Nash was only able to sell 826 cars. This meant the end for this worthy company. Only Rambler remained as an independent make.

Nash cars

COUNTRY OF ORIGIN: USA

Nash 600

MODEL YEAR: 1945-1948

NUMBER MADE: 182,850

SPECIAL REMARKS: The 600 was designed in 1941 but was modern enough post-war to sell well.
It had independent front suspension and all-round coil springs.

Nash Airflyte Ambassador

MODEL YEAR: 1949-1955

NUMBER MADE: Unknown

SPECIAL REMARKS: The Airflyte series were designed by the famous Italian Pinin Farina. In 1949, the Ambassador was the largest Nash with an overall length of 209$^3/_4$ in (5,330 mm), making it 9 in (230 mm) longer than the Airflyte 600.

Nash Rambler

MODEL YEAR: 1950-1956

NUMBER MADE: Unknown

SPECIAL REMARKS: The Rambler was far ahead of its time as a "compact" car. The first examples were only 176 in (4,470 mm) long, which is remarkable for that era. When the Rambler became a marque of its own in 1956, it grew to 199 in (5,050 mm).

The 1949 Airflyte Ambassador was a spacious 6-seater with 3,855 cc six-cylinder ohv engine of 114 bhp.

The Nash-Healey was a joint effort of Nash, Healey, and Pininfarina. Nash provided the mechanical parts, Pininfarina produced the bodies of the second series, and Healey assembled the cars.

Nash-Healey

MODEL YEAR: 1951-1954

NUMBER MADE: 506

SPECIAL REMARKS: The first 104 cars had an aluminium body built in Britain. The remainder had a steel body by Pininfarina.

Nissan (Datsun)

It took a long time for the car to become popular in Japan. In 1908 there were only twenty in Tokyo and a mere three in Yokohama. These cars had been imported by wealthy Japanese, although a Japanese car was made, based on US mechanical engineering, from 1902.

Masijiro Hashimoto returned to Japan from the USA in 1911 where he had studied as an engineer and been especially interested in automobiles. Back in Japan he set up a factory with friends where in 1914 he built his first DAT car. Production was limited for the car remained a toy for wealthy Japanese. The factory mainly produced lorries and buses.

This 1951 car was named Datsun Thrift. It looks like a Jeep but was designed as a private car.

Datsun specialised in building small cars. This 1951 DX was a four-seater with four doors and four-cylinder engine.

A number of cars were produced before World War II as Datsuns. These were small cars the size of an Austin Seven. After the war, the cars remained too small for Westerners and it was a long time before the dimensions were amended.

In 1948 the Datsun DB was launched to the Japanese market. The car was the spitting image of an American Crosley but was barely large enough for four small Japanese.

Nissan cars

COUNTRY OF ORIGIN: Japan

181

The Datsun DB looked precisely like the US Crosley but was only suitable for the narrow Japanese roads.

Datsun DB

MODEL YEAR: 1948-1954

NUMBER MADE: Unknown

SPECIAL REMARKS: This midget car had a four-cylinder side-valve engine of 860 cc that produced 20 bhp at 3,600 rpm.

Datsun A110

MODEL YEAR: 1955

NUMBER MADE: Unknown

SPECIAL REMARKS: The Datsun A110 was based on an Austin built by Nissan under licence. The engine was a 860 cc four-cylinder unit.

It is hard to believe this is an Austin A110 with a Japanese body. The car had fixed axles front and back and was powered by a 25 bhp side-valve engine.

NSU

NSU built cars from 1906 to 1928 before switching to motorcycles. Part of the company was sold to Fiat in 1929 and this company produced Fiat cars under licence and sold them as NSU-Fiat. The NSU name did not return with a car of its own until 1957.

The NSU Prinz was very successful. It had an air-cooled twin-cylinder engine which was rear-mounted in the car at a tilt. In contrast with the engines of most small German cars, the power unit was a four-stroke. Its capacity was 583 cc but because its valves were operated by an overhead camshaft, the power output was in the region of 20 bhp.

The body was of unitary construction resulting in a four-seater weighing a mere 476 kg (1,047 lb). The Prinz was continuously improved and the engine more highly developed. Eventually the twin-cylinder unit produced 30 bhp.

When the body was adapted and enlarged, the Prinz IV was born, which looked slightly

Felix Wankel (1864-1948).

like a Chevrolet Corvair from a distance. Its 598 cc engine supplied power of 30 bhp to the rear wheels. The car easily exceeded 100 kph (62 mph) and was consequently also available after 1964 with disc brakes on the front wheels. The final Prinz family car appeared in 1965. This was the 1000 TT and TTS, which were sheep in wolf's clothing, which managed to embarrass competitors on racing circuits. The engines varied from 996-1,177 cc and power ranged from 55-70 bhp. These were still four-seater cars that looked like family saloons despite their sportive performance unlike the Sport-Prinz which was a two-seater sports coupé designed by Bertone.

Felix Wankel was given the opportunity in 1964 to install his rotary motor, on which he had worked for decades, in an NSU. This resulted in the Wankel Spider which was at first a rather unreliable milestone in automotive history. The larger family car with a Wankel engine was the Ro80 which was an extremely modern front-wheel drive car with spacious monocoque body. Unfortunately it took too long to get rid of all the teething problems with this car.

NSU sports cars

COUNTRY OF ORIGIN: Germany

NSU Prinz

MODEL YEAR: 1958-1962

NUMBER MADE: 94,549

NSU cars are restored and lovingly cared-for by enthusiasts, especially in Germany.

SPECIAL REMARKS: The Prinz was larger than the German midget cars and was therefore in a class apart. It had a top speed of 65 mph (105 kph) and was very economical on fuel at about 60-75 miles per gallon (4-5 litres pr 100 km).

NSU Prinz 4

MODEL YEAR: 1961-1973

NUMBER MADE: 576,023

The Prinz 4 was only sold with a 30 bhp engine.

SPECIAL REMARKS: The Prinz 4 was 300 mm (11³/₄ in) longer than its forerunner at 3,440 mm (135 in). This also made the car more attractive which was reflected in the sales figures.

NSU 1000 TT/TTS

MODEL YEAR: 1965-1971

NUMBER MADE: 63,289 & 2,404

SPECIAL REMARKS: The TT had a 1,177 cc four-cylinder engine of 65 bhp. The TTS had

The NSU 1000 TT was to German buyers what the Mini Cooper was for the British, the Gordini for the French, and Fiat Abarth for the Italians.

The Sport Prinz was the great success of the 1958
Frankfurt motor show. The 2+2 was as fast as the
VW Karmann Ghia but cost a third less.

The NSU Spider was a fine car but no-one dared to
buy it.

a smaller 996 cc engine for 1-litre class races.
It produced 70 bhp at 6,200 rpm.

NSU Sport Prinz

MODEL YEAR: 1959-1967

NUMBER MADE: 20,831

SPECIAL REMARKS: The body of the Sport
Prinz was designed by Franco Scaglione
when he still worked for Bertone. The Sport
Prinz was delivered with two different
engines: 583 cc/30 bhp or 598 cc/32 bhp.

NSU Wankel Spider

MODEL YEAR: 1964-1967

NUMBER MADE: 2,375

SPECIAL REMARKS: The rotary Wankel engine
produced 50 bhp at 5,000 rpm which easily
took the car to a top speed in excess of 94
mph (150 kph).

NSU Ro80

MODEL YEAR: 1967-1977

NUMBER MADE: 37,389

SPECIAL REMARKS: Once the teething problems were finally solved the Ro80's engine
proved to be as reliable as any other four-
stroke. Unfortunately it remains thirsty with
fuel.

The Ro80 was certainly the best-looking German car of its day. With its top speed of 112 mph (180 kph) it was also
fast enough.

Oldsmobile

Oldsmobile too was small once. Ransom Eli Olds built himself a three-wheeler in 1891, complete with steam engine, to create America's first ever car. Olds became famous in 1901 with his "Curved Dash" which he sold for $650 and of which he sold 2,500 in 1902.

When William Capo Durant established General Motors in 1908, the first company he wanted to take over was Oldsmobile. He acquired the business for $17,000 and shares in GM worth $3,000,000. This was a good decision for Durant for Oldsmobile built its two millionth car in 1941. In that year 230,703 cars rolled off the production lines. In July 1945, the American forces were still occupied with the war with Japan when the first "post-war" Oldsmobile exited the factory. Customers could choose from three models: the Special Series 60, Dynamic Series 70, and the Custom Cruiser 90. In addition to the sedan, the models were available as coupé, convertible, and station wagon. The series 60 and 70 had 3,902 cc six-cylinder side-valve engines while the 70 was also available with the 4,210 cc eight-cylinder in-line engine of the 90 series. The demand for new cars was tremendous and Oldsmobile sold as many as they could make.

Charles "Boss" Kettering, who invented the electric starter motor, designed a new Oldsmobile V-8 engine in 1947, which was fitted in the more expensive models. This overhead valve unit was 4,974 cc and its output was 136 bhp, increasing after 1952 to 162 bhp. Oldsmobile advertised the engine as "The Power Sensation of the Nation." In reality this Rocket motor did prove to have an almost infinite capacity for further development. Oldsmobiles won NASCAR races and the Carrera Pan-America road race

A "98" Holiday Coupé achieved a top speed of 90 mph (140 kph) in 1951. The Rocket V-8 engine did less than 12 miles per gallon (25 litres per 100 km).

over 3,000 km (1,875 miles) across Central America. Kettering also designed a new overhead valve six-cylinder engine. In addition to these new motors, the cars were also given new bodies and the demand for Oldsmobiles continued to climb with more than 400,000 being sold in 1950. The cars got bigger and the engines more powerful. Automatic transmission replaced manual gearboxes and more and more cars were equipped with servo-assisted braking and power-steering. Air conditioning became standard in virtually every model and so was a radio. When American cars started to sprout tail fins, Oldsmobile joined in, albeit with more modest versions.

Oldsmobile also joined in when Detroit moved into "compact" cars. The Oldsmobile model was an F-85 but it was not a small car. It kept Americans happy though and they bought 76,394 of them in its first year of 1961.

The Oldsmobile Toronado of 1966 had banner headlines in the newspapers. It was the first post-war American car with front-wheel drive to be built in large numbers. The five-seater coupé had a brilliant V-8 engine of 6,965 cc and after 1968 even 7,446 cc to produce at first 390 then 406 bhp. The Toronado was little used for racing though. For this the works had the F-85 in 4-4-2 version. The figures have the following significance: 400 cu. inch (6.5 litres), quadruple carburettors, and twin exhaust. These engines produced 370 bhp and that usually proved sufficient for a place on the winner's rostrum.

The 1972 Toronado had lost much of its charm. It was still the most expensive Oldsmobile and at 226³/₄ in (5,760 mm) the longest.

Oldsmobile cars

COUNTRY OF ORIGIN: USA

Oldsmobile Sixty-Six

MODEL YEAR: 1946

NUMBER MADE: 30,556

SPECIAL REMARKS: The Sixty-Six series (six for six-cylinders) was the cheapest Oldsmobile in 1946. The basic version in the USA cost $1,108. For another $26 the car could be bought with four doors.

Oldsmobile Eighty-Eight

MODEL YEAR: 1949

NUMBER MADE: 99,276

The new Eighty-Eight was the official pace car for the Indianapolis 500 in 1949 which provided valuable publicity.

SPECIAL REMARKS: By installing the new Rocket V-8 engine of the Ninety-Eight in the chassis of the lightweight Seventy-Six, Oldsmobile created the new Eighty-Eight.

Oldsmobile Ninety-Eight

MODEL YEAR: 1951

186

The Ninety-Eight series was the top-of-the-range in 1947. Three versions were available: convertible, 4-door sedan, and Club Sedan (illustrated).

NUMBER MADE: 90,975

SPECIAL REMARKS: Oldsmobile could provide three different models in 1951: the 88, Super 88, and 98. The 98 had a longer wheelbase and therefore had more room for passengers.

Oldsmobile Super Eighty-Eight

A 1955 Super 88 4-door hardtop which Oldsmobile called a Holiday Sedan. They sold 47,385 of them.

This Super 88 in 1957 was named Fiesta. It had space for nine and their luggage.

MODEL YEAR: 1955

NUMBER MADE: 242,192

SPECIAL REMARKS: The Super 88 was launched in 1955, powered by the most powerful motor Oldsmobile had: a V-8 that produced 202 bhp at 4,000 rpm, which was 17 bhp more than the engines of the 88 and 98.

Oldsmobile Starfire

MODEL YEAR: 1961

NUMBER MADE: 7,800

A 1961 six-seater Starfire convertible weighed 4,345 lb (1,975 kg). Its V-8 engine had a capacity of 6,466 cc.

SPECIAL REMARKS: A new model, named the Starfire, appeared in 1961. This top-of-the-range Oldsmobile (the most expensive of its time) was only available as a convertible. The tuned engine produced 330 bhp, which was slightly more than other models.

By the 1963 model year the F-85 at 192 in (4,880 mm) had grown 4 in (100 mm) compared to 1961 when it was launched.

Oldsmobile F-85

MODEL YEAR: 1961

NUMBER MADE: 69,609

SPECIAL REMARKS: The F-85 was the "small" Oldsmobile. It had a new aluminium V-8 engine which was also fitted in Buick and Pontiac (and much later also in British Rover cars).

Oldsmobile F-85, 4-4-2

MODEL YEAR: 1965

NUMBER MADE: Unknown

Only coupé and convertible versions of the 4-4-2 type of F-85 were available.

SPECIAL REMARKS: The 4-4-2 package consisted of a 400 cubic inch motor with quadruple carburettors and twin exhausts. The engine produced 345 bhp.

Oldsmobile Toronado (1966)

MODEL YEAR: 1966

NUMBER MADE: 40,963

SPECIAL REMARKS: Oldsmobile proved with the Toronado that front-wheel drive was not just suitable for small cars.

Oldsmobile Toronado (1973)

MODEL YEAR: 1973

NUMBER MADE: 55,921

SPECIAL REMARKS: In 1974 the Toronado

only had one choice of motor but what a motor! The V-8 with a capacity of 7,446 cc output power of 253 DIN bhp to the front wheels.

A new era was begun with the Toronado. For the first time since the Cord of the 1930's a big American car had front-wheel drive.

The Toronado had everything the America buyer could want in a sporting car. It was a coupé with an endless motor hood or bonnet.

Opel

The Adam Opel company made sewing machines and cycles for many years before the five brothers decided to start making motor cars. They started in a low risk way by making Lutzmann cars under licence. The first Opel-Lutzmann emerged from their Rüsselsheim works in 1898 but it was not successful and so Opel tried to gain a licence to build French Darracq cars. They started to build their own car in 1902, initially with a two-cylinder motor but later with a four-cylinder unit. When the Opels appeared to sell better than the Opel-Darracqs, they ceased producing the French marque. Opel was very successful with its Laubfrosch, which was a German version of the Citroën Trèfle. In 1929, Opel became part of General Motors and from then on the company's fortune's flourished.

In 1935, Opel was one of the first to produce a car with a monocoque body, without a chassis. This was the Olympia which was produced once more from 1947. Some ten

Adam Opel (1837-1895).

In 1958 the Kapitän acquired a fashionable panoramic front windscreen. The lowered roof line was impractical because head room in the rear was significantly marred.

years later the body was still modern but the overhead valve engine of 1,488 cc that produced 37 bhp at 3,500 rpm could also still hold its own. The Opel Kapitän of 1939 also returned in 1949 except that it now had round headlights instead of the pre-war rectangular ones.

Ford was very successful in 1952 with is Taunus 12M so Opel responded with the Rekord which was available in late 1953. There was also a renewed Kapitän in 1953 with improved monocoque body and space for six people. The Kapitän was powered all this time by a 2,473 cc overhead valve six-cylinder engine. In those cars just after the war the output was 55 bhp and this rose to 75 in 1953 and by 1955 Opel had coaxed 82 bhp from the unit. The Kapitän got an entirely new body in 1959 and although the engine was still 2,473 cc the power was now 100 bhp!

Towards the end of the 1960s Opel moved further into the luxury car market with cars such as the Commodore, the Admiral, and the Diplomat, that had to help prevent customers from switching to a Mercedes. This was partially successful since the Diplomat was a fine car with its 5,354 cc Chevrolet V-8 engine. Opel did not forget the "common man" though. For the masses there was the Opel Kadett in various versions, including GT and sporting models. The sports model was a two-seater coupé with a body that was built in France.

Opel cars

COUNTRY OF ORIGIN: Germany

Opel Olympia (1947)

MODEL YEAR: 1947-1949

NUMBER MADE: 25,952

The Olympia was a very modern car before World War II so that it had no problem in reappearing in post-war markets.

SPECIAL REMARKS: The four-cylinder overhead valve engine of the first post-war Olympia produced 37 bhp.

Opel Olympia (1950)

MODEL YEAR: 1950-1952

NUMBER MADE: 161,103

SPECIAL REMARKS: The Olympia got a new grille and modernised wings for the 1950 model.

The Olympia as it was built from 1950-1952. It was available as saloon, convertible, and estate car.

The post-war Kapitän could be told apart from the pre-war model by its rounded headlights.

Opel Kapitän

MODEL YEAR: 1948-1951

NUMBER MADE: 30,431

SPECIAL REMARKS: The first post-war Kapitäns had a floor-mounted gear lever. In the 1950 model there was a column gear change. The 2,473 cc six-cylinder engined produced 55 bhp at 3,500 rpm.

Opel Rekord P1

MODEL YEAR: 1957-1960

NUMBER MADE: 787,835

SPECIAL REMARKS: The Rekord P1 was available with a choice of two different engines: a 1.5-litre unit giving 45 bhp and a 1.7-litre motor for 55 bhp.

The fashion followed America in the 1950s so it was two-tone paintwork, panoramic windscreen, and lots of chrome. This is a 1959 Rekord.

This 1967 Rekord C has the biggest four-cylinder engine at 1,897 cc for 90 bhp at 5,100 rpm.

Opel Rekord C

MODEL YEAR: 1966-1971

NUMBER MADE: 1,276,681

SPECIAL REMARKS: The Rekord got a new body in 1966 to become the Rekord C. This model was available with either four-cylinder or six-cylinder engines of 1,492 or 2,239 cc.

Opel Kadett A

MODEL YEAR: 1962-1965

NUMBER MADE: 649,512

SPECIAL REMARKS: A new factory was built in Bochum for the Opel Kadett A. This four-seater was 3,990 mm (157 in) long.

The coupé version of the Kadett A appeared in 1963 with a 993 cc engine that produced 48 bhp.

Opel Kadett B

MODEL YEAR: 1965-1973

NUMBER MADE: 2,610,650

A Kadett B estate car with room for five and their luggage.

SPECIAL REMARKS: More than 2.5 million Kadett B cars were sold in eight years. The Kadett B was a successful and very good car. The engines had capacities of 1,078-1,897 cc and power ranging from 45-90 bhp.

Opel GT

MODEL YEAR: 1968-1973

NUMBER MADE: 103,463

SPECIAL REMARKS: Of the total, 3,573 were sold with a 1,078 cc engine while the remainder had a four-cylinder 1,897 cc unit with power of 90 bhp.

In total more than 100,000 Opel GT cars were built. Production ceased in 1973 when the Opel factory in France where the car was built was sold to Renault.

Despite the countless jokes about the Manta and their owners, it remains an attractive car. This is a 1900 from 1973.

Opel Manta A

MODEL YEAR: 1970-1975

NUMBER MADE: 498,533

SPECIAL REMARKS: The Manta had to compete with the Ford Capri which it did quite happily. In common with the Capri, the Manta had a wide choice of power units. There were four-cylinder motors from 1,196-1,897 cc which could also be tuned up in a variety of way.

Opel Commodore B

MODEL YEAR: 1972-1977

NUMBER MADE: 140,827

The fastest version of the Commodore B was the GS/E. Its fuel-injected 2.8-litre engine produced 160 bhp at 5,400 rpm.

SPECIAL REMARKS: The six-cylinder engines of the Commodore B were 2,490 or 2,784 cc and they delivered 115 or 160 bhp.

Opel Diplomat

MODEL YEAR: 1969-1977

NUMBER MADE: 11,108

SPECIAL REMARKS: This was the most expensive of Opel's biggest three cars (Kapitän, Admiral, and Diplomat). It was given a new body in 1969 and remained with little external change until 1977. The car was powered by a 5,354 cc V-8 engine.

The Diplomat, such as this 1973 example, had much in common in both size and mechanics with smaller American cars. It had a Chevrolet V-8 engine and Turbo-Hydra-Matic transmission.

Packard

The year of 1941 was not too good for Packard. The company had only managed to build 69,653 cars with the best-selling model being the Clipper. This car had been designed by Howard "Dutch" Darrin in the record time of ten days. For the first time ever, a Packard was wider than it was high and no other manufacturer could advertise seats as broad as those of this car. Fewer cars still were built in 1942 but Packard earned a great deal of money building aircraft engines for the British Mosquito and Lancaster bombers among others. When the war was over, Packard had earned $16,600,000 from this work.

The first post-war car came of the line on 19 October 1945 and once again the Clipper was successful. Packard wanted to build 100,000 of them but events prevented them. There were regular strikes among the employees and if the strikes were not in their own factory then there were strikes at those of suppliers of parts, tyres, wheels, batteries etc. Work stopped forty-seven times during 1946 and when workers at General Motors went on strike Packard had to sent their workers home for fifteen days. If there was no strike in the car factory then it would be at Briggs who built the car bodies. There were even six strikes at Briggs within three days.
The consequence of this industrial unrest was that Packard only built 30,793 cars for the 1946 model year. These were two and four-door Clippers with huge 4,621 cc straight-eight engines. It was not until April 1946 that customers could get a car with a 4,015 cc six-cylinder engine and in May 1946 a 5,834 cc eight-cylinder engine became available. In June 1946 Packard was able to introduce Custom Super Eight sedans to their range. Packard also fell far short of its intended production totals in 1947. If the US government had not paid a few of its outstanding bills the company would have been in difficulties. To win new customers, Packard introduced a new body in 1949

with a horizontal grille instead of a vertical one. With these new cars and virtually no more strikes, Packard made a profit of $15,000,000.
Packard celebrated its fiftieth anniversary in May 1949. At that time it had 11,665 workers whose average pay was $1.65 per hour.

Packard dealers received new models on 24 August 1950. These were the Series 24 designed by John Reinhart with modern lines. The Series was divided into 200, 200 Deluxe, 250, 300, and 400 Patrician models. The higher the range number, the higher was the price of the car. Customers got a great deal for their money of course. The straight-eight engines had capacities of 4,719 or 5,358 cc. Packard got a new President, James Nance, on 1 May 1952 who was lured away from General Electric for an annual salary of $150,000. General Electric bought 25,000 Packard shares in the conviction that their value would increase. Unfortunately Nance was far less successful than anticipated. He did give all the models new names. The cheapest Packard was once more a Clipper, then there was Clipper Deluxe, and Clipper Sportster. The slightly more expensive range became Cavalier, Mayfair, Caribbean, and Patrician. In 1953 Packard had twelve differ-

James Ward Packard was born in 1863.

ent base models with thirteen different body types. The wide range of models was too numerous for the factory to produce profitably and things got worse for the company. When Packard managed to sell 71,079 cars in 1953, Nance built a new factory for about $50,000,000. When the factory was ready, sales had slumped to 38,396 cars.

To survive against the big three, Nash and Hudson had merged to form American Motors Corporation in 1954. In 1954, Packard joined together with Studebaker but the merger was not successful. Packard sold only 38,969 cars that year. Packard finally managed to bring out its V-8 engine in 1955. There were two versions: the "small" one with capacity of 5,237 cc and 228 bhp, and the bigger 5,773 cc and power output of 248 or 279 bhp.

The new engine was fitted in a modernised body which pulled production back up to 52,000 but this dropped once more to 28,396 in 1956. Packard could no longer be prevented from going under. The drop in demand had dramatic consequences. Only 5,189 cars were sold in 1957 and production was halted in 1958 after only 2,599 cars had been made. It was the end of another historic marque.

Packard cars

COUNTRY OF ORIGIN: USA

Packard Clipper (1946)

MODEL YEAR: 1946-1947

NUMBER MADE: 80,379

SPECIAL REMARKS: The Clipper could be bought with six or eight-cylinder in line engines. It was mounted on a heavy chassis and was finely trimmed.

The Clipper was the final Packard with a classic high grille. It was designed before World War II by Howard "Dutch" Darrin.

A 1948 Station Sedan from the Standard Eight Series. This was a luxurious car that was 30 % dearer than the four-door Standard Eight.

Packard Standard Eight

MODEL YEAR: 1948

NUMBER MADE: 12,803

SPECIAL REMARKS: A straight-eight engine with capacity of 4,610 cc and power output of 132 bhp purred under the hood or bonnet of the Standard Eight. The range was available as sedan, limousine, or station wagon.

Packard Patrician

MODEL YEAR: 1951

NUMBER MADE: 9,001

SPECIAL REMARKS: The lengthy eight-cylinder engine was 5,358 cc and the unit produced 157 bhp, making it Packard's most powerful motor.

The Patrician was the top model in 1951 and it was only available as a four-door limousine.

Packard Clipper (1953)

MODEL YEAR: 1953-1954

NUMBER MADE: 86,995

SPECIAL REMARKS: The Clipper name, discarded since 1947, returned for the cheapest Packard. Customers could choose between two eight-cylinder engines of 4,719 or 5,358 cc.

Packard Caribbean

MODEL YEAR: 1956

NUMBER MADE: 539

The 1956 Caribbean was the most expensive Packard. The convertible cost $5,995 – twice the price of a 4-door Packard Clipper.

SPECIAL REMARKS: The Caribbean was the most expensive Packard in 1956 but it was also the least sold. Only 263 coupés and 276 convertibles found owners.

Packard Hawk

MODEL YEAR: 1958

NUMBER MADE: 588

SPECIAL REMARKS: The final Packard was a Hawk; in reality it was a Studebaker with extra equipment and an attractive name. Its V-8 engine had a capacity of 4,738 cc, giving power for the rear wheels of 210 bhp or 275 bhp with a McCulloch turbo.

Panhard

The company founded by René Panhard and Emil Levassor started one of the first automobile factories. Cars with their name on the radiator were driving through Paris in 1891. The company did not specialise in a certain type of car but made racing and sports cars as well as small personal cars and limousines.

Panhard grasped during World War II period that there would be a shortage of small and inexpensive cars. Before even the surrender agreement was signed they decided to build a small car. Panhard consulted Jean Albert Grégoire about the project – he was one of the first proponents of front-wheel drive. Grégoire did the first drawings for a post-war Panhard in 1943. This Dyna Panhard was a modern four-seater with a steel body but the four doors and bonnet were of aluminium. The air-cooled twin-cylinder engine was front mounted and drove the front wheels. The first car of the type was premiered at the Paris motor show in 1946. It had a 610 cc 24 bhp engine but this quickly rose to 745 and then 850 cc with power output increasing to 38 bhp.

The small Dyna was replaced in 1954 by the Dyna 54 which was mechanically identical to its predecessor but with a larger aerodynamic body. Instead of separate seats there were bench seats front and back. The Dyna 54 had power steering and was a genuine six-seater.

The car was given a facelift in 1959 to form the Panhard PL17. Little was changed mechanically and the new model was mainly detected on the outside by new bumpers and headlights.

Panhard cars were not cheap and the Panhard 24B, which was added in 1963, was even more expensive. It was a four-seater coupé and the most expensive twin-cylinder engined car in the world. This model was available in various versions: the standard 24B, slightly cheaper 24BA. The 24C had a shorter wheelbase and was really a 2+2. Those who wanted the version with the more powerful Tigre engine had to order a BT or CT.

Panhard continued to be too expensive to sell well and so the company's board felt obliged to sell their shares to Citroën. This was the beginning of the end for Panhard, even though everything seemed to be going well. Panhard could used Citroën's big network of dealers and Citroën's engineers helped with teething problems with the Panhard twin-cylinder engines. But Citroën had other plans for the company. In 1967 Citroën bought the remaining shares and allowed Panhard to wither away.

The Dyna as a 2+2 cabriolet.

Panhard cars

COUNTRY OF ORIGIN: France

Panhard Dyna

MODEL YEAR: 1946-1954

NUMBER MADE: Approx. 55,000

Weight was spared wherever possible with the Dyna. It had aluminium doors, bonnet, bumpers, and grille.

SPECIAL REMARKS: Because the Dyna weighed only 550 kg (1,210 lb) as a four-door saloon it was economical with expensive French petrol.

The PL17 had room for six with its front and back bench seats.

Panhard PL17

MODEL YEAR: 1959-1965

NUMBER MADE: Approx. 130,000

SPECIAL REMARKS: The air-cooled 850 cc twin-cylinder of the Dyna was also used for the Pl17. The standard motor produced 42 bhp but the Tigre motor managed 50bhp at 5,570 rpm.

The PL17 was also available as cabriolet. Only 600 were sold though because the car was too expensive.

The final Panhard was a coupé. This is a 24BT with Tigre engine.

The last pre-war and first post-war Peugeot was the 202, available as saloon, estate, or cabriolet (as shown).

Panhard 24B

MODEL YEAR: 1963-1967

NUMBER MADE: 23,245

SPECIAL REMARKS: This four-seater had a top speed of 94 mph (150 kph) but was 6 mph (10 kph) faster with the Tigre 50 bhp engine.

Peugeot

The Peugeot family firm made itself famous at first for its cycles, tools, coffee-grinders, and other household items before building its first car in 1889 with help from Léon Serpollet. Production of cars got under way quickly after that and 29 cars were sold in 1892, 40 in 1894, 500 in 1900, and by 1917 it had risen to 5,000. Peugeot introduced the 202 four-door saloon in 1938 with an 1,100 cc engine. An unusual feature of the car were the way the headlights were placed close together behind the grille. This model reappeared in February 1945 and more than 14,000 of them were sold that year. Work had gone on during the war on a post-war car so that the 203 was ready to introduce in the autumn of 1947. The 203 was an extremely modern car with stream-lined monocoque body and a fine four-cylinder overhead valve engine that produced 42 bhp from a capacity of 1,300 cc. Although the 203 was built for many more years, a

successor appeared in 1955. The body of this new 403 had been designed by Pininfarina in Turin. The car was more spacious than the 203 although mechanically the cars had much in common. The 403 though had a 1,468 cc engine that produced 58 bhp. In common with the 203, this model was available in different body forms.

Peugeot introduced their 404 in May 1960. Once again the body was designed by Pininfarina. Although the car appeared bigger than the 403 it was at 4,420 mm (174 in) actually 50 mm (2 in) shorter and also 60 mm ($2^{3}/_{8}$ in) lower. A variety of engines were available for the car, from 1,468-1,816 cc, with the latter having petrol-injection. There were also two diesel engines. Peugeots had built a reputation for fuel economy, the space in their cars, and good road-holding. This road-holding was improved further when the 504 got independent rear suspension in September 1968. This was also Peugeot's first model with power-assisted disc brakes on all four wheels. The coupé or cabriolet versions had fuel injection and from October 1974 the

Peugeot sold 60,186 304 coupés and 18,647 cabriolets.

cars could also have a V-6 engine. The new V-6 was a joint development with Renault and Volvo.

The Peugeot 204 took the company into front-wheel drive in April 1965. The 204 was a small four-seater designed by Pininfarina. It was powered by a transversely-mounted four-cylinder engine of 1,130 cc and 53 bhp. The same approach was used for the 304 in 1969. This 4,140 mm (163 in) long car filled the gap between the smaller 204 and larger 504. This model was also successful. The S version was launched in October 1972. The 204S had twin Solex carburettors and produced 69 bhp.

Peugeot cars

COUNTRY OF ORIGIN: France

The Peugeot 202 could be recognised at a distance by its headlights, close together beneath the grille.

Peugeot 202

MODEL YEAR: 1945-1949

NUMBER MADE: Unknown

SPECIAL REMARKS: The 202 was still built on a separate chassis but had independent front suspension and a 1,133 cc overhead valve engine that produced 30 bhp at 4,000 rpm.

Peugeot 203

MODEL YEAR: 1947-1960

NUMBER MADE: 685,828

The Peugeot 203 could be bought as an estate in 1950 with a 200 mm (8 in) longer wheelbase than the saloon.

SPECIAL REMARKS: The engine of the 203 was a wonder to behold. It had a bore/stroke relationship of 75 x 73 and hemispherical combustion chambers in the aluminium cylinder head.

The cabriolet or convertible was called "découvrable" by the French. The sides of the car were fixed but the entire roof could be rolled back. This is a 1950 203.

The Peugeot 404 remained in production for fifteen years and can still be widely seen on French roads.

Pininfarina was responsible for the shape of the Peugeot 403.

Peugeot 403

MODEL YEAR: 1955-1966

NUMBER MADE: 1,121,510

SPECIAL REMARKS: The 403 was the first car with which Peugeot sold more than 1,000,000. The car was also available with a diesel engine after 1959.

Peugeot 404

MODEL YEAR: 1960-1975

NUMBER MADE: 2,779,926

SPECIAL REMARKS: The 404 was sold in great numbers. The model was also available as a cabriolet (3,728) and coupé (6,837). These were designed by Pininfarina.

Peugeot tended to produce a convertible or cabriolet of every model they brought out. This included the 403.

The Peugeot 504 was a spacious car and 4,490 mm (176³/₄ in) long. The 1.8-litre injected motor gave a top speed of 109 mph (175 kph).

The 504 coupé was really a 2+2 with a wheelbase 190 mm (7¹/₂ in) shorter than the saloon.

Peugeot 504

MODEL YEAR: 1968-1983

NUMBER MADE: 2,871,001

SPECIAL REMARKS: Customers for the 504 had a choice from seven four-cylinder power units. The motors had overhead camshafts with the smallest 1,796 cc producing 50 bhp and the largest 2,112 cc yielding 136 bhp. A 2,664 cc V-6 engine that produced 136 bhp was added in 1975.

Peugeot 204

MODEL YEAR: 1965-1977

NUMBER MADE: 1,387,473

SPECIAL REMARKS: The 204 was a very modern car in mechanical terms. The engine had an overhead camshaft and all-four wheels had independent suspension. There were Girling disc brakes on the front wheels.

The 204 came out in 1966 as a cabriolet and coupé. Peugeot sold 18,181 open tops and 42,765 coupés.

Peugeot 304

MODEL YEAR: 1969-1980

NUMBER MADE: 1,334,309

SPECIAL REMARKS: The first 304 had power-steering in common with the 204. The engine of 1,288 cc produced 60 bhp at 5,750 cc but the S-version developed 69 bhp at the same rpm.

Plymouth

In 1928, Walter P. Chrysler bought Dodge for $170,000,000, to make Chrysler at one stroke one of the largest US automobile manufacturers. Chrysler's most expensive model was the Imperial and in order to broaden his new company's market reach, Chrysler created Plymouth as a cheap Chrysler and De Soto as a cheap Dodge. The new Plymouth marque was successful so it reappeared after World War II.

Plymouth stood at number three in 1931 for the number of cars sold and it managed to defend this position successfully until 1954. Chrysler still sold 650,451 cars in 1953 but this dropped to 463,148 in 1954. The Plymouth brand slipped to fifth place.
One of the models which sold badly was the Belvedere five-seater convertible which man-

New bodies for the 1955 model such as this Belvedere saw sales shoot up.

the Camara. Pontiac then responded three years later with the Firebird.

New bodies for the 1955 model such as this Belvedere saw sales shoot up.

Plymouth cars

<small>COUNTRY OF ORIGIN:</small> USA

Plymouth Belvedere Convertible

<small>MODEL YEAR:</small> 1954

<small>NUMBER MADE:</small> 6,900

aged only 6,900 in 1954. Something had to happen and Virgil Exner was ordered to design new models to regain Chrysler's position. His efforts were successful for in 1955 705,455 cars were sold. This was a compliment for Exner but also for the new engine for at last Plymouth could offer its customers a V-8.

Plymouth constantly strived to retain its position with the top marques. When Ford brought out the Mustang, Plymouth responded with its Barracuda. Chevrolet took another six months before it followed with

<small>SPECIAL REMARKS:</small> The Belvedere was the most expensive Plymouth and the convertible the highest priced Belvedere, costing $2,281 compared with $1,933 for a four-door sedan.
The six-cylinder side-valve engine had a capacity of 3,569 cc with an output of 101 bhp (SAE) at 3,600 rpm. The three-speed gearbox had no synchromesh for first gear.

Plymouth had a good year in 1954. Their most expensive model at the time was this Belvedere convertible.

The Belvedere was no performance car. The six-cylinder engine's 101 bhp was really too little for a 1¹/₂ ton car.

Column gear-change was quite normal still in 1954 and it enable three people to seat on the front bench seat.

When the Belvedere got a new body the sale shot up once more.

Plymouth Belvedere

MODEL YEAR: 1955

NUMBER MADE: 276,965

SPECIAL REMARKS: The Belvedere was available for the first time in 1955 with a V-8 engine. This had a capacity of 4,261 cc to give 169 bhp (SAE) at 4,400 rpm. This engine was installed in more than sixty per cent of all the cars sold.

Plymouth Belvedere Sports Coupe

MODEL YEAR: 1957

NUMBER MADE: 67,268

SPECIAL REMARKS: Things were better again for Plymouth in 1957 when 762,231 cars were sold in the model year. Plymouth customers could choose from two six-cylinder and four V-8 engines. The smallest V-8 was 3,975 cc and the biggest was 5,220 cc. This latter unit produced 294 bhp (SAE) at 5,400 rpm.

Plymouth Valiant

MODEL YEAR: 1960-1976

NUMBER MADE: Unknown

SPECIAL REMARKS: Plymouth had its "com-

Plymouth's answer to smaller imported cars was the Valiant.

The Valiant could also be bought as a convertible from 1964.

There was room for the entire family in a "small" Valiant. The car was 188 in (4,780 mm) long in 1964.

pact" just as Ford and Chevrolet did. These cars were intended to stem the tremendous tide of imported cars. The Valiant was at first only available with a 2,789 cc six-cylinder engine but had a V-8 also from 1964. The "small" Plymouth sold 251,504 in its first year compared with 607,956 Ford Falcons and 338,687 Chevrolet Corsairs.

Plymouth Barracuda

MODEL YEAR: 1964-1974

NUMBER MADE: 265,819

SPECIAL REMARKS: Although the Barracuda was an extremely attractive car it varied little from the Valiant. The floor pan was the same as was the body from the front bumper to the doors. Customers could choose from a thrifty six-cylinder or a powerful 235 bhp (SAE) V-8 unit.

A 1969 Barracuda Fastback. Its 340 cubic in (5.6 litre) V-8 with quadruple Carter carburettors produced 279 bhp (SAE) at 5,000 rpm but only did about 15 miles per gallon (1 litre to 5 kilometres).

Pontiac

General Motors introduced a new make to the New York motor show in January 1926. It was intended that the new Pontiac marque should fill the gap between the most expensive Chevrolet and cheapest Buick and the concept worked. Pontiac cars with a six-cylinder engine and enclosed body cost a mere $825. In their first year of existence, Pontiac cars sold 76,695 and by 1928 this had risen to 203,701.

The 1946 Pontiac cars were identical to the 1942 models. These were good but not too expensive cars that were nothing exceptional. They had six or eight-cylinder in-line motors with side-valves. Pontiacs could be spotted by the wide strip of chrome on the motor hood or bonnet and this remained a feature for a long time. The marque also used native American titles. There were Chieftains, Star Chiefs, and Super Chiefs from the Michigan factory.

The cars got new bodies in 1949. These were in reality stretched Chevrolet bodies. Mechanically there were no changes. The Streamliner and Chieftain, as the models were now called, were powered by the same elderly side-valve engines which now had capacities of 3,920 and 4,396 cc. Pontiacs got a thorough work over for the 1953 model year. The wheelbase was lengthened from 120 in (3,050 mm) to 122 in (3,100 mm) and

The Catalina, such as this 1951 example, was a 2-door hardtop coupé in the Chieftain range. It was available with either six or eight cylinder engines.

The Americans call the Pontiac Tempest a small car. In 1961 it was certainly shorter 15³/₄ in (400 mm) shorter at 189 in (4,810 mm) than other Pontiacs.

the new bodies had windscreens of one piece of curved glass. The six-cylinder motor now produced 119 bhp to give a top speed of 84 mph (135 kph). The time of the side-valve engine was now really over. Their competitors could provide more economical overhead valve engines but Pontiac customers had to wait until 1955 for them. The wait proved worth while though for the new ohv V-8 produced 183 bhp from a 4,706 cc unit.

Each year, the cars got a minor or major facelift and about every other year there were new bodies. After the native American names came descriptions such as "Special Deluxe" or "Custom" that indicated the standard of equipment and amount of chrome trim. Pontiacs first appeared without the broad chrome bands on the motor hood or bonnet in 1957. In its place there was the new body known as "Star Flight Styling". From 1955 onwards all Pontiacs sold in the USA had a V-8 engine. Cars destined for export, and those built in Canada, had the older six-cylinder unit. The 1957 V-8 could be tuned in a number of ways. The standard V-8 from the Chieftain had a capacity of 5,690 cc and power of 230 or 255 bhp. This engine in the Super Chief and Star Chief produced 242 and 275 bhp. Fitted in the Sports Bonneville, which was not exported and had fuel injection, the output climbed to 300 bhp.

Most American cars of the era had tail fins on the rear wings and Pontiac followed this trend with their cars became increasingly impressive. Pontiac also successfully joined in the battle for more horsepower. The V-8 engines were given a capacity of about 7 litres and had outputs of around 400 bhp. The cars also grew out of their garages and

got as long as 236 ft in (6 m), which the Americans thought was wonderful. It was impossible to imagine the cars without automatic transmission, power steering, and air conditioning. Of the around 100,000 Bonnevilles that were supplied in 1967, only 278 had manual gearboxes.

In 1961, General Motors gave both the Buick Special and Oldsmobile F-85 the same body. When this was also added to a Pontiac it was named the Tempest. It was surprising that the heavy Pontiac Tempest was available with a four-cylinder engine. This had a capacity of 3,185 cc and power of 112, 120, 140, or 170 bhp, depending on the compression ratio and carburettors. If a V-8 Tempest was preferred, this had a 3,531 cc unit with power of 165 or 188 bhp. The GTO in 1964 was based on the Tempest. The motors in the GTO were Detroit's most powerful units. The smallest of them was 6,364 cc with power of 259 bhp and the biggest was a 7,462 cc unit that produced 365 bhp. The GTO was only sold as convertible and coupé.

In 1967, Chevrolet introduced the Camaro. Pontiac followed with the Firebird. Both cars had the same body but differed from each other in the details. Customers here too could select a motor from a choice. For those who wanted it, the Firebird was available with a six-cylinder 3,769 cc power unit of 167 bhp output. The faster Firebirds proved to be quite dangerous. Customers in 1970 could choose from Standard Six or V-8, Esprit, Formula 400, or a Trans-Am. This latter model without tuning had a 6,558 cc V-8 that delivered 350 bhp at 5,000 rpm under its hood.
Pontiac guaranteed a top speed in excess of 125 mph (200 kph) but did not speak about road-holding.

Pontiac cars

COUNTRY OF ORIGIN: USA

Pontiac Streamliner Six

MODEL YEAR: 1946-1948

Pontiac only offered an 8-seater station wagon in the Streamline range in 1946.

NUMBER MADE: Unknown

SPECIAL REMARKS: Pontiac had two ranges of cars until 1948. The cheaper range were the Torpedo models with more expensive cars in the Streamliner range. They were all available with six-cylinder and eight-cylinder engines.

Pontiac Torpedo

MODEL YEAR: 1948

NUMBER MADE: 84,622

SPECIAL REMARKS: Slightly more than half (49,262) the Torpedo cars built had 3,920 cc six-cylinder engines. Hydra-matic automatic transmission was fitted to 25,326.

Pontiac Chieftain

MODEL YEAR: 1951

NUMBER MADE: Unknown

SPECIAL REMARKS: The long eight-cylinder engine of the Chieftain had a capacity of 4,396 cc but only produced 116 bhp at 3,600 rpm. The compression ratio was 7.5:1.

A 1948 Torpedo Silver Streak. The streaks can be seen as three chrome strips across the motor hood or bonnet. The sun visor was a popular accessory at that time.

Pontiacs such as this Chieftain Deluxe got new bodies in 1953, with a one piece curved windscreen.

The Pontiac Starchief came out in 1954. It was available as 4-door sedan (Star Chief Deluxe) or 2-door convertible (Star Chief Custom).

Pontiac Starchief

MODEL YEAR: 1954

NUMBER MADE: 115,088

A 1956 Star Chief convertible of which 13,510 were built.

The chrome was not spared in 1956 when this Star Chief Custom hardtop coupé was built.

SPECIAL REMARKS: The Starchief was new for the 1954 model year. The car had a eight-cylinder engine and 2 in (50 mm) longer wheelbase of 124 in (3,150 mm) instead of 122 in (3,100 mm). Gear-change was by Hydra-Matic automatic.

Pontiac Catalina

MODEL YEAR: 1959

NUMBER MADE: 231,561

The 1959 Catalina 2-door Sports Coupé had room for six and plenty of luggage.

SPECIAL REMARKS: The Catalina was the cheapest model in the Pontiac range. The car was stretched in 1959 to a length of 213³/₄ in (5,430 mm). The 6,364 cc V-8 engine produced 304 bhp at 4,600 rpm.

Pontiac Tempest

MODEL YEAR: 1961-1962

NUMBER MADE: 243,976

SPECIAL REMARKS: The Pontiac Tempest shared a body with Chevrolet and Buick but the Pontiac was the most interesting of them mechanically. The gearbox and differential were moulded as one piece to aid weight distribution.

Pontiac Bonneville (1963)

MODEL YEAR: 1963

NUMBER MADE: 110,316

The twin headlights were placed one above the other in the 1963 Bonneville instead of next to each other.

SPECIAL REMARKS: The Bonneville was based on the same chassis as the Star Chief. The smallest V-8 engine's capacity was 6,364 cc and it produced 238 bhp. The most powerful unit was 6,899 cc for 370 bhp.

Pontiac Tempest GTO

MODEL YEAR: 1964

NUMBER MADE: Unknown

SPECIAL REMARKS: The "untuned" V-8 engine

The Tempest GTO in 1964 had a top speed of 125 mph (200 kph).

of the GTO had a single quadruple choke carburettors by Carter. The more powerful versions had triple twin-choke units by Rochester.

Pontiac Firebird

MODEL YEAR: 1967

NUMBER MADE: 82,560

The Firebird like this 1967 model had the same body as the Chevrolet Camaro but a distinctive Pontiac nose.

SPECIAL REMARKS: The Firebird customer could choose from two six-cylinder engines both of 3.8 litres but either 165 or 215 bhp. In addition there were three V-8 units: two at 5.3 litres with output of 250 or 285, and a 6.6 litre for power of 325 bhp.

Pontiac Le Mans (1969)

MODEL YEAR: 1969

NUMBER MADE: 100,001

SPECIAL REMARKS: The Tempest Le Mans was

The 205 1/2 in (5,220 mm) length of the Le Mans was considered a "medium" car in the USA.

The Grand Prix, like this 1970 example, was Pontiac's priciest model and it was only available as a hardtop coupé.

available in 1969 with either a 4.1-litre six-cylinder engine or 5.8-litre V-8 unit.

Pontiac Grand Prix

MODEL YEAR: 1970

NUMBER MADE: 65,750

SPECIAL REMARKS: The 6,558 cc V-7 engine was equipped with quadruple Rochester

carburettors to produce power of 355 bhp. On request a 6,998 cc could be installed for higher power of 375 bhp.

Pontiac Bonneville (1972)

MODEL YEAR: 1972

NUMBER MADE: 50,293

SPECIAL REMARKS: The Bonneville was both big and heavy. It weighed more than 2 tons

The 1974 Le Mans with its 7.5-litre V-8 engine had a top speed of 131 mph (210 kph).

A 1972 Bonneville Grand Safari that weighs 5,280 lb (2,400 kg).

and was 224¾ in (5,710 mm) long. The
station wagon was even longer at 230 in
(5,850 mm).

Pontiac Le Mans (1974)

MODEL YEAR: 1974

NUMBER MADE: Unknown

SPECIAL REMARKS: The Le Mans was available as four-door hardtop or station wagon.
Customers could choose from a 4.1-litre six-
cylinder engine or 5.8, 6.6, or 7.5-litre V-8
motors.

Pontiac Firebird Trans Am

MODEL YEAR: 1975

NUMBER MADE: 26,417

SPECIAL REMARKS: Only 6,140 Firebird Trans
Ams were supplied with manual gearboxes.
The standard 6.6-litre engine produced 225
bhp (DIN). Enthusiasts could opt for a
7.5-litre V-8 with output of either 253 or 290
bhp.

Brute force: a 1975 Pontiac Firebird.

Pontiac Grand Am

MODEL YEAR: 1975

NUMBER MADE: 10,679

SPECIAL REMARKS: The 7.5-litre V-8 that
Pontiac introduced was intended solely for
the Grand Am. It developed 203 bhp to DIN
norms which was ample for a top speed of
119 mph (190 kph).

The 1975 Grand Am was available as 2 or 4-door coupé. It was the most expensive medium-sized Pontiac.

Reliant

Three-wheeler cars were very popular in Britain, because of cheaper road tax for them and the fact they could be driven on a motorcycle licence (provided they had no reverse gear). Reliant was founded in 1935 by a Mr. T. Williams to make small three-wheeled delivery vehicles. It seems this concept was very successful. In 1952, the company expanded its range by building a car on the chassis of a delivery van to create the Reliant Regal, which was in production for many years. This four-seater was powered by various engines such as the 747 cc unit from an Austin Seven, and similar sized Ford Anglia motor. The bodies were made of glass-fibre reinforced polyester after 1956.

Then in 1961, Reliant introduced a sports car, the Sabre, powered by a four-cylinder Ford Consul engine. The car was also available as a kit. The following year with a new body and six-cylinder Ford Zephyr/Zodiac engine the Sabre Six was born. These were also built under licence in Israel as a Sabra.

Reliant has built more than 100,000 of these tri-cars. They are still an every day sight.

When Princess Anne bought a Reliant Scimitar GTE the firm could not wish for better publicity.

The Reliant Scimitar was a 2+2 designed by David Ogle, originally under commission from Daimler. This car was also powered by a 2,553 cc unit from the Ford Zodiac. When Ford brought out their V-6 engine, Reliant were also able to offer it. The most interesting offspring from the Reliant family was the Reliant Scimitar GTE. This true sports car with the space of a two-door estate car was a concept that was imitated by both Lancia and Volvo. Reliant introduced a new small car at the London motor show in 1975. The car was called a Kitten but it was just a four-wheeled Robin. The mechanical parts all originated with the three-wheel Robin. Since the car weighed a mere 1,111 lb (505 kg), its 848 cc Mini engine took it to a top speed of 75 mph (120 kph). In 1975, the Kitten was also introduced as an estate car.

Reliant cars

COUNTRY OF ORIGIN: United Kingdom

Reliant Regal

MODEL YEAR: 1952-1973

NUMBER MADE: More than 100,000

SPECIAL REMARKS: In contrast with the midget car of Germany, the Regal had a four-stroke, four-cylinder engine. The first series had 748 cc Austin Seven units which

A 1968 estate car version of the Reliant Regal, also known as Supervan.

The Scimitar's body was built of glass-reinforced polyester. Depending on the motor fitted the car's top speed was 109-122 mph (175-195 kph).

gave a top speed of more than 62 mph (100 kph).

Reliant Sabre

MODEL YEAR: 1961-1966

NUMBER MADE: 135

The Reliant Sabre is no longer available as a kit car. It was not successful, in part because it cost as much as an Austin-Healey.

SPECIAL REMARKS: Reliant was less successful with its sports cars than their three-wheelers. The first Sabres had a 1,703 cc/91 bhp Ford Consul engine. The final 77 had a 2,553 cc six-cylinder from the Ford Zephyr with power output of 120 bhp.

Reliant Scimitar GT

MODEL YEAR: 1964-1970

NUMBER MADE: 1,003

SPECIAL REMARKS: Three different engines were fitted to the Scimitar GT. Initially there

was a choice from two six-cylinder units of 2,553 and 2,995 cc. Subsequently a V-6 of 2,495 cc was available. The power outputs in order were 120, 146, and 121 bhp.

Reliant Kitten

MODEL YEAR: 1975-1982

NUMBER MADE: 4,074

Reliant advertised the Kitten as the world's most economical car with fuel. It did about 60 miles per gallon (4.7 litres to 100 km).

SPECIAL REMARKS: The Kitten's wheelbase was 84 in (2,140 mm) with an overall length of 131 in (3,330 mm). Its 41 bhp power took it to a top speed of 75 mph (120 kph).

Renault

Renault was already one of France's biggest industrial concerns before World War II. In 1939, more than 40,000 employees built

almost 18,000 cars. In 1940, the company was forced to switch over to constructing military trucks for the Germans, making the Billancourt factory a regular target for Allied bombing. When Paris was liberated in August 1944, the 13,000 still working for Renault got to work in clearing the debris. At first the factory repaired tanks and made Jerry cans for the Allies. When the war was over Renault returned to making cars. The first model to roll of the line again was the pre-war Juvaquatre. During the war Renault's design department had worked on a modern car. This Renault 4CV was shown for the first time at the Paris motor show in October 1946 and proved to be just what everyone was waiting for. It was small but with space enough for four adults, economical with fuel but with a good turn of speed. The orders streamed in and the waiting time quickly rose to two years. The first 4CV cars were all sprayed with paint left by the Germans which had been destined for trucks

intended for the Afrika-Corps. The half-million 4CV rolled out of production in 1954 with production ending finally on 6 July 1961, when more than a million had been sold.

Before the war, Renault had built big cars as well as small ones, and when demand increased for more luxury cars, they brought out the Frégate in 1950. This was a spacious six-seater with a conventional front-mounted 2-litre four-cylinder engine that drove the rear wheels. The car was modern mechanically though, with independent suspension of the rear wheels as well as the front. There was a four-speed gearbox. The car's top speed was 81 mph (130 kph) with average fuel consumption of 30 miles per gallon (1 litre to 10 km).

The big news at the Geneva motor show in March 1956 was the Renault Dauphine, replacement for the old 4CV. Renault even built a new factory at Flins, twenty-five miles (40 km) from Paris. The Dauphine was 300 mm (11³/₄ in) longer than the 4CV and had much more space. The engine was rear mounted but was more powerful – initially 27 then later 49 bhp. The first Dauphines were produced in the spring of 1956 and

The Renault 4CV like this early model, recognisable by the aluminium trim stripes at the front, was also available as a "décapotable" with which the centre part of the roof could be rolled back.

more than 100,000 of them drove out of the factory in that first year. The Dauphine's motor was developed by Amedée Gordini, a magician in coaxing more power from an engine. This led to the famous Dauphine-Gordini for motor-sport enthusiasts. The millionth Dauphine was produced in 1960 and the last of some 2,100,000 plus left the Flins works in December 1967. It continued in production elsewhere for a while longer. The Dauphine was built in at least eleven different countries. In addition to the four-door saloon versions of the Dauphine, there was also a sporting two-door convertible, and a Floride coupé (known as Caravelle after 1962). The final 4 CV was made in August 1961, to be replaced by the Renault 4. This looked nothing like its predecessor. The engine was front-mounted and had front-wheel drive. The car had more in common with the Citroën 2CV than the former Renault 4 CV models.

Renault brought out its Renault 8, sometimes called the big Dauphine. This in turn was replaced by the larger Renault 10 in 1965 when the successful Renault 16 was also launched. This larger car replaced the Frégate in a convincing manner. This car also had front-wheel drive and was very comfortable. An innovation was the fifth door or rear hatch, which was a novelty at the time. The European public discovered the advantages of the space and accessible body and ordered the car in great numbers. Renault introduced the TS version of the R16 in 1968. This had a 1,565 cc motor instead of the 1,470 cc unit and had power output of no less than 88 bhp (SAE).

To bridge the gap between the Renaults 4 and 16, the Renault 6 appeared in 1968. The following year the Renault 12 emerged. This looked like a Renault 16 from the front but had a conventional boot at the back instead of a hatch-back. The Renault 15 and 17 followed in 1971. These sportive-looking cars were intended to compete with the Ford Capri and Opel Manta. The R15 had a 1,289 cc engine while the R17 had a 1,565 cc unit. Both motors had four-cylinders. The much-loved Renault 5 first emerged on the market in 1971. The sporting Alpine and Alpine Turbo version of the Renault 5 have written motor-sport history.

Renault cars

COUNTRY OF ORIGIN: France

Renault Juvaquatre

MODEL YEAR: 1939-1948

NUMBER MADE: 40,681

The post-war Juvaquatre can be recognised by the boot lid. In 1939 models the boot can only be accessed via the back seat. The 1946 version also had hydraulic brakes.

SPECIAL REMARKS: Estate car versions of the Juvaquatre were particularly popular with French proprietors of small businesses. The estate was built until 1960. Its 1,003 cc side-valve engine produced 24 bhp at 3,500 rpm.

Renault 4CV

MODEL YEAR: 1947-1961

NUMBER MADE: 1,105,543

SPECIAL REMARKS: The first Renault 4CV cars had a 747 cc/18 bhp at 4,000 rpm engine. In later cars drivers had 42 bhp at their disposal at 6,000 rpm from a 760 cc engine.

Renault Dauphine

MODEL YEAR: 1956-1968

NUMBER MADE: 2,120,220

SPECIAL REMARKS: The Renault Dauphine was a huge success and not just in France.

The 4CV was successful but almost twice as many Dauphines were sold. The Dauphine was larger, faster, and more modern than its forerunner.

It was built in Italy under licence by Alfa Romeo. The car was excellent for motor-sport too and Renault built more than 2,500 of the special Dauphine 1093 cars specially for this purpose.

Renault Dauphine Floride/Caravelle

MODEL YEAR: 1959-1968

NUMBER MADE: More than 180,000

SPECIAL REMARKS: The Dauphine Floride looked fast but was intended for the road rather than the track. The body was designed in Italy by Piero Frua. This car was called a Caravelle in the USA and also in Europe after 1962.

The Floride was the sports version of the Renault Dauphine. It was available as coupé or convertible and had room for three plus their luggage.

Renault Frégate

MODEL YEAR: 1951-1960

NUMBER MADE: 177,686

SPECIAL REMARKS: Renault returned to making more luxurious cars with the Frégate, which could also be supplied with an automatic gearbox or with a pre-selector gear-change.

Renault 4

MODEL YEAR: 1961-1992

NUMBER MADE: More than 8,000,000

The Renault 4, with its four-cylinder water-cooled engine, was a more luxurious competitor for the Citroën 2CV. The R4 had more space than the Renault 4CV but lacked much of that car's charm.

SPECIAL REMARKS: The exterior of the Renault 4 had nothing of its predecessor but the public seemed ready for a new concept as the sales figures prove. At first the engine was 603 cc but this was increased to 747, then 845, 956, and finally to 1,108 cc.

Renault 8

MODEL YEAR: 1962-1972

NUMBER MADE: 1,329,372

SPECIAL REMARKS: The design of the Renault 8 with the rear-mounted engine seemed like its forerunner, the Dauphine. The body was more angular though and at the time more up-to-date. The Gordini R8 could be recognised by the two fog-lights incorporated in the front of the car. The engine produced 95 bhp at 6,500 rpm.

The successor of the Dauphine was the Renault 8 which also had its engine in the back. The car was available with four-speed manual or an automatic gearbox. The manual was operated by a lever in the dashboard.

Renault 16

MODEL YEAR: 1965-1979

NUMBER MADE: 1,846,000

The Renault 16 had the space of a large estate car. The TS version not only had a more powerful engine but also a tachometer which were only found in sports cars in those days.

SPECIAL REMARKS: The Renault 16 was in many respects an enlarged version of the Renault 4. Its fifth door provided the utility and space of an estate car. First examples had a 1,470 cc engine, increased later to 1,565 and then 1,647 cc. Power went up from 55 to 93 bhp.

Renault 12

MODEL YEAR: 1969-1980

NUMBER MADE: More than 2,800,000

SPECIAL REMARKS: The Renault 12 had a 54 bhp 1,289 cc engine. The Gordini version's

tuned 1,647 cc Renault 16 engine produced 125 bhp at 6,000. The Gordini model was sold between 1971-1974.

Renault 15/17

MODEL YEAR: 1971-1979

NUMBER MADE: 207,854 & 92,589

SPECIAL REMARKS: Renault sold the R15 and R17 as competitors for the Ford Capri and Opel Manta. These were not really sports cars but they had sporting lines and had enough space for smaller families. Engine capacity ranged from 1,289-1,565 cc for power of 60-108 bhp.

Riley

The first Riley tri-car was made in Coventry in 1898. The final Riley emerged from the factory in 1969. In those intervening seventy years Riley produced some delightful cars, many conservative ones, but also very successful sports cars. Financial matters were somewhat different though. Riley was taken over by Lord Nuffield in 1938 to become a part of his Nuffield group.

Riley was one of the few manufacturers to bring out an entirely new car in 1946. The body had no connection whatever with pre-war cars. The car was also quite advanced for its time. The One-Point-Five had hydraulic brakes and independent front suspension. The car did still have a chassis and its engine was pre-war but in no way was it old-fashioned. On the contrary, the 1.5 Litre had twin camshafts mounted high on the engine and hemispherical combustion chambers. The engine developed power of 55 bhp at 4,500 rpm. The car's roof was covered with vinyl, which was imitated years later by the Americans. The top speed of the Riley 1.5 Litre was 75 mph (120 kph). When customers demanded better performance, the wheelbase was extended from $112^{1}/_{2}$ to $118^{3}/_{4}$ in (2,860 to 3,020 mm) and a 2.5-litre engine was installed under the longer bonnet. Power increased from an 90 to bhp, giving the 1952 model a top speed of 94 mph (150 kph).

Austin also joined the Nuffield group in 1952 to create the British Motors Corporation. Riley continued with its distinctive identity until 1954 but when full-width bodies were introduced in Europe and America, Riley too followed suit but sharing bodies, so that the new Riley Pathfinder was based on the Wolseley 4/44. This was the very beginning of what later became "badge engineering". The Pathfinder retained its chassis and renowned engine. Rileys were never cheap cars, costing three times as much as a Renault 4CV of its day. BMC brought out a newly-developed six-cylinder engine in 1957 which was first installed in the Wolseley 6/90 and new Riley 2.6. Both these cars had the same body but differed in the details although both had superb quality internal trim with walnut and leather. The 1957 Riley One-Point-Five was aimed at a broader market with a more affordable price. The car still incorporated plenty of luxurious touches though. The engine had the same twin carburettors installed in the MGA of the same

year. The 1957 Riley 1.5 was the first Riley with a monocoque body. It had a kerb weight of 2,090 lb (950 kg) and a top speed of 90 mph (145 kph). A subsequent small Riley was the Elf to compete with the Mini from in house. Since not everyone wished to be seen in a Mini, some elected instead to have a Riley Elf parked in front of their cottages. When BMC expanded the Mini concept to form the 1100/1300 range, the Riley Kestrel and Riley 1300 followed. The only external differences of these cars were the Riley grille. The Rileys were more expensive than the Austin and Morris Minis.

The final large Riley was the 4/72 with a body designed by Pininfarina. The car had a 1,622 cc four-cylinder engine with twin carburettors and power output of 70 bhp at 5,000 rpm. It goes without saying of course that this same body was also used by Wolseley and for the MG Magnette.

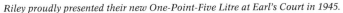

Riley proudly presented their new One-Point-Five Litre at Earl's Court in 1945.

Riley cars

COUNTRY OF ORIGIN: United Kingdom

Riley One-Point-Five Litre (1946)

MODEL YEAR: 1946-1954

NUMBER MADE: 13,950

SPECIAL REMARKS: The Riley 1.5 Litre was 178 in (4,520 mm) long and had two leather seats at the front and leather bench seat in the back.

Riley Two-Point-Five Litre

MODEL YEAR: 1947-1953

NUMBER MADE: 8,959

SPECIAL REMARKS: The initial 2.5-litre engine had power output of 90 bhp; this became 100 bhp after 1948. The car was equipped with hydraulic brakes in 1952.

The Two-Point-Five looked almost identical to the One-Point-Five. The difference lay under the bonnet and in a longer wheelbase.

Riley brought a quality car in reach of many more with the new One-Point-Five four-door saloon.

Riley Pathfinder

MODEL YEAR: 1953-1957

NUMBER MADE: 5,152

SPECIAL REMARKS: This model was identical mechanically to its predecessors but had a new chassis and body, now entirely made of steel, with no wood.

Riley One-Point-Five Litre (1957)

MODEL YEAR: 1957-1965

NUMBER MADE: 39,881

SPECIAL REMARKS: The 1957 1.5 Litre had a four-cylinder engine of 1,489 cc that developed 69 bhp (SAE), overhead valves, twin SU carburettors, four-speed gear box, and was the first Riley with monocoque body.

Riley Elf

MODEL YEAR: 1961-1969

NUMBER MADE: 30,912

The Riley Elf, this is a 1968 Mk II, was 10$^{1}/_{4}$ in (260 mm) longer than the Mini. This was mainly due the additional boot space.

SPECIAL REMARKS: The Riley Elf had the 998 cc Cooper engine but detuned to 39 instead of 56 bhp. The engine was transversely-mounted in the front of the car as in the Mini.

Riley 4/72

MODEL YEAR: 1961-1969

NUMBER MADE: 14,191

Almost all Riley 4/72 cars had two-tone paint finish. The engine was shared with Wolseley and the MGA.

The Silver Shadow convertible was known as a Corniche from 1971. The hood alone took 40 man-hours to make.

SPECIAL REMARKS: The 4/72 was a big car with a relatively small engine. It weighed 2,508 lb (1,140 kg) and had a top speed of 87 mph (140 kph).

Rolls-Royce

Hobbyist Henry Royce built his first car for the "man of the world", playboy, and publicist Charles Rolls.
Rolls-Royce cars are undoubtedly the finest automotive engineering and quality anyone can demand. The first Rolls-Royce was built in 1904. The company, which started in Manchester and then later moved to Derby and Crewe, be-

Henry Royce (1863-1933)

Charles Rolls (1877-1910)

came world famous for cars of exceptional quality. There are of course other makers of first-class prestige cars (some may even make better cars) but no other marque has the cachet of a Rolls-Royce. It is the exclusivity of Rolls-Royce cars that only the wealthy can afford which sets them apart.

The final model in 1939 was the Wraith and this reappeared in 1946 as the Silver Wraith. The cars in those days were only supplied as rolling chassis which were fitted with bodies by specialist coachwork companies to the client's individual requirements. The engine in the Silver Wraith was a six-cylinder unit with inlet valves in the cylinder head and exhaust valves in the cylinder block. The car could be supplied with an automatic gearbox from 1952 onwards. The Silver Wraith was designed to be driven by a personal chauffeur but the Silver Dawn of 1949 was an "owner-driver" car.
The Silver Dawn was virtually identical in mechanical terms to the Silver Wraith but was slightly smaller and also less expensive. In addition, most customers purchased the car with the standard works body, which was very similar to the Bentley Mk VI. This body was replaced from 1952 on with the more modern Bentley R-type coachwork.

The Silver Dawn was replaced by the Silver Cloud which was available with short or long wheelbase. Some superb cars were built on this chassis. The Silver Cloud was also the last Rolls-Royce with a six-cylinder engine. Its successor, the Silver Cloud II was fitted with a 6,230 cc V-8 engine beneath its long aluminium bonnet.

The Silver Shadow heralded a new era for Rolls-Royce in 1965 by being the first Rolls-Royce with a monocoque body. This car too was available in two different lengths and sat full of gadgets and equipment. Air conditioning was standard and had the capacity of sixty refrigerators. The heating system provided as much warmth as that of four central heating boilers. The Frankfurt motor show in 1967 saw a Silver Shadow convertible on display. The press pack revealed that the car was made up out of 85,000 separate parts. The Shadow was replaced in 1971 by the Corniche with clear differences in styling. The Corniche was also available as a coupé or convertible but only the open version was sold after 1982. Among the most magnificent and also rarest of Rolls-Royce cars are the Phantoms.

The first Phantom appeared in 1925 and the most recent Phantom VI in 1993. The final pre-war Phantom was the III which was powered by a colossal V-12 engine. The first post-war Phantom was the IV, first delivered in 1950. This car was made at the request of H.M. The Queen. After she took delivery, orders streamed in from other crowned heads and other rulers but most were disappointed for only eighteen were built.
The lucky owners included the Shah of Persia (who bought two), the Emire of Kuwait (who like General Franco, bought three), and the Aga Khan. More (516) were built of the successor Phantom V between 1959–1968.

This car cost about half as much as the Phantom IV but was still enough to buy a fine country mansion. The Phantom VI was the last of these ultra-expensive cars. It appeared first in 1969 with a 6,230 cc V-8 engine that was replaced in 1979 by a 6,750 cc unit. The

The final Phantom VI was supplied in 1990. The car illustrated was built in 1979 and was still in use as a works demonstrator and courtesy car in 1990 when photographed.

Phantom VI was also available with an aluminium "Special Landaulette" body by Mulliner Park Ward that was longer than 19ft (6 m).

Rolls-Royce cars

COUNTRY OF ORIGIN: United Kingdom

Rolls-Royce Silver Wraith

MODEL YEAR: 1946-1959

NUMBER MADE: 1,783

SPECIAL REMARKS: Up to 1951, the six-cylinder engine had a capacity of 4,257 cc. This increased to 4,566 and then after 1955 to 4,887 cc.

With more than 500 built, the Phantom V was not as rare as its predecessor.

The Silver Wraith can be mistaken for a pre-war car with is almost separate headlights.

The Silver Dawn was a Bentley Mk VI with a Rolls-Royce radiator grille and emblem.

A 1974 Rolls-Royce Silver Shadow, weighing 4970 lb (2,259 kg), 203¹/₂ in (5,170 mm) long, and with fuel consumption of 13-16 mpg (18-22 litres/100 km).

Rolls-Royce Silver Dawn

MODEL YEAR: 1949-1955

NUMBER MADE: 761

SPECIAL REMARKS: Most of the cars were supplied with standard works bodies by Pressed Steel.

Rolls-Royce Silver Cloud

MODEL YEAR: 1955-1965

NUMBER MADE: 7,373

SPECIAL REMARKS: When the Silver Cloud got a V-8 engine it became the Silver Cloud II. The Silver Cloud II can be recognised by its twin headlights.

Rolls-Royce Silver Shadow

MODEL YEAR: 1965-1980

NUMBER MADE: 14,611

SPECIAL REMARKS: A total of 1,075 convertibles were made of the Silver Shadow. These cars had all-round independent suspension and four disc brakes. The model was available with either long or short wheelbase. The longer version was known as Silver Wraith after 1977.

This Rolls-Royce Silver Cloud III belonged to the film star Curt Jürgens.

Rover

Rover's factory in Coventry had built both cycles and an electric car (in 1888). It was sixteen years later in 1904 before the first petrol-engined car was made there. At first only small cars were produced but in the 1930s this included medium-sized cars. Rover cars were always of better quality than most of their competitors but not always as up-to-date. Electric starter motors could first be ordered as an optional extra in 1923. Until then all Rovers had to be hand cranked. On the other hand, Rover had an overhead valve engine in 1926 and brought out a car in 1928 with an overhead camshaft. The first post-war models were utterly conservative.

These were the Ten, Twelve, Fourteen, and Sixteen. The figures relate to the old British horsepower ratings. The Ten and Twelve both had four-cylinder engines of 1,389 and 1,496 cc but the bigger cars had 1,901 and 2,147 cc six-cylinder power units. These were the last Rovers with the old horsepower indicated in their names. In 1948 there were new engines and new model designations. These new engines had the inlet valves in the cylinder head and the exhaust valves in the block, as used by Rolls-Royce. The 1948 series was termed P4 and consisted of the Rover Sixty and Seventy-Five.

The Sixty had a 1,595 cc four-cylinder engine that produced 51 bhp and the Seventy-Five a 2,103 cc six-cylinder unit of 73 bhp at 4,000 rpm. The range was extended during the 1950s with the Rovers 90, 100, and 105 with six-cylinder engines. Only the Rover 80 by then had a four-cylinder engine.

In 1958, Rover introduced their 3-litre P5 as a competitor for both Daimler and Jaguar. Some unkindly gave the car names suggesting it was rather too big. It was Rover's first car with a monocoque body and it was powered by a 2,995 cc six-cylinder engine with output of 117 bhp. When Rover put a V-8 engine in the car it became the Rover 3.5. The new aluminium engine was developed by General Motors for the Buick Special and Oldsmobile F85.

The Rover 2000 which arrived on the scene in 1963 was a thoroughly modern car in every respect and was chosen by a panel of

This 1947 Rover Sixteen has a 6-cylinder engine and a longer 115 in (2,920 mm) wheelbase.

international motoring writers in 1964 as "Car of the Year". The 1,978 cc four-cylinder engine had an overhead camshaft and it input 100 bhp to the rear wheels which were mounted on a De Dion axle.

Front and back brakes were equipped with discs. Various versions of the car were produced with both 2,205 cc and even a 3,528 cc V-8 engine.

Rover cars

COUNTRY OF ORIGIN: United Kingdom

Rover Ten

MODEL YEAR: 1946-1948

NUMBER MADE: 2,640

The doors opened the wrong way in the first post-war Rovers like this 1946 Rover Ten.

SPECIAL REMARKS: The first Rovers still had rigid front and back axles. The engine was still a side-valve unit.

Rover P4-75

MODEL YEAR: 1950-1964

NUMBER MADE: 130,342

SPECIAL REMARKS: The P4-75 was supplied with both four and six-cylinder engines of

The first of the P4 type Rover stood out because of the spotlight in the centre of the grille. This "Cyclops" look was removed in 1952.

1,997-2,625 cc. All models had the same 111 in (2,820 mm) wheelbase and were $178^3/_4$ in (4,540 mm) long overall.

Rover 3 Litre

MODEL YEAR: 1959-1967

NUMBER MADE: 48,541

SPECIAL REMARKS: This luxury car had a 3-

The Rover 3 Litre was a big and heavy car with length of $181^1/_2$ in (4,740 mm) and kerb weight of 3,801 lb (1,728 kg).

The Rover 3 Litre was also available as a 4-door, 4-seater coupé. Surely the designers did not spend long over the model.

litre six-cylinder engine which initially produced 117 and later 136 bhp. Depending on the version, they had top speeds of either 100 (160 kph) or 109 mph (175 kph).

Rover 2200 TC

MODEL YEAR: 1966-1977

The various cars with the Rover 2000 body varied little externally. That this is a 2200 TC can be seen by the spare wheel mounted on the boot lid.

NUMBER MADE: Unknown

SPECIAL REMARKS: The TC indicates that this model, with a 2,205 cc four-cylinder engine, is equipped with twin carburettors. The power unit produced 110 bhp at 5,500 rpm.

Rovin

The Rovin brothers, Robert and Raoul, built midget cars in Paris before World War II and a prototype of another small car was constructed during the German occupation. The Rovin was extremely primitive in appearance yet very modern mechanically. It had a monocoque body and all-round independent suspension. The small single-cylinder four-stroke engine was rear mounted and at first had a capacity of 240 then later 275 cc. Export versions of the car had twin-cylinder water-cooled engines of 425, then 462 cc. The gearbox had three ratios and was operated by a column-change gear shift.

Rovin cars

COUNTRY OF ORIGIN: France

Rovin D2

MODEL YEAR: 1947-1948

NUMBER MADE: Unknown

SPECIAL REMARKS: The Rovin was truly a midget car with its length of 2,850 mm (112 in). There were no doors or a boot.

Rovin D4

MODEL YEAR: 1951-1958

NUMBER MADE: Unknown

SPECIAL REMARKS: The final Rovin had a 462 cc twin-cylinder power unit producing 13 bhp at 3,200 rpm. Once Citroën introduced their 2CV everybody stopped buying Rovin cars.

Rovin built a total of about 3,000 cars. This is a 1948 D2.

Saab

Saab was founded in Trollhättan, Sweden in 1937 to build aircraft. The initials are short for the company name in Swedish (Svenska Aeroplan AB). Saab jet fighters have become world famous and form the backbone of the Swedish air force.

When World War II was over, Saab moved into other areas because the demand for aircraft had diminished, and the company wished to retain its personnel. Other aircraft manufacturers also moved into making cars, such as Bristol, Heinkel, and Messerschmitt. The first cars betrayed that they had been designed by aeronautical and aerodynamic specialists.

The first bodies were designed by Gunnar Ljungström and Sixten Sasanover whose department drew outlines of the body and made clay and later wooden models. These were then tested for aerodynamic properties in a wind tunnel.

The first prototype, designated 92001 by the factory, was first driven in 1946 and a further three prototypes were made in 1947, which resembled 92001 but had mechanical differences. Once these cars had driven 100,000 kilometres, they were finally shown to the press on 10 June 1947. There was a twin-cylinder two-stroke engine under the bonnet, which was transversely-mounted and drove the front wheels. The car was named a Saab 92 but it was not available to buy until December 1949.

The right to sell the cars in Sweden were granted to Philipsons Automobil AB who ordered 8,000 of them and helped Saab's start-up finance by paying a deposit for the cars. Production was slow to get going and at first only four cars were being built each day. By the end of 1948, only 1,246 Saabs had been delivered, all of which were sprayed green. Saab owners quickly discovered their new cars were extraordinarily suitable for driving through deep snow and over poor roads. A key reason was the entirely smooth floor pan which helped the car slide over snow instead of ploughing its way through. This property became valuable in later rallying and other motor sport. Saab gave the car a face-lift in December 1952 after 5,300 cars had been made. For a few months it was possible to buy a Saab in another colour than

A 1947 Saab prototype which the development team called "Ursaaben".

green. More importantly, the much too small rear window had been enlarged and there was now a boot lid. With the first cars luggage had to be placed in the boot from the rear seat.

The 10,000th Saab rolled off the line on 6 March 1954 and in the summer of 1955 the type 92 was replaced by type 93. At first the 93 looked precisely like its predecessor but there was now a three-cylinder two-stroke engine under the bonnet. Demand for the blue-smoke emitting and coughing two-stroke engine waned so Saab fitted a four-cylinder Ford Taunus engine from 1967 to create the Saab 96. The following year Saab cars were only available with four-stroke engines.

The original body remained unchanged until 1980, even though a new 99 model was added in 1968. This car no longer had the typical Saab look but retained the sound engineering of the other Saabs. This model also shared front-wheel drive of course which has subsequently become the norm with almost all manufacturers. Saab and DKW were pioneers in the field.

Saab cars

COUNTRY OF ORIGIN: Sweden

Saab 92

The first Saab production model was the 92 which had a divided windscreen, single rear window but no boot lid.

MODEL YEAR: 1949-1956

NUMBER MADE: 20,128

SPECIAL REMARKS: The Saab's body remained unchanged for many years but the cars were continuously improved. From 1953 they got access to the boot.

Saab 93

MODEL YEAR: 1955-1960

NUMBER MADE: 52,731

The Saab 93 was a great step forward for the company. It now had a three-cylinder engine.

SPECIAL REMARKS: The Saab 93 had a three-cylinder power unit instead of the former twin. It was still a two-stroke engine but was no longer transversely-mounted. The new engine had a capacity of 748 cc with output of 33 bhp at 4,200 rpm.

Saab 96

The basic shape is still recognisable in this 1963 Saab 93.

MODEL YEAR: 1960-1980

NUMBER MADE: 547,221

SPECIAL REMARKS: The successor to the 93 was the 96 (the 95 was the estate car version). The three-cylinder engine was now 841 cc with output of 38 bhp at 4,250 rpm. A Ford V-4 unit of 1,498 cc could be installed from 1967. Its output was 68 bhp at 5,500 rpm.

Saab 99

MODEL YEAR: 1968-1984

NUMBER MADE: 588,643

The Saab 99 appeared in 1968 with an entirely new body. Enthusiasts could still buy the old shape until 1980.

SPECIAL REMARKS: Everything was different with the Saab 99. There was a new body and a four-cylinder Triumph engine with overhead camshaft that had an option with fuel injection from 1969 onwards.

Salmson

Salmson established its reputation during World War I for aircraft engines for fighters. When that war ended and the aircraft market slumped, the company decided to make sports cars. They made small two-seaters,

The first post-war Salmsons had pre-war bodies with headlights still mounted outside the front wings.

known as cycle-cars but also sporting saloons powered by engines with a single or twin overhead camshaft.

When the company restarted production at Billancourt on the river Seine, the cars were identical to the pre-war models. The S4 was available with two different four-cylinder engines: 1,730 and 2,320 cc. Both engines had cylinder heads with twin overhead camshafts with power output of 50 and 70 bhp. The front wheels had independent suspension and most cars were fitted with an electrically-operated Cotal gearbox. The brakes were still mechanically-operated and the body was of pre-war design. The headlights still stood outside the body until 1948 when they were replaced with lights incorporated into the front wings, next to the

In common with many French and Italian sporting cars from the 1940s and 1950s, the Salmson had the steering on the right.

The S4 was Salmson's best-seller. This is a 1949 4-seater convertible. Note the chains on all 4 wheels.

radiator grille. By the time Salmson had produced more than 1,000 cars in 1950, a new model, named Randonnée, was introduced to replace the S4. The body was modern with headlights now within the wings. The engine at 2,200 cc was slightly smaller yet more powerful with 71 bhp. The company found itself in financial difficulties in 1951 but these were quickly resolved by a new owner. Two years later, a further new model appeared called the 2300 Sport. By the time this car was launched at the Paris Motor Show the company had run into further financial difficulties. Salmson was taken over by Renault in 1955 and its founder died soon afterwards in 1957.

Salmson cars

The Salmson was a luxury car with sporting inclinations.

COUNTRY OF ORIGIN: France

Salmson S4

MODEL YEAR: 1946-1952

NUMBER MADE: 2,983

SPECIAL REMARKS: On the plus side were independently suspended front wheels and a twin overhead camshaft. On the negative side were the inadequate mechanical brakes.

A Salmson S4-E Berline. This 4-door car was 4,610 mm (181 1/2 in) long, weighed 1,200 kg (4,400 lb) and had a top speed of 84 mph (135 kph).

Salmson Randonée

MODEL YEAR: 1951-1952

NUMBER MADE: 545

SPECIAL REMARKS: The Randonée's twin overhead camshaft engine had a capacity of 2,200 cc and power output of 71 bhp at 4,000 rpm.

Simca

Simca stands for Société Industrielle de Mécanique et Carosserie Automobile. Its founder was Henri T. Pigozzi, who built Fiat cars, starting in the Nanterre factory in 1935 with exact copies of the Fiat 508 Balillaof and 518 Ardita.

After World War II in 1946 the Simca Cinq appeared as counterpart of the Fiat Topolino and the Simca Huit, precisely like the Fiat 1100. Both cars had four-cylinder engines of 589 and 1,089 cc and power outputs of 14 and 32 bhp. These cars sold well and by 1951, when 20,000 cars had been built, Simca was the fourth largest car maker in France, behind Renault, Citroën, and Peugeot. Simca introduced a model of their own, called Aronde, in 1951, which had a modern monocoque body. The Aronde was the start of a golden era for Simca, which sold more than 52,000 cars in 1952. In 1954,

Pigozzi bought Ford's factory at Poissy. Because Ford had made the Vedette there, the car was now sold as a Simca Vedette. This was a spacious six-seater with side-valve V-8 engine. In the Spring of 1957, the Vedette and Simca Ariane were being produced. This latter car combined the spacious body of the Vedette with the more economical four-cylinder engine from the Aronde.

The Aronde was continuously improved mechanically and in appearance. In 1951, the four-cylinder overhead valve engine had a capacity of 1,221 cc and power output of 45 bhp at 4,500 rpm. By the following year power had increased to 51 bhp and in 1955 the cylinder capacity was increased to 1,290 cc to produce 55 or 57 bhp from this relatively small engine. The Aronde P60, which appeared in 1958, had both an entirely new body and a new power unit of 1,290 cc and 60 bhp. Such an engine gave it a top speed capability of 87 mph (140 kph).

Chrysler started to buy shares in Simca in 1958 and it was not long before the American company took over the control of the company.

An entirely new Simca was to be seen in 1961 at the Paris motor show: the Simca 1000. This was the first Simca with a rear-mounted engine and the body style had no link with the previous Simcas. The final Arondes were made in 1963 to be replaced by the Simca 1300 and 1500 with the same four-

The Simca Aronde, like this 1956 Elysée was an extremely reliable car which also broke many records, including first to complete 100,000 km at an average speed of 100 kph (62 mph).

door bodies but different 1,290 or 1,475 cc engines under the bonnet.

When front-wheel drive became in vogue, Simca followed suit. The Simca 1100 was introduced in 1967 with a new three-door or five-door body and engines of 944, 1,118, 1,204, or 1,294 cc. From 1970 onwards the Simca name was increasingly pushed into the background with the new models of that year being sold as Chrysler 160 and 180. By the following year people spoke of French Chrysler and then later the company became Talbot Simca.

Simca cars

COUNTRY OF ORIGIN: France

Simca Huit

MODEL YEAR: 1946-1951

NUMBER MADE: 89,457

With its headlights on stalks, the 1946 Huit was almost the same as its pre-war counterparts.

SPECIAL REMARKS: The Simca Huit had a 1,089 cc motor producing 32 bhp until 1949. The motorist then got a 1,221 cc unit with 40 bhp available for a top speed of 75 mph (120 kph).

Simca Aronde

MODEL YEAR: 1951-1960

NUMBER MADE: 1,014,355

The Aronde was available in various forms, including this Ranch 3-door estate.

SPECIAL REMARKS: The Aronde was the first true Simca. It had a monocoque body with a 1.3-litre engine with power initially of 45 and later 57 bhp.

Simca Aronde P60

MODEL YEAR: 1959-1963

NUMBER MADE: 260,504

SPECIAL REMARKS: The final version of the Aronde was the P60, available with a choice

The P60 Etoile was the cheapest Aronde. This is a 1960 example. Its 1,089 cc engine had power of 48 bhp at 5,200 rpm.

of either a 1,089 cc/48 bhp or 1,290 cc/57 bhp engine.

Simca Vedette

MODEL YEAR: 1955-1961

NUMBER MADE: 166,895

When Simca took over Ford's French factory, the Vedette became a Simca car. This is a 1959 Chambord version.

SPECIAL REMARKS: The V-8 engine of the Vedette was a pre-war side-valve unit of 2,351 cc that had output of 80 bhp at 4,400 rpm.

Simca 1000

MODEL YEAR: 1961-1978

NUMBER MADE: 1,642,091

SPECIAL REMARKS: The Simca 1000 was the best-selling Simca. Inside its monocoque body was a rear-mounted four-cylinder engine. The car was a much-prized rally entrant.

The Simca 1000 was rear-engined and had space for five and plenty of boot space.

The 1300/1500 and 1301/1501 Simcas replaced the Arondes. These were roomy cars that sold well. This is a 1301.

Simca 1300/1500 & 1301/1501

MODEL YEAR: 1963-1976

NUMBER MADE: 1,075,342

SPECIAL REMARKS: This total includes 437,809 cars from the first series. The remaining cars were sold as 1301/1501. The bodies were virtually identical.

Simca 1100

MODEL YEAR: 1967-1982

NUMBER MADE: More than 2,000,000

SPECIAL REMARKS: The Simca 1100 was a five-seater car at the lower end of the medium car market. The engine was transversely-mounted at the front and drove the front wheels.

The most powerful version of the 1100 range was the 1204 illustrated intended for the US market. Its 1,204 cc engine had output of 63 bhp at 5,800 rpm.

Singer

Singer began life making cycles and motorcycles, in common with numerous other English car makers, when they gambled on making their first car in 1905. The first Singer was a tri-car but they quickly switched to making four-wheeled cars. By the late 1920s, Singer was number three in Britain behind Morris and Austin. The company specialised in sports cars and sporting saloons and established a reputation for making cars of quality.

After World War II the demand was for cheap cars such as a Morris or Austin rather than more expensive models and this caused Singer financial difficulties. The firm was taken over in 1956 by the Rootes Brothers and when Chrysler took over Rootes, Singer became part of the US concern in 1967. By 1970, the Singer name had vanished.

Back in 1949, Singer brought out the Singer Nine, Super Ten, and Super Twelve. These were relatively small cars with powerful four-cylinder engines with an overhead camshaft, plus twin SU carburettors for the sports cars. Both front and rear axles of these cars were rigid and there were still mechanical brakes. Singer was first of the British companies with an entirely new design in 1949. It was the SM 1500 (the SM was for Singer Motors) with a strikingly modern body.

When Singer was taken over by Rootes Brothers, the heady days of sports cars came to an end. The Singer Gazelle of 1956 had the same body as the Hillman Minx and the Singer Vogue of 1961 was really a Hillman Super Minx. When the Hillman Imp was launched in 1963 as a competitor for the

The 1949 Singer Nine Roadster with 1,074 cc engine had an overhead camshaft and SU down-draught carburettor to yield 35 bhp at 5,000 rpm.

Mini, loyal customers could buy the same car the following year as a Singer Chamois, which remained in production until 1970.

Singer cars

COUNTRY OF ORIGIN: United Kingdom

Singer Super Ten

MODEL YEAR: 1946-1949

NUMBER MADE: 10,497

SPECIAL REMARKS: The Super Ten's engine was a 1,193 cc unit that delivered 39 bhp at 4,900 rpm. In contrast to the Nine, the Ten had a four speed gearbox, instead of three speed.

Although the SM 1500 had an entirely new body, its sports car version retained the old Singer Nine body.

The SM 1500 dashboard: a tachometer was found unnecessary.

Singer SM 1500

MODEL YEAR: 1949-1954

NUMBER MADE: 22,648

SPECIAL REMARKS: In addition to its new body, the SM 1500 also had independently suspended front wheels and a four-cylinder engine producing 48 bhp, increasing to 58 bhp from 1953.

Singer Hunter

MODEL YEAR: 1954-1956

NUMBER MADE: 4,772

SPECIAL REMARKS: The Singer Hunter was the last true Singer. The car was identical mechanically to the SM 1500 but provided more luxury. The Hunter even had a heater and a clock.

Skoda

Skoda is one of Eastern Europe's oldest car makers and also one of the largest industrial concerns that made armaments and built locomotives. They began making the famous Hispano Suiza cars under licence in 1923. Two years later Skoda purchased Laurin & Klement whose factory had made motorcycles and cars since the turn of the nineteenth and twentieth centuries.

233

The Skoda 110R coupé looked faster than it was. It took effort to reach 90 mph (145 kph).

The first Skoda cars were based on Laurin & Klement designs, such as the famous Popular, Favorit, and Rapid.
Skoda were one of the first European car production plants to deliver cars in 1945, and although these were still to pre-war designs, they sold well in a number of European countries.

The chassis of the 1101 consisted as pre-war of a central tube. The front wheels had independent suspension and a 1,089 cc four-cylinder overhead valve engine produced 32 bhp at 3,800 rpm. Skoda cars were specially developed for the poor roads of Eastern Europe and were virtually indestructible. The 1200 series followed in 1952 with an entirely new body with no use of wood. The car appeared similar mechanically to its forerunners but the engine was now increased to 1,221 cc to achieve 36 bhp. The estate car version of this series remained in production until 1970.

In 1955, the Skoda 440 was introduced at the Brussels motor show. This had a new body but the mechanical side was unaltered. When this model was given a facelift, Skoda called it Octavia. The Octavia also incorporated improved mechanical engineering. The 1,098 or 1,221 cc engines had outputs of 43 or 47 bhp. The Felicia was the convertible version of the Octavia. The 1,089 cc engine of this model had power output of 54 bhp. By the time Skoda decided to install their engines in the rear of their cars this was then out of fashion, making the 1000 MB less popular in the west. The 1000 MB now had a monocoque body big enough for four adults. The 110 R sports version was successful in rallies in East bloc countries.

Today Skoda is part of the Volkswagen concern and the Felicia and Octavia names are once more in use.

Skoda cars

Country of origin: Former Czechoslovakia/ Czech Republic

Skoda 1101

Model year: 1945-1952

Number made: 81,140

The Skoda 1101 was available in various forms. This is a 4-door saloon with front doors that open the wrong way.

Special remarks: The first post-war Skoda had a 2,480 mm (97$\frac{1}{2}$ in) wheelbase and was 4,050 mm (159$\frac{1}{2}$ in) long overall. With a top speed of 62 mph (100 kph) they were not fast but certainly very robust.

Skoda 1200

Model year: 1952-1970

Number made: 93,741

Special remarks: Everything had got bigger with the 1200. The wheelbase was now 2,690 mm (106 in) and the overall length now

4,500 mm (177 in). The engine was now 1,221 cc with output of 36 bhp at 4,000 rpm.

Skoda Octavia

MODEL YEAR: 1959-1964

NUMBER MADE: 227,258

SPECIAL REMARKS: The Octavia was the first Skoda to have coil springs instead of leaf springs. There were 2,273 cars made of the TS version with twin carburettors.

Skoda Felicia

MODEL YEAR: 1958-1964

NUMBER MADE: 15,864

There was also a polyester hardtop version of the Felicia designed by Ghia in Turin.

SPECIAL REMARKS: The Felicia was the open roadster version of the Octavia. There was room for four but the car looked more sportive than it was with its top speed of 78 mph (125 kph).

The 1000 MB was the first rear-engined Skoda. It was launched when this concept was over-the-hill.

Skoda 1000 MB

MODEL YEAR: 1964-1977

NUMBER MADE: 1,239,327

SPECIAL REMARKS: The 1000 MB was available with either a 988 cc/45 bhp engine or one of 1,107 cc with output of 52 bhp. The four-cylinder units had overhead valves, an aluminium cylinder head, and cast iron cylinder block.

Standard

Reginald Walter Maudsley (1871-1934) started his involvement with cars in 1903. His first cars had a single-cylinder engine but these were quickly followed by twins and four-cylinder units. His Standard Motor Company not only built its own cars but also the engines for the first SS sports cars (later to become Jaguar) of William Lyons. During World War II Sir John Black became a director of the company and in 1945, Black managed to take over the Triumph company. He hoped to create a stronger, more competitive position by this means but he was only partially successful. By 1961, Black felt forced to join British Leyland and all went well until 1964 when the Standard marque disappeared into the history books.

Standard had cleared the debris from the bombing of Coventry before the end of the war and were able to produce their first car in 1945. The first post-war model was the Standard Eight which was a small car with a 1,009 cc engine that produced a mere 28 bhp. This was soon followed by the Twelve and Fourteen which had engines of 1,609 and 1,766 cc. Like the pre-war models, the Twelve and Fourteen still had chrome-plated headlights on stalks outside the wings.

The first truly new post-war model was the Vanguard, introduced in 1948. This was a big car, which for the first time had a monocoque body, with a 2-litre overhead valve engine. The three-speed gearbox was fully synchronised and was operated by a column-change gear-lever. The Vanguard was very

A Standard Eight takes a corner at Zandvoort circuit. The car needs a great of work to turn it into a competitive motor-sport car.

The post-war Eight as convertible. It had a top speed of 59 mph (95 kph). Note the trafficator above the rear wing.

Dashboard of the post-war Eight. The wipers were operated by the round knobs on either side. The catch in the centre allows the windscreen to be opened.

successful and remained in production, with various changes, until 1963. The final 9,953 were sold as Vanguard Luxury Six with a six-cylinder engine.

The Standard Eight got a new body in 1953, which looked like a smaller version of the Vanguard. This was still a cheap car in which the works had spared every possible penny, by not having a boot lid, for example, so that luggage had to be put in through the back seat. The later Ten did have a boot lid but was otherwise, apart from its engine, identical with the Eight. The Ten had a 948 cc engine instead of the Eight's 803 cc unit. When Standard showed their new models at the London motor show in October 1957 the Vanguard appeared to have changed its name to Ensign. This new version had a smaller four-cylinder engine than the Vanguard.

There was a choice of 1,670 or 2,136 cc units for power output of either 61 or 75 bhp. The Ensign was the final Standard to leave the factory in 1964 before Standard disappeared.

Standard cars

COUNTRY OF ORIGIN: United Kingdom

Standard Eight (1945)

MODEL YEAR: 1945-1948

NUMBER MADE: 53,099

SPECIAL REMARKS: Unlike the Ten and Four-teen, the 1945 Standard Eight had a rigid front axle. All the cars now had a four-speed manual gearbox with floor-mounted gear-lever.

Standard Vanguard

MODEL YEAR: 1948-1963

NUMBER MADE: 341,289

SPECIAL REMARKS: The four-cylinder engine had a capacity of 2,088 cc and power output of 69 bhp at 4,200 rpm. The final 9,953 had 1,998 cc six-cylinder engines of 81 bhp at 4,400 rpm.

The Standard Vanguard was one of the first European cars with a completely new post-war body.

The Vanguard Mk II was made from 1953-1955. This is a 5-door estate.

Standard Eight/Ten (1954)

MODEL YEAR: 1954-1961

NUMBER MADE: 172,500

SPECIAL REMARKS: The Eight/Ten had a monocoque body and a larger 948 cc four-cylinder engine in the Ten that produced 37 bhp. The Eight retained the 803 cc unit of the earlier Standard Eight. An overdrive could be added to the four-speed box as an optional extra.

Standard Ensign

MODEL YEAR: 1957-1963

NUMBER MADE: 21,170

SPECIAL REMARKS: The Ensign had a choice of 1,670 or 2,136 cc engine for power outputs of either 61 or 75 bhp, to give top speeds of 75 mph (120 kph) or 87 mph (140 kph).

Steyr-Puch

When the demand for armaments dropped following World War I, the Osterreichische Waffenfabriks Gesellschaft AG, Steyr decided to switch to making cars, with the help of famous engineer Hans Ledwinka. Some fine large cars resulted and Ferdinand Porsche also designed several models for the company, which merged in 1935 with Daimler and Puch to form Steyr-Daimler-Puch. This company still exists and now builds the Chrysler Voyager and Mercedes G320

Steyr has also worked successfully with Fiat and a number of Fiat models have been built under licence. Finally the company developed a model of its own, the Steyr-Puch 500, yet this too was a Fiat 500 with a different engine block. This was the secret though of the car's success for the air-cooled twin-cylinder had become a boxer engine of 493 cc and power of 16 bhp at 4,600 rpm. The

A quick demount for the engine before a race at Zandvoort.

The Final Steyr-Puch had a 600 cc engine for output of 30 bhp at 5,500 rpm.

This race-prepared Steyr-Puch is almost too small for the race numbers at the Nürburgring.

Fiat 500 also had a 28 IBMS-Weber carburettor which appears to have been ideal for race tuning the car. There were also more powerful version with 643 and 660 cc engines that had an output of 40 bhp. The excellent roadholding of the Fiat 500 made it convincingly successful and races are still being won by a Steyr-Puch.

Steyr-Puch cars

COUNTRY OF ORIGIN: Austria

Puch 500

MODEL YEAR: 1956-1969

NUMBER MADE: 54,300

SPECIAL REMARKS: The engine had an oversquare bore diameter to stroke of 70x64 mm. This car was also available in an estate version.

Studebaker

Studebaker expired after a long illness as a result of a whole series of bad mistakes in December 1963, with the closure of its South Bend factory. There had been a final unsuccessful effort to save the company by moving to Canada. The loss of the Studebaker marque was greatly missed, with the passing of the oldest maker of means of transport in the world. Brothers Henry and Clem Studebaker built their first wagons and carriages in 1852. By 1875 the company already had a turnover of $1,000,000. The first car was built in 1902 which they sold through a wide dealer network of 5,000 outlets across America. No more coaches were built from 1920 onwards when Studebaker concentrated on building cars, resulting in a turnover in 1922 of $100,000,000.

Studebaker made a great deal of money during World War II. They produced 260,000 trucks, 64,000 aircraft engines, and 15,000 Weasels (an amphibious troop carrier). Ford

Studebakers re-emerged from a face-lift in 1950 with the "bullet nose" that some called a "jet aircraft".

was able to restart supplying cars on 3 July 1945 but because Studebaker were required to continue making Weasels for the war against Japan, its customers had to wait. There were 651 cars for the 1946 model year made in 1945. These Skyway Champions had both two-door and four-door bodies and the same 2,785 cc six-cylinder side-valve engine fitted in the military Weasels.

Although Studebaker could have sold its old models for a few years, they introduced an entirely new model in April 1946, designed by Raymond Loewy, famous for his design of the Coca-Cola bottle. In reality, the drawings had been produced by Virgil Exner. It was a striking car, sold as Champion, Commander, or Land Cruiser. All these cars had six-cylinder engines. In the Champion it was a 2.8-litre unit of 80 bhp while the other two shared 3.7-litre motors of 94 bhp. The Champion was the smallest of the three with a wheelbase of 112 in (2,840 mm), the Commander's wheelbase was 119 in (3,020 mm) and the Land Cruiser length between axle centres was 4 in (100 mm) longer.

Studebaker launched a new car in 1953 that really was designed by Raymond Loewy, also known as Champion or Commander. These were superb cars with a height of 56 in (1,420 mm) that was unusually low for its time.

The sports versions were the Starlight and Starliner hardtop coupés. Studebaker also re-introduced the pre-war name of President in 1955 for a luxury version of the Champion and Commander. There was

a special version known as the President Speedster finished in a three-colour paint job and with all the gimmicks the factory could think of. This car led to the Golden Hawk in 1956 and GT Hawk in 1962. These were the final Studebakers.

When Compacts became in vogue with Detroit, Studebaker brought out the Lark with a choice of six-cylinder or V-8 engine. Studebaker and Packard entered into a co-operation arrangement in 1954 in an effort to compete with the big three makers of Detroit but unfortunately this prove ultimately impossible. This is in spite of the fact that Loewy designed the Avanti in record time in 1962. The Avanti had an eye-catching polyester body and was available with a selection of V-8 engines. There was even a version with twin Paxton turbochargers that produced more than 330 bhp.

It seemed that Studebaker's days had gone. In spite of the new Avanti, sales figures continued to slump. Packard had succumbed in 1958 and in a final attempt to save Studebaker from financial ruin, the works was moved to Hamilton in Canada where all the 1964 model year cars were built. But there were too few of them. Only 29,969 cars were sold in 1964.

Studebaker's reaction was to scrap the big GT Hawks from its range but the sales continued downwards with then only 17,000 cars being sold. The stocks of big engines had been used up and because no big engines could be turned out in Canada, the necessary motors were purchased from General Motors. These 3,186 cc six-cylinder units from the Chevrolet Chevy II and 4,637 cc V-8 now found their way to the Studebaker Larks, which were renamed Challenger, Commander, Dayton, and Cruiser in 1964. The out-

The Daytona was a slightly more expensive version of the compact.

look was even more bleak in 1966 so finally the decision was taken on 17 March to quit. The final car to leave the South Bend works on that day is housed in the Studebaker Historical Collection.

Studebaker cars

COUNTRY OF ORIGIN: USA

Studebaker Champion (1946 pre-war version)

MODEL YEAR: 1946

NUMBER MADE: 19,275

SPECIAL REMARKS: The immediate post-war Champion was the 1942 model yet it was a modern car still with independent front suspension and a 2,786 cc six-cylinder engine of 78 bhp.

Studebaker Champion (1946 new post-war version)

MODEL YEAR: 1946-1949

NUMBER MADE: 291,364

SPECIAL REMARKS: This Studebaker Champion was the first truly new post-war car.

A 1947 Champion. Despite only 2 doors there was room for 6 people.

Studebaker Commander

MODEL YEAR: 1950-1951

NUMBER MADE: 158,834

SPECIAL REMARKS: The "bullet nose" was intended to make the Studebaker look like an aircraft. The Commander had a choice of two six-cylinder engines: 2,786 or 4,024 cc, or a 3,811 V-8 unit.

Studebaker Champion (1953)

MODEL YEAR: 1953-1954

NUMBER MADE: 145,069

Raymond Loewy excelled himself with the design of this 1953-1954 model.

SPECIAL REMARKS: There was little mechanical change in these cars but the body was entirely new and very attractive.

Studebaker President Speedster

MODEL YEAR: 1955

NUMBER MADE: 2,215

SPECIAL REMARKS: The Speedster had the new Pacemaster V-8 engine of 4,249 cc capacity and power output of 188 bhp.

Studebaker Golden Hawk

MODEL YEAR: 1956-1958

NUMBER MADE: 9,305

SPECIAL REMARKS: For those in a hurry there was also a Golden Hawk with V-8 engine equipped with Paxton compressors that produced 275 bhp (SAE).

Studebaker built the President Speedster in 1955. The car is recognised by the fog lights in the front bumper and three-colour paintwork.

The successor to the President Speedster was the Hawk. It had a new grille and fashionable tail fins.

Brook Stevens took the Golden Hawk and created the GT Hawk.

The imposing instrument panel of the GT Hawk. Studebaker kept harking back to aircraft.

Studebaker GT Hawk

MODEL YEAR: 1962-1964

NUMBER MADE: 15,517

SPECIAL REMARKS: The Gran Turismo had a top speed of 87 mph (140 kph), with its 2,779 cc six-cylinder engine but with the 4.7-litre V-8 speeds of more than 106 mph (170 kph) could be achieved or 125 mph (200 kph) with turbocharger.

The Studebaker Lark, like this six-cylinder engined model, was the competitor for the Ford Falcon, Chevrolet Corvair, and Plymouth Valiant.

Studebaker Lark

MODEL YEAR: 1959-1964

NUMBER MADE: 534,102

SPECIAL REMARKS: Unlike its competitors, the Lark was available from its launch with a choice of various engines. The smallest was a 2.8-litre six-cylinder unit and the biggest was a 4.2-litre V-8.

Studebaker Avanti

MODEL YEAR: 1963-1964

NUMBER MADE: 4,643

SPECIAL REMARKS: The Avanti customer could choose from a broad range of engines. There were several V-8 units, with and without turbochargers and with single or quadruple carburettors. The top speed was given in publicity material as 156 mph (250 kph).

The Avanti was supposed to have prevented Studebaker's demise but the plan failed. Avantis have continued to be built, but not as a Studebaker.

Stutz

Although the Stutz Motor Company has not made cars since 1935, they are still regarded as some of the finest cars ever made in the USA. Harry C. Stutz built his first racing car in 1913 but made his name for his sports cars. To own a Bearcat Speedster of 1914 is still the dream of many collectors and car museums. Stutz cars were extremely expensive and could only be bought by a small group of enthusiasts. When this group lost its money during the Great Depression it also spelled the end for the Stutz Motor Company.

A cunning businessman purchased the rights to the Stutz name in 1970 and brought out a range of cars bearing the name. These had nothing to do with the original Stutz cars of course and were no longer made in Indianapolis but by Padana near Modena in Italy. The cars are based on a slightly adapted Pontiac floor pan with tuned Pontiac V-8 power units. The body was designed by Virgil Exner and hand made by Padana. When completed, the cars are shipped to Stutz in New York where they are sold as Bearcat, Victoria, or Blackhawk. These models are all two-door coupés. There is also a Stutz IV Porte four-door sedan, on a Cadillac chassis.

In spite of the nostalgic styling, the new Stutz cars were not replicas such as the Excalibur but were in any even striking. The first car was purchased by Elvis Presley and Muhammad Ali the boxer also had one. The company has change owners at regular intervals but is still in business.

Stutz sports cars

COUNTRY OF ORIGIN: USA

Stutz Blackhawk

MODEL YEAR: 1970-present day

NUMBER MADE: Unknown

The Stutz Blackhawk, like this 1971 example, was a neo-classic without copying a former model. It was certainly striking.

SPECIAL REMARKS: The Blackhawk has the floor-pan and running gear of the Pontiac Grand Prix with a 6,558 cc V-8 engine of 425 bhp output. The wheelbase is 118 in (3,000 mm) and 207 in (5,260 mm) overall length.

Subaru

Subaru has become famous for its four-wheel drive cars. The company forms part of the enormous Fuji Heavy Industries Ltd concern but builds mainly more compact cars. Subaru started its car experience with small cars. The

The 2,990 mm (117 in) Subaru fits any parking place.

Subaru 360 was the first car to leave the factory in 1958. It was the size of a Fiat 500 but four-wheel drive had not been dreamed of by Subaru's engineers so the engine was rear-mounted and drove the back wheels. The car was successful and 5,111 were sold in 1959. In 1961, 22,319 of them were produced. With Subaru as with everyone else, cars grew in size. In 1966, Subaru cars changed to front-wheel drive and to four-wheel drive in 1974. Since then the company has remained loyal to four-wheel drive.

Subaru cars

COUNTRY OF ORIGIN: Japan

Subaru 360

MODEL YEAR: 1958-unknown

NUMBER MADE: Unknown

SPECIAL REMARKS: In contrast with modern Subaru cars, the 360's engine was mounted in the back. It was a 356 cc twin-cylinder two-stroke unit with output of 16 bhp.

243

The Subaru 360 had a monocoque body and all-round independent suspension.

troduced first in 1971, followed by a saloon in February 1972. The 1,361 cc four-cylinder boxer engine drove the front wheels with output of 80 bhp (SAE) at 6,400 rpm.

Sunbeam

John Marston started a cycle works in Wolverhampton in 1887 and business flourished. Since Marston wished to move with the times he built his first car in 1899. Local people in Wolverhampton trusted the firm, which from 1905 on became the Sunbeam Motor Car Company Ltd. Production climbed but then dropped back. Sunbeam amalgamated with Talbot and Darracq in

Subaru Leone

MODEL YEAR: 1972-unknown

NUMBER MADE: Unknown

SPECIAL REMARKS: The Leone coupé was in-

The Subaru Leone was sold in Europe. This 1975 model was 4,000 mm (157 in) long, weighed 750 kg (1,650 lb), and had a top speed of 100 mph (160 kph).

1920 to form STD but this new company was in its turn taken over in 1935 by the Rootes Brothers. From then the cars were sold as Sunbeam-Talbot. Talbot cars were only produced in France after World War II but the Sunbeam-Talbot name was used for some time in the United Kingdom. The pre-war Sunbeam-Talbots reappeared in 1945 as the Ten and Two Litre. Both cars had four-cylinder side-valve power units of 1,184 and 1,944 cc. When these engines got new cylinder heads with overhead valves in 1948, the cars became the Sunbeam-Talbot 80 and 90. These cars had new bodies designed by Ted White. There were hydraulic brakes but both front and rear axles were rigid. The Eighty was taken off the market in the autumn of 1950 and replaced by a Ninety with independent suspension and a more powerful engine. The same chassis was also used for the Sunbeam Alpine sports convertible in 1953. Drivers such as Stirling Moss had many rally successes with this car, including the Rallye des Alpes, from which the new car gained its name. The Sunbeam Alpine was consistently improved and remained a serious competi-

A 1946 Sunbeam Alpine in the Alps from which it got its name.

The Mk III was the final version of the Sunbeam-Talbot Ninety. It could be recognised by the three nacelles in the bonnet.

tor for sports cars such as the MGA and Triumph TR until the late 1960s. There was also a small-scale production of a sporting 2+2 coupé built in Italy by Touring of Milan from Sunbeam parts, known as the Sunbeam Venezia. A subsequent sporting saloon was the Sunbeam Rapier, based on the Hillman Minx, for which the American designer Raymond Loewy designed the body. The Rapier got steadily more powerful engines. It started with a 1,395 cc four-cylinder unit and capacity grew via 1,494 and 1,592 cc to 1,725 cc. The most powerful engine was used in the final version of the Rapier. This roomy five-seater coupé was introduced at the London motor show in October 1967.

When Rootes were enjoying success with the Hillman Imp and Singer Chamois, the Sunbeam customer was offered the Sunbeam Chamois and Sunbeam Imp. The Sunbeam Imp was the sporting model. Both cars had 875 cc four-cylinder engines that had outputs of 42 in the Chamois and 55 in the Imp. There was also a coupé version of the Hillman Californian that was known as the

The Sunbeam Imp Sports had the same engine as the Stiletto but was 90 lb (41 kg) heavier at 1,652 lb (751 kg).

Sunbeam Stiletto. The 55 bhp engine was to be found in the rear of this 2+2.

When Chrysler took over the Rootes Group, all the sports cars disappeared. Instead there were cars such as the Sunbeam 1250 which shared body and mechanicals with the Hillman Avenger. There were still Sunbeam cars produced until 1974, such as the Imp, 1300, Alpine, and Rapier. Then the marque disappeared but there was no real sadness at the demise for the real Sunbeams had long since ceased to be made.

Sunbeam cars

COUNTRY OF ORIGIN: United Kingdom

Sunbeam-Talbot Ten

MODEL YEAR: 1945-1948

NUMBER MADE: Unknown

SPECIAL REMARKS: The Ten had a four-cylinder side-valve engine that produced 40 bhp

at 4,400 rpm. The "sporty" open roadster could also go no faster than 69 mph (110 kph).

Sunbeam-Talbot Ninety

MODEL YEAR: 1950-1957

NUMBER MADE: 5,249

An open Ninety like this Mk II of 1954 won the Rallye des Alpes for Stirling Moss.

SPECIAL REMARKS: The 1950 Ninety was a modern car with independent front suspension and an overhead valve 2,267 cc engine that produced 70 bhp at 4,000 rpm.

All the doors opened the wrong way in 1948. This is the Sunbeam-Talbot Two Litre.

A 1956 Sunbeam Rapier hardtop coupé. There was also a convertible version.

A 1972 Sunbeam Rapier of the type introduced in 1967.

Sunbeam Rapier

MODEL YEAR: 1955-1967

NUMBER MADE: 68,809

SPECIAL REMARKS: The first Sunbeam Rapier was the first Sunbeam with a monocoque body, shared with the Hillman Minx. The car was powered by a 1,395 cc four-cylinder engine that produced 62 bhp.

Sunbeam Venezia

MODEL YEAR: 1964-1965

NUMBER MADE: 143

Touring of Milan built the Venezia on a tubular chassis, specially for the Italian market.

SPECIAL REMARKS: The Venezia differed from the Sunbeam Alpine in various ways. It was built on a tubular chassis and had a 1,592 cc engine that produced 94 bhp.

Sunbeam Chamois

MODEL YEAR: 1964-1966

NUMBER MADE: Unknown

The small Singer Chamois was available in several versions, such as this Stiletto with a motor that can be tuned to yield 51 bhp at 5,800 rpm.

SPECIAL REMARKS: The 875 cc engine of the small Sunbeam had an overhead camshaft. The block and cylinder head were aluminium and power output 42 bhp.

Sunbeam Hunter

MODEL YEAR: 1966-1976

NUMBER MADE: Unknown

SPECIAL REMARKS: The 1,725 cc engine had an aluminium cylinder head. Power output was 75 bhp, which was enough with the car weighing only 2,057 lb (935 kg) for a top speed of 90 mph (145 kph).

The Sunbeam Hunter was an export version of the Hillman Hunter. It was shown in 1966 at the Paris motor show. The car illustrated is a 1968 Mk II.

Talbot

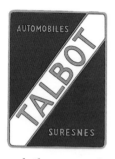

The Talbot name was well known by motorsport enthusiasts in the immediate pre- and post-war years. Clement-Talbot was a British firm, based in France that was founded in 1902. It was taken over by Darracq, also British owned in 1919 and the group bought Sunbeam in 1925. When Rootes purchased the group in 1935, Antonio Lago, a Venetian living in France, bought Darracq and the cars made by Lago were sold as Darracq in Britain and Talbot in France. The Darracq name disappeared after World War II and the cars were known as Talbot-Lago and also Lago-Talbot. When Lago took over Darracq, he got the firm to build racing and sports car because of his great love of motor sport. Although Talbots were feared opponents on the circuits of Europe, it was not possible to exist on sporting cars alone and so saloon cars were also made. These Talbots were able to compete with the cars made by Delahaye, Delage, and Hotchkiss. They shared the same high prices but also the same excellent quality.

All the makers of expensive cars experienced difficulties following World War II, with many having to close down or in danger of doing so.
The first Talbot models in 1946 were Talbot-Lagos, which closely resembled the 1939 cars. This was not such a disadvantage since the car was still technically very advanced for its time. They had independent front suspension and 4.5-litre six-cylinder engines with overhead valves operated by two camshafts mounted high on the engine but not overhead.
Lago was a great proponent of the Wilson pre-selector gearbox and used it in all his cars except the racing and sports cars.
Many Talbot-Lagos were sold as rolling chassis for specialist coachwork companies like

Figoni & Falaschi, Graber & Saoutchik to complete with a body. There were also works four-door saloons, coupés, and convertibles available. Lago motors derived their petrol from twin Zenith-Stromberg carburettors. When three of these were installed in 1947, power increased from 170 to 190 bhp. The company called this car a Talbot-Lago Grand Sport. The wheelbase of this car was reduced from 3,130 mm (123 in) to 2,650 mm (104 in) to make it more sporting.

When demand for expensive cars fell away even further, Lago tried a less expensive engine to form the Talbot-Lago Baby, powered by a four-cylinder engine. This four-door car also had a manual four-speed gearbox to lower the price further.

Meanwhile Lago had not ignored motorsport. On the contrary, although the company could ill afford it, Talbots competed successfully in Grand Prix races, winning the 1947 French Grand Prix, the 1949 Belgian

The Swiss car body builder Hermann Graber imported much of the Talbot output as rolling chassis into Switzerland where they were given mainly 2+2 bodies. This is a 1948 Lago Record.

Grand Prix, and 1950 Dutch Grand Prix at Zandvoort. Furthermore, Louis Risier won Le Mans in 1951. But things were getting worse with saloon cars. Only 453 cars were sold in 1950 and fewer than 80 were sold in 1951. Lago tried with new bodies and by reducing the prices but none of this had the desired result. Fortunately, the French government gave him an order for tank engines.

Talbot offered three models in 1953: the Lago Baby, Lago Record, and Lago Grand Sport. A year later the Baby was no more and the last Lago Record was made in 1955. That same year there was an entirely new Talbot Lago 2500 with a 2.5-litre four-cylinder engine and a manual four-speed gearbox. An attempt was made with a second new model, the Talbot-Lago America to save what might be saved. The fine-seeming twin camshaft engine that Talbot had developed for this car was a flop and hence the company had to change to the BMW 2.5-litre V-8 engine: there was still no interest in the car. Financial matters were so bad that the company had to be sold. Simca took over the shares in 1958.

The Talbot-Lago America was built once more with a tuned Simca V-8 side-valve engine but this remained a prototype. The Talbot marque was at an end. Talbots appeared after this, from Peugeot, in the 1970s, but they had nothing in common with the marque that was gone.

Talbot cars

COUNTRY OF ORIGIN: France

Talbot-Lago Record

MODEL YEAR: 1946-1956

NUMBER MADE: Approx. 750

SPECIAL REMARKS: The Lago Record was one of the best cars to come from the French car industry.
The most famous coachwork companies used the rolling chassis as the starting point for their creations.

Talbot could also make finished cars of course but these lacked the style of the specials. This is a 1948 works 4-door Lago Record saloon.

A 4-seater convertible Lago Record by the firm of Graber in Switzerland. Rear passengers must make do without a view to retain the attractive lines.

Talbot-Lago Baby

MODEL YEAR: 1948-1954

NUMBER MADE: Unknown

SPECIAL REMARKS: The Baby was initially powered by a 2,690 cc four-cylinder engine, producing 110 bhp. From 1951 it was also available with a 2,694 cc six-cylinder engine for the same 110 bhp but this engine was much smoother and quieter.

Talbot-Lago Grand Sport

MODEL YEAR: 1952-1955

NUMBER MADE: Unknown

SPECIAL REMARKS: This car's 4,482 cc six-cylinder engine produced output of 210 bhp

A 1953 Talbot-Lago Grand Sport 4-seater convertible.

at 4,500 rpm with its triple carburettors. It was Talbot's most powerful engine which was also used for motor-sport.

Talbot-Lago 2500 Sport

MODEL YEAR: 1955-1956

NUMBER MADE: 54

SPECIAL REMARKS: The 2500 Sport was the last true Talbot with a factory-developed engine. Unfortunately the four-cylinder engine was unreliable and had to be replaced by a BMW V-8.

Talbot-Lago America

MODEL YEAR: 1957-1958

NUMBER MADE: 12

One of the final "true" Talbots to come from the works: a 2500 Lago Sport with 4-cylinder Talbot engine. he car was sold as Lago America with a BMW V-8 engine.

SPECIAL REMARKS: This car was powered by a BMW V-8 engine that had its cylinder capacity reduced from 2,580 to 2,476 cc for fiscal reasons. The power of this overhead valve power unit was 90 bhp.

Tatra

The first cars were built by the Nessel-dorfer Wagenbau-fabrik in 1897. The model was known as President and had a twin-cylinder 5 hp Benz engine. The succeeding cars were quite modern for 1906, with four-cylinder engines and overhead camshafts designed by Hans Ledwinka. When the borders were redrawn following the Armistice after World War I, Nesseldor-fer was no longer a part of Austria but now formed part of Czechoslovakia and was renamed Koprivnice. The name of the cars too was changed in 1923 from Nesseldorfer to Tatra. Once again Ledwinka designed cars that made automotive history. Cars were constructed on a tubular steel chassis and fit-ted with an air-cooled boxer engine to create cars such as the superb streamlined Type 77 of 1934, with its rear-mounted V-8 air-cooled motor. These cars formed the basis for the larger post-war Tatra cars.

The Tatra factory became state controlled in 1945 and production of private cars started again. The Tatra 57B of 1939 was put back on the market with a 1,256 cc four-cylinder, air-cooled boxer engine that output 25 bhp. In addition to this small -two-door car, there was also a successor for the larger Type 77, now called Type 87. As before the war, this car was powered by an air-cooled V-8 engine.

Interesting features of this rear-mounted 3-litre unit were the air-cooling and twin over-head camshafts. The car was also available with a 1,749 cc four-cylinder engine and the Type 97 Tatra was also fitted with a similar engine. The Type 87 was succeeded in 1947 by the Tatraplan 600. This model was chiefly intended for export. The four-cylinder engine was now more run-of-the-mill, without an overhead camshaft, and produced barely 52 bhp from a capacity of 1,950 cc.

A Tatra 603 (left) with a Tatraplan with simple windscreen and only two headlights.

Then in 1956, the Tatra 603 was introduced for the party bosses of the USSR and surrounding Russian satellite countries. The body was similar to its predecessors and there was an air-cooled V-8 engine once more at the back. The camshaft was in the cylinder block but twin carburettors helped increase power to 100 bhp from the 2,545 motor.

All the post-war Tatra cars had all-round independent suspension in common with all cars designed by Ledwinka. The 603 was the first with a monocoque body. There were three headlights mounted behind a piece of translucent flexible plastic. This model was built for twenty years, though it was of course restyled from time to time.
During this time the three headlights became four (in 1961) and power output was increased to 105 bhp after the compression ratio was increased from 6.5:1 to 8.2:1 in 1962. The 603 was not replaced until 1971, by the 613, with a modern body designed by Vignale in Italy. It was several years though before there were any supplies of this new car, so the 603 remained in production until 1975.

Tatra cars

COUNTRY OF ORIGIN: Former Czechoslovakia/
Czech Republic

Tatra 57B

MODEL YEAR: 1938-1949

NUMBER MADE: 6,469

Remember that this 57B was designed in 1939. Its lines were still modern after World War II.

SPECIAL REMARKS: This smaller medium-class car had an air-cooled four-cylinder boxer engine that provided power of 25 bhp to the rear wheels.

Tatra 87

MODEL YEAR: 1947-1950

NUMBER MADE: 3,023

The Tatra 87 was quite an eye-catcher. Note the panoramic windscreen and third headlight.

The louvres in the engine compartment cover gave some restricted rear visibility for the driver. This was the final model with the rear fin.

SPECIAL REMARKS: The Tatra 87 was a big car at 4,740 mm (186 in). All but first gear were synchronised in the four-speed gearbox.

Tatra Tatraplan 600

MODEL YEAR: 1947-1952

NUMBER MADE: 6,342

SPECIAL REMARKS: This was the simplest version of the big Tatra. The 600 was powered

All manner of advertising was created for the Tatraplan. There were post cards such as this in which the distinctive shape was associated with happy, elegant people, to suggest carefree motoring in a car that combined power, speed, and elegance.

by a 1,950 cc four-cylinder boxer engine with output of 52 bhp at 4,000 rpm.

Tatra 603

MODEL YEAR: 1955-1975

NUMBER MADE: 20,422

The 603 was a popular taxi in Czechoslovakia because it had room for six.

The final version of the 603 had four headlights.

The 2-603 had a top speed of 100 mph (160 kph).

SPECIAL REMARKS: The 603 was sold with one of two V-8 engines: 2,472 cc/95 bhp or 2,545 cc/105 bhp.

Tatra 613

MODEL YEAR: 1975-present day

NUMBER MADE: Unknown

Vignale designed the Tatra 613 in 1973 but it was two years before the first of these cars could be delivered.

SPECIAL REMARKS: This was Eastern European luxury: a 3,495 cc V-8 with four overhead camshafts that output power of 165 bhp at 5,200 rpm for a top speed of approximately 119 mph (190 kph).

Thunderbird

One of the reason why the Chevrolet Corvette sold poorly at first was the Ford Thunderbird. Ford introduced the Thunderbird at the Detroit motor show of 10 February 1954. At this time it was still a wooden model, compared with Corvettes that were ready-to-run on the Chevrolet stand, yet it still spoiled things for Chevrolet. Ford handed out thousands of brochures for people to study at home, which put many off buying a Corvette. The first T-bird rolled of the line on September 9, 1954. This 1955 model had much to offer. The two-seater had a 4,785 cc Mercury V-8 engine with manual gearbox but there was also an amazing list of optional extras. Buyers could choose an automatic gearbox, power-assisted brakes, power steering, electrically-operated windows, and plastic hardtop. The V-8 engine had quadruple carburettors and produced 193 bhp to enable a top speed of 115 mph (185 kph). The T-bird's body was of steel, which was another plus point, since there were few body shops in those days able to repair polyester body shells after an accident. The cars also sold well in Europe.

The Thunderbird did have one big problem, in common with the Corvette: it was a true

Only 1,882 Sports Roadsters were sold thanks to its high price. The cars cost $5,439, which was $651 more than the price of a standard convertible.

An interesting variant was the Sports Roadster of 1962 and 1963, said to be a creation of Lee Iacocca.

It was only sold for two years and was in reality just a four-seater convertible with a plastic cover for the rear seat. The car had chrome spoked wheels. In contrast to this "two-seater", Ford produced the Four Door Landau in 1967.

This 212½ in (5,400 mm) long car managed a top speed in excess of 125 mph (200 kph) thanks to its 7,536 cc V-8 engine.

two-seater with no space for a small child or third passenger. Ford quickly acknowledged this problem and although the two-seater sold well, they planned a larger model. The 1956 and 1957 Thunderbirds were virtually identical to the launch model but the 1958 version, to the dismay of enthusiasts, retained nothing of the famous and much loved predecessors. The "Squarebird", as Americans quickly dubbed the new car, was a spacious four-seater with monocoque body.

The small two-seater was181½ in (4,610 mm) long but its big replacement was 205½ in (5,220 mm) between bumpers. Many owners of the previous T-bird part-exchanged their cars for a Corvette but Ford suffered little from this because of the thousands of new customers who had always wanted a T-bird but did not want to leave the family at home. If we compare the sales figures, we can see that Ford's managers, who thought in dollars, were ultimately right.

Two-seater T-birds:
1955   16,155
1956   15,631
1957   21,380

Four-seater Squarebirds
1958   37,892
1959   67,456
1960   92,843
1961   73,051

Thunderbird became a separate marque within Ford, like Mercury and Lincoln in 1959. The big birds get regular facelifts, appear in different versions, and are sold better in some years than others. For example, 92,465 were sold in a successful year such as 1964 but only 63,313 in the trough of 1963.

No more convertibles were made in 1967. This Landau was the most expensive Thunderbird but this 4-door car had little in common with its forerunners.

The 1973 T-bird weighed 4,300 lb (2,150 kg). To get such mass to a top speed of 128 mph (205 kph) required a 7,033 cc V-8 producing 214 bhp.

Thunderbird cars

COUNTRY OF ORIGIN: USA

Thunderbird Two-Seater

MODEL YEAR: 1955-1957

NUMBER MADE: 53,166

A 1956 T-bird. The hardtop was an extra and could be with or without porthole.

SPECIAL REMARKS: Customers for the 1955 model had a choice of either one 3,654 cc V-6 or two V-8 engines of 4,457 or 4,785 cc (175 and 203 bhp). In 1956 and 1957 there was only a choice between a 4,785, or 5,112 cc V-8 engine of 209 and 269 bhp output.

Thunderbird Squarebird

MODEL YEAR: 1958-1960

The second generation of Thunderbirds were nothing like the two-seaters of 1955. This is a 1959 five-seater convertible.

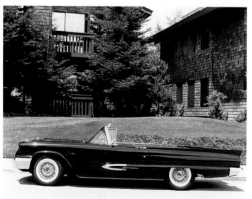

NUMBER MADE: 198,191

SPECIAL REMARKS: The new Squarebirds got new 5,436 or 5,766 cc engines of 233 or 304 bhp output. They had become luxury cars and were no longer sports cars. Most of them were sold with automatic transmission.

Toyota

Sakichi Toyoda (with a "D") was a well-known maker of textile machinery when he turned to making cars in 1933. His son Kiichiro was ordered to develop a car industry and he did this successfully. The first prototypes A-1 was completed in May 1935, looking obviously like the Chrysler Airflow and with a six-cylinder engine that might have come from Chevrolet in Detroit.

Before the war Toyota (now written with a "T" built only a few private cars. Between 1935-1944 just 1,913, since the government preferred to see army vehicles being made.
After the war, Toyota started up again slowly. General MacArthur banned the Japanese from making private cars but the ban was softened in 1947 and Japan was allowed to build 300 cars. Of these, 110 originated from the Toyota works. These cars, designated type SA, looked somewhat like the VW Beetle and they remained in production until

The Toyota SD of 1949 was developed as a taxi. It had 5 doors and space for 5 adults.

1952. Since public transport was more important than private cars, Toyota introduced the SD in 1949, specially developed as a taxi. This was the first four-door Toyota. The engine was identical to the one in the SA.

Toyota cars

COUNTRY OF ORIGIN: Japan

Toyota SA

MODEL YEAR: 1947-1952

NUMBER MADE: 215

SPECIAL REMARKS: The SA was powered by a

The Toyota SA looked somewhat like the VW Beetle. The car was sold in Japan as a Toyopet.

955 cc four-cylinder engine with output of 27 bhp. The length was 3,800 mm (149¹/₂ in) width 1,590 mm (62¹/₂ in) and wheelbase 2,400 mm (94¹/₂ in).

Toyota SD

MODEL YEAR: 1949-1951

NUMBER MADE: 176

SPECIAL REMARKS: The SD was a big car in Japanese terms with its length of 4,230 mm (166¹/₂ in). It was not fast though with a top speed of about 47 mph (75 kph).

This 1959 Crown is an export model with left-hand steering. Its mass of chrome is to impress the US market.

Toyota Crown

MODEL YEAR: 1955-unknown

NUMBER MADE: Unknown

SPECIAL REMARKS: The Crown was the most expensive car Toyota had ever made at the time. It had a monocoque body with space for six persons and a 1,453 cc four-cylinder engine of 55 bhp output.

Trabant

When the former DKW designed IFA F8 became too old for even the East Germans, a new model appeared in 1950 known as the Trabant P50. The car had a modern body with wings incorporated and, as a first for Germany, it was constructed in glass-reinforced polyester. Little thought appears to have been given to mechanical matters.

There was still a twin-cylinder two-stroke engine under the bonnet with a capacity of 500 cc and output of 18 bhp. A larger version of the P60 appeared in 1960 with a engine that output 20 bhp. The first renewal was in 1961 when the Trabant 601 was introduced. Some 2,500,000 of this model were to be built by 1990.

When Volkswagen took over the Zwickau factory some Trabants (or Trabis as the German's call them) were fitted with VW Polo engines.

Trabant cars

COUNTRY OF ORIGIN: Former German Democratic Republic (East Germany).

Trabant P50

MODEL YEAR: 1958-1962

NUMBER MADE: Unknown

SPECIAL REMARKS: The twin-cylinder two-stroke engine had proved itself for years in the IFA, East Germany's successor to the DKW. The capacity was 500 cc and power output was 18 but later 20 bhp.

A dream once for every East German, to own a Trabant 601. It needed patience with a waiting time of some years.

The 601 Universal estate version of the Trabant was available from 1965.

Trabant P601

MODEL YEAR: 1961-1990

NUMBER MADE: Approx. 2,500,000

SPECIAL REMARKS: The 594 cc twin of the Trabant 601 was boosted to 26 bhp output. The 1,043 cc Volkswagen engine gave 40 bhp and took the car to a dangerous top speed of 78 mph (125 kph).

Triumph

If Triumph had still be in existence in 1993 the company could have celebrated a number of anniversaries. It would have been the seventieth year since Triumph was founded and precisely forty-five years since the famous TR series was first introduced. It would also have been the ninetieth anniversary of the Standard Motor Company, which owned Triumph at that time. Instead, the famous marque was abandoned on 9 June 1984. In the final years, only the Triumph Acclaim was built, which was in reality a Honda Ballade with a different emblem on the front.

In 1883, Siegfried Bettmann, left Nuremberg in Germany where he was born to seek his fortune in England. He found a job with another former German, Mauritz Johann Schulte, with whom he later established a cycle works in Coventry. The company was later to become world famous for motorcycles. Until the Japanese brought their motorcycles to the market, Triumph was the biggest volume producer of motorcycles in the entire world.

Bettmann introduced his own car in 1923 but was less successful with it than with cycles and motorcycles. The car factory changed ownership several times and then in November 1944 it was taken over by Sir John Black who also owned the Standard Motor Company. The Triumph Company introduced two new cars in 1946, the Roadster, which was a 2+2 with which the rear seat passengers sat in the boot, and a saloon with a 1,776 cc four-cylinder engine. This spacious five-seater's body was designed by Walter Belgrove and Frank Callaby. This had sharp angular edges in its design that some

called "razor edge" or "knife edge". This model remained in production for nine years, first as the TD series with an 1,800 cc engine and later with 2-litre engine as the TDA.

These first post-war Triumph saloon cars had much in common mechanically with sports cars. They had the same tubular chassis and had bodies partially built in aluminium. The cars were sold under the Renown name in 1949 but now had the same chassis and engine as the Standard Vanguard.

A smaller version of the Renown also appeared in 1949, known as Triumph Mayflower. This was the first British car with monocoque body. Beneath its angular bonnet was the same engine that powered the 1939 Standard Ten. The three-speed gearbox was also not new. Virtually all Triumph cars were half sports cars and the Mayflower was no exception. A European motoring review of the time called the car "an American soap-box" and said it was dangerous to exceed 40 mph (65 kph) in the car because its centre of gravity was too high. Production of the

Mayflower ceased in 1953 and Triumph continued only with the larger Renown and smaller TR sports cars. The other saloon also disappeared in 1959 so that Triumph dealers only had sports cars to offer until 1959. It was in that year that the Herald appeared as a small car to replace the Standard Ten. The body was designed by Giovanni Michelotti.

Sharp angles from every viewpoint: a 1951 Triumph Renown.

Triumph cars

COUNTRY OF ORIGIN: United Kingdom

Triumph 1800

MODEL YEAR: 1946-1954

NUMBER MADE: 6,691

The Triumph Mayflower (this is a 1950 example) was the first British car with monocoque body.

The Herald was available as a saloon or 2+2 coupé, and as a convertible. The 948 cc overhead valve engine was from the Standard Ten and it produced 38 bhp in the saloon but 48 bhp in the coupé. It was surprising that these cars were not monocoque but had a real chassis as previously. The four wheels had independent suspension and the car had a turning circle of less than 24 ft (8 m), which is smaller than that of a London taxi.

A Herald look-alike with a six-cylinder engine appeared in 1962, called the Vitesse. The engine was now 1,596 cc, a smaller version of the Vanguard motor.

The chassis of the Standard Vanguard formed the basis of the Triumph 2000 which had to compete with the successful Rover 2000. The car remained in production until 1975. The engine was later enlarged and fitted with fuel injection to power the Triumph 2.5 PI. The driver could count of power of 106 bhp and later 132 bhp from this 2,498 cc six-cylinder engine.

A smaller Triumph was also introduced using Herald parts, known as the 1300. This was also available with the Triumph Spitfire engine. This 1,493 cc four-cylinder engine produced 76 bhp for the rear wheels. A striking car was the Dolomite Sprint. This was a four-door saloon that won both rallies and races. This car was introduced in 1973 with an engine fitted with an overhead camshaft and four valves per cylinder. This is commonplace today but exceptional at the time.

SPECIAL REMARKS: This model had independent front suspension and a modern overhead valve engine. The four-speed gearbox was operated by a column-change gear-lever.

Triumph Mayflower

MODEL YEAR: 1949-1953

NUMBER MADE: Approx. 35,000

SPECIAL REMARKS: The Mayflower was a

The front end and doors of the Herald convertible were identical to the saloon.

small car with an overall length of 154³/₄ in (3,930 mm) making it 10¹/₂ in (270 mm) shorter than the VW Beetle.

Triumph Herald

MODEL YEAR: 1959-1971

NUMBER MADE: 525,767

SPECIAL REMARKS: The Herald did not have a monocoque body. Michelotti designed it so that the seven body panels bolted together instead of being welded. This is an advantage for body repairs.

Triumph Vitesse

MODEL YEAR: 1962-1971

The Triumph Vitesse was available as saloon and convertible. It looked much like the Herald but had a six-cylinder engine and twin headlights.

NUMBER MADE: 51,182

SPECIAL REMARKS: Until 1966 the Vitesse had a 1,596 cc six-cylinder engine then received a 1,998 cc motor which increased power from output from 70 to 90 bhp.

Triumph 2000

MODEL YEAR: 1963-1975

NUMBER MADE: 219,816

SPECIAL REMARKS: The six-cylinder engine had capacity of 1,998 cc and produced 91 bhp. The car had a four-speed fully-synchronised manual gearbox which could incorporate an electric overdrive as an optional extra. The Triumph 2000 had disc brakes on the front wheels.

The Triumph 2500 PI like this 1972 Mk II, was a spacious and luxurious 5-seater.

Triumph 2.5 PI Mk II

MODEL YEAR: 1968-1969

NUMBER MADE: Unknown

SPECIAL REMARKS: The Triumph 2.5 PI Mk II was a Triumph 2000 with the petrol injection engine from the TR-5 sports car. The 2,498 cc engine produced power of 106 bhp at 4,700 rpm.

Triumph Dolomite

MODEL YEAR: 1973-1980

NUMBER MADE: 22,941

SPECIAL REMARKS: The Dolomite was supplied with four different four-cylinder engines of 1,296, 1,493, 1,854, and 1,998 cc with power outputs ranging from 59-129 bhp. The top speeds ranged from 85-117 mph (137-187 kph).

The Dolomite Sprint was a wolf in sheep's clothing. It had the body of the Triumph 1300 but a highly-developed engine with 4 valves per cylinder and 129 bhp power.

Tucker

Among the interesting post-war cars to emerge in America must surely be the Torpedo of Preston Tucker. Tucker was mainly involved in developing motor-sport cars before World War II but he introduced his Torpedo in 1945. It was a dream of a car with aerodynamic body, designed by Elex Tremulis, who had been senior engineer at Duesenberg.

The prototype had a gigantic 9.6-litre aluminium boxer engine with six-cylinders. This was mounted at a slant in the rear of the car and the steering wheel was in front of the centre of three seats.

The production model was slightly less futuristic, although the engine was still in the back, but was now a six-cylinder water-cooled boxer motor used for helicopters. Although this engine was more reliable than the one used in the prototype, it had so many teething problems that they were almost impossible to fix.

Tucker borrowed money wherever he could get it and ran into big financial difficulties. He had to close his factory on 9 July 1948. His 2,000 employees had only made 51 cars. The 1,872 Tucker dealers who had paid deposits for the cars on order, according to contract, lost their money, as did the 50,000 shareholders who had collectively invested $25,000,000.

Tucker cars

COUNTRY OF ORIGIN: USA

The Tucker was in 1947 very modern in both appearance and concept.

The Tucker Torpedo dashboard: note the small column-change gear-lever to the right of the steering-wheel.

Tucker Torpedo

MODEL YEAR: 1947-1948

NUMBER MADE: 51

SPECIAL REMARKS: The Tucker was a big car. It had a 128 in (3,250 mm) wheelbase and was 219 in (5,570 mm) long. All four wheels had independent suspension.

Vanden Plas

The coachwork company of Guillaume Vanden Plas and his three sons established an extraordinarily good name. At the beginning of the twentieth century they built special bodies in Brussels, and not just on Belgian chassis. There were 850 personnel in 1913 who built more than 750 bodies that year. These bodies were predominantly much appreciated in Britain. The British importer Captain Teho Masui decided to change the name of his firm in 1913 to Vanden Plas (England) Ltd. The firm produced Belgian bodies under licence, specialising in coachwork for the more expensive makes. They became a main supplier for Bentley and others. During the war the factory turned out wooden Mosquito fighter-bombers.
Austin sought a new coachbuilder in 1946 who would work exclusively for them and Vanden Plas agreed to the proposal and became a part of the Austin company. One of the first fruits of this co-operation was the Austin A-135 Princess which was shown at Geneva in 1947. In 1958, Vanden Plas

became a marque in its own right. It built expensive cars such as the 4-litre R which had a Rolls-Royce engine and also special editions of cheaper Austins, such as the Vanden Plas 1500. This was a luxury version of the Austin Allegro. In 1968 the British Motor Corporation was formed and there was no room for the big Vanden Plas models. These were seen as harmful competition for the prestigious Jaguars and Daimlers of the group. Hence not only the 4-Litre R disappeared but also the large Princess with its six- and eight-seater bodies. Vanden Plas from now on could only offer the most luxurious versions of the 1300 and 1500 in their class. The last of the models of this marque were made in 1980.

Vanden Plas Cars

COUNTRY OF ORIGIN: United Kingdom

Vanden Plas 3-Litre Princess

MODEL YEAR: 1959-1964

NUMBER MADE: 12,615

SPECIAL REMARKS: This model shared its body and mechanical parts with the Austin A-99 Westminster and Wolseley 6/99. It was finished to a much higher standard and incorporated many luxury touches.

Vanden Plas 4-Litre Princess

The 4-Litre Princess like this 1964 example offered as much luxury as a Rolls-Royce or Bentley but cost half as much.

The windscreen of the 4-Litre was still divided and flat in 1966.

MODEL YEAR: 1959-1968

NUMBER MADE: 2,100

SPECIAL REMARKS: This car was originally sold as the Austin A-135 Princess in 1952. It was available as a six- or eight-seater from Vanden Plas. The 3,993 cc six-cylinder engine produced output of 122 bhp.

Vanden Plas 4-Litre R

MODEL YEAR: 1964-1968

This superb 4-Litre R of 1965 had a top speed of 100 mph (160 kph), which was quite something for a car weighing more than 2 tons.

The inlet valves of the 3,909 cc Rolls-Royce engine were in the aluminium cylinder head and the exhaust valves in the cylinder block. Power output was of the order of 175 bhp at 4,800 rpm.

NUMBER MADE: 6,555

SPECIAL REMARKS: The body of the 4-Litre R was designed by Pininfarina. The engine came from Rolls-Royce and the automatic gearbox was by Borg-Warner from the USA.

Vanden Plas 1300 Princess

MODEL YEAR: 1967-1974

The Princess 1300 could not be compared to an Austin or Morris 1300. The Vanden Plas not only had a different grille but also an entirely different and far finer interior with ample walnut.

NUMBER MADE: 23,734

SPECIAL REMARKS: When Vanden Plas had made 16,007 of the Princess 1100 (1963-1968) it was followed by the 1300 with a 1,275 cc four-cylinder engine with output of 66 bhp at 5,750 rpm.

Vanden Plas 1500

MODEL YEAR: 1974-1980

NUMBER MADE: 11,842

SPECIAL REMARKS: Except for the grille, the 1500 was little different to the Austin Allegro except for the far more exceptional luxury of its interior trim with wood and leather.

Vauxhall

The Scottish engineer Alexander Wilson was building steam engines for ships back in 1857. His company was then known as Vauxhall Iron Works Ltd and was based in London. At the start of the twentieth century the company moved into producing motor cars and sold 43 cars in 1903. This number rose to 76 in 1904 and from then on continued to flourish. The business moved in 1905 to Walk near Luton where it is still based. Among the outstanding Vauxhall cars are the 30/98 sports cars of the 1920s which can be compared with today's Ferraris and Lamborghinis. The company became a part of General Motors in 1925 and ceased making fast sports cars and racing cars, which might gain valuable publicity but did not generate profits. Today Vauxhall build identical cars to the GM Opel range of Germany. These are mainly for the United Kingdom domestic market.

When World War II broke out there were 12,000 people working for Vauxhall in Luton. In the first year after the war instead of cars the factory produced five million Jerry cans, a quarter of a million Bedford trucks, almost six thousand Churchill tanks and most of the parts for post-war jet fighters. The first cars rolled off the line again in 1946. These now almost all had monocoque bodies. These were sold as Vauxhall Ten, Twelve, and Fourteen. The Ten and Twelve had 1,203 and 1,442 cc four-cylinder engines

(in that order) but the Fourteen had a 1,781 cc six-cylinder overhead valve engine. The first truly new models appeared in late 1948. These were the Wyvern and Velox. Both had the same monocoque bodies of their predecessors but were now powered by 1,442 cc four-cylinder and 2,275 cc six-cylinder engines. The more expensive Velox was externally recognised by the cream coloured wheels and overriders on the bumpers. These did not remain on sale long as they were replaced in August 1951 by entirely new bodies with the wings incorporated within the body in the style of the big American cars. The Cresta appeared in the 1955 model year as a luxurious version of the Velox, recognisable by a different grille and improved dashboard.

After investment of $100,000,000 in a new factory at Luton, new models appeared from the production line such as the Victor which had much in common with the German Opel Rekord. This had its press launch in February 1957, The Victor replaced the Wyvern and had an entirely new four-cylinder engine of 1,507 cc and power of 55 bhp at 4,200 rpm. The three-speed gearbox was now at last fully synchronised. The external appear-

1903 *1953*

Leaders

through

four

reigns

Vauxhall Motors Limited

VAUXHALL MOTORS LIMITED · LUTON · BEDFORDSHIRE

The Vauxhall Firenza "Droopsnout" is a popular sight on the racing circuit. Apart from its front end it otherwise looks precisely like an Opel Manta.

The final version of the Vauxhall Victor was this FE, like this 1975 example. It had a choice of 4 and 6-cylinder engines.

ance of the cars had regular face-lifts and the engines got steadily bigger and more powerful. Automatic transmission and four-speed manual gearboxes with electrical overdrive became commonplace. Gradually Vauxhall worked increasingly closer with Opel in Germany.

They are both part of the American General Motors concern. This co-operation led to the Vauxhall Viva in 1963 which was an exact copy of the Opel Kadett. Much was expected of this model and a new factory was built at Ellesmere Port near Liverpool. The high unemployment in the area meant it was easy to find workers. The Viva engine was 1,057 cc with output at first of 45 bhp and later of 54 bhp, which was slightly better than its German counterpart. The Viva's body was also ³/₄ in (20 mm) longer, 1¹/₂ in (40 mm) wider, and 1¹/₄ in (30 mm) lower than the Kadett. There was also a four-seater Viva GT with a four-cylinder engine with overhead camshaft and twin carburettors. The capacity of the unit was 1,975 cc and power output was 106 bhp at 5,500 rpm. This car was only available in a two-door version that had a top speed of 100 mph (160 kph).

When Opel introduced the Manta, Vauxhall followed with the Firenza. This had a slightly different front end and a real spoiler at the rear. This gave it the name of "Droopsnout". There was also an estate car on the same floor pan and running gear, the Magnum Sports Hatch. The Vauxhall Magnum Coupe filled the gap between the Victor and Viva but was in reality a Viva with a bigger engine. This was available with either a 1,759 or 2,279 cc four-cylinder engine. Both engines had an overhead camshaft and produced power of 78 or 111 bhp.

A further new Vauxhall appeared in 1975. The Chevette made its debut in March 1975 at the Geneva motor show. It was a three-door car with a 1.25-litre engine. Vauxhall's range in 1975 consisted of this Chevette, the Viva in various forms, the Magnum, the Firenza, the Victor, the VX 4/90, and the Ventora. The final two models were luxurious versions of the Victor. The Vauxhall Cavalier appeared in late 1975. This was identical to the Opel Ascona with the front end from the Manta and Vauxhall Viva engine. The car was built in Belgium for two years before production moved to Britain.

Vauxhall cars

COUNTRY OF ORIGIN: United Kingdom

Vauxhall Fourteen

MODEL YEAR: 1946-1948

NUMBER MADE: 30,511

SPECIAL REMARKS: The Fourteen was still typically pre-war with stand-up headlights on stalks. It did though have independent front suspension, an overhead valve engine, and monocoque body.

Vauxhall Wyvern

MODEL YEAR: 1948-1951

The Wyvern and Velox got new bodies in 1951 with doors
that opened the normal way. Note the sun visor which
was a popular accessory then.

NUMBER MADE: 55,409

SPECIAL REMARKS: The Wyvern was no fleet
of foot with its weight of 2,178 lb (990 kg)
and 1,442 cc/35 bhp motor. Its top speed
was in the region of 62 mph (100 kph).

Vauxhall Victor

MODEL YEAR: 1957-1975

After two years in production, the Victor got a face-lift in
1959 to create the Mk 2 shown. This car was assembled
at Biel in Switzerland.

The exterior of the Vauxhalls was regularly renewed.
This is a 1961 Victor with slightly different grille to
its predecessors.

NUMBER MADE: More than 1,000,000

SPECIAL REMARKS: The Victor was first powered by a 1,508 cc.55 bhp four-cylinder
engine. This grew to 1,599 cc and finally to a
six-cylinder 3,294 cc unit that developed 124
bhp.

Vauxhall Velox

MODEL YEAR: 1957-1960

NUMBER MADE: 81,841

SPECIAL REMARKS: The 1957 Velox was comparable with the Opel Kapitän. Its six-cylinder engine had a capacity of 2,262 cc and
produced power of 68 bhp for the rear
wheels.

Vauxhall Cresta

MODEL YEAR: 1964-1965

NUMBER MADE: Unknown

The Cresta was a more expensive version of the Velox.
From 1960, it had a 2,651 cc engine of 115 bhp, in
common with the Velox.

The 1964 Cresta had a 6-cylinder engine of either
2,651 or 3,299 cc. Because these engines produced 115
and 130 bhp the top speed was about 100 mph (160 kph).

SPECIAL REMARKS: The Cresta and Velox had front disc brakes. They were also available with overdrive as an optional extra. The three-speed gearbox was operated by a column-mounted gear-lever.

Vauxhall VX 4/90

MODEL YEAR: 1961-1964

NUMBER MADE: Unknown

The front occupants sat in bucket seats in the VX 4/90 (4 cylinders/90 bhp (SAE). This car had a floor-mounted gear-lever and disc brakes on the front wheels.

SPECIAL REMARKS: The VX 4/90 was the sporting version of the Victor. Twin Zenith carburettors and a higher compression ratio of 9.3 instead of 9:1 provided true brake horsepower of 75 bhp.

Vauxhall Firenza (Droopsnout)

MODEL YEAR: 1973-1975

NUMBER MADE: 204

SPECIAL REMARKS: The Droopsnout was the quick version of the Firenza and was developed for motor-sport with a 2,279 cc engine that produced 132 bhp.

Vauxhall Cavalier

MODEL YEAR: 1975-1981

NUMBER MADE: 238,980

SPECIAL REMARKS: The Cavalier had the four-cylinder Viva engine of 1,584 or 1,897 cc (70 or 90 bhp). The more powerful unit gave

The Cavalier has similarities with the Opel Manta and Ascona. It was a serious competitor for the Ford Cortina.

acceleration of 0-60 in 11 seconds (0-100 kph in 11.5 seconds).

Vespa

The Vespa name immediately conjures up thoughts of the world-famous scooters made by the Piaggio company. These "motorcycles" which can be ridden wearing one's Sunday suit were invented by Coradina D'Ascanio. Until this time Piaggio had only built bomber aircraft. At the Paris motor show in 1957 there were cars for the first time alongside the scooters. The public called them "autoscooters" but the factory in Pontedara, between Livorno and Florence called them "the smallest cars in the world". This Vespa 400 was built in Piaggio's French factory. The competition for midget cars was fierce though and it quickly became obvious that the car would not become as popular as the scooter. To look at, the Vespa looked

The roll-back roof was standard equipment. The first cars only had quarter lights in the doors.

Unlike the Fiat 500 that had space at least for a child on the back seat, the Vespa 400 was a pure two-seater.

something like the Fiat 500 Topolino which had ceased production in 1957. The Vespa was smaller though and only had room for two. The car weighed a mere 370 kg (814 lb) and had a top speed of 55 mph (88 kph) despite its tiny 13 bhp engine. It fuel consumption was rated at a constant 50 kph (39 mph) as 69 miles per gallon (1 litre per 23 kilometres). This dropped with the foot flat on the floor to 45 mpg (1 litre per 15 kilometres).
The Vespa 400 with its 393 cc engine was available in two versions: the deluxe model with two windscreen wipers instead of one, chrome-plated bumpers and nave plates, and better upholstery trim. Sliding windows in the doors were added in 1959 and a four-speed gearbox in 1960. The following year production ceased. The Vespa could not compete with cars offering much more but costing less.

The crankshaft operated the inlet valves in the Vespa engine.

Vespa cars

COUNTRY OF ORIGIN: Italy

Vespa 400

MODEL YEAR: 1957-1961

NUMBER MADE: Approx. 34,000

SPECIAL REMARKS: The twin-cylinder two-stroke engine had a capacity of 393 cc and it was rear-mounted in the car. It produced 13 bhp for the rear wheels.

Vignale

Various Italian car body companies have had a go at marketing their own car. This equally applies to companies such as Ghia, Zagato, and Vignale. Alfredo Vignale (1913-1969) had a car body works in the Italian village of Grugliasco, which is a stone's throw from Bertone's home town of Turin. Vignale built superb cars for Maserati, Ferrari, Lancia, and Fiat, often designed by his friend Giovanni Michelotti.

The Vignale Gamine though was all Alfredo Vignale's own work. It was built on the floor-pan of the Fiat 500 and had a 499 cc twin-cylinder engine. The two-seater car had something of the look of a Fiat 508 Balilla Coppa d'Oro from the 1930s. It was intended for the Italian market or at least for countries with a good climate. Vignale was killed in a car accident in November 1969 and the company was taken over by De Tomaso.

Vignale cars

COUNTRY OF ORIGIN: Italy

Vignale Gamine

MODEL YEAR: 1967-1970

The Vignale Gamine was a fine weather car without hood or side panels.

The "urchin's" dashboard was as simple as that of the Fiat 500. The rubber knob under the speedometer operates the windscreen washers.

NUMBER MADE: Unknown

SPECIAL REMARKS: The Gamine (or street urchin) was based on the Fiat Nuova 500 chassis. Its wheelbase was 1,840 mm (72$^{1}/_{2}$ in) with overall length 3,020 mm (118$^{3}/_{4}$ in).

Volkswagen

At the mention of the Volkswagen name, young people think of the Golf GTi, while older generations think of the VW Beetle. This latter is not surprising since they were made by the millions and are still made. The experts at Volkswagen in Wolfsburg have built other cars, some of which have brought the good name of the company into disrepute.

The first design for the Beetle was offered by Ferdinand Porsche to Adolf Hitler on 17 January 1934. Production of the "strength-through-joy people's car" (Kraft-durch-Freude Wagen) did not get started though until 1938. The factory was in the village of Fallersleben, now known as Wolfsburg. The Volkswagen name originated with Dr. Ferdinand Porsche who called his design a "people's car". The man in the street did not see the car though for the few that were built went to the party hierarchy and the factory was mainly busy producing all-terrain vehicles.

When British troops reached Fallersleben, Major Ivan Hirst renamed the factory "Motor

The VW Beetle continues to be much loved. Thousands often turn up at special Beetle club meets and events.

The millionth VW Beetle was delivered in 1955, the ten millionth in 1967, the fifteen millionth in 1972, and the twenty millionth in 1981!

Today the Beetle is made in Mexico. A larger engined version, the VW 1500 with rear-mounted air-cooled engine of 1,493 cc that produced 45 bhp joined the stable in 1961. This was followed in 1965 by the VW 1600 with a 1,584 cc engine of 54 bhp. Although these cars were still made in Europe until 1973, a different large VW was launched in 1968 under the name 411 and 412 for the estate version. The concept of a rear-mounted air-cooled boxer engine had not changed but this new model was bigger in every respect than its predecessors. These new cars were supplied with two different engines: a 1,679 cc and after 1973 with a 1,795 cc unit.

An unusual vehicle was the VW 181 built for the Germany army but also sold to the public. This was a terrain vehicle but with rear-wheel drive only. The body was not unlike that of the Kübelwagen of the war. The first examples had a 1,493 cc engine from the Beetle but after 1 August 1970, the 1,584 cc engine was also available.

The K70 of 1970 was originally designed by NSU but since Volkswagen took the company over before its launch, it appeared as a VW. In mechanical terms this car owed more to NSU than Volkswagen, for instance it had front-wheel drive and a water-cooled engine. Production of the K70 was moved to a specially-built new factory at Salzgitter, fifty kilometres south-west of Wolfsburg. Volkswagen had done better to save their money for only 200,000 of these cars were sold.

Works" and had his motor pool revived. He had cars built from the supplies of spares and 1,785 cars left the factory in 1945 that got named Volkswagen after the event. Production rose to 10,000 in 1946 and the first exports were shipped to The Netherlands in 1947.

The car was exhibited in 1948 at the Amsterdam motor show. These early Beetles had a 985 cc air-cooled four-cylinder engine that produced 20 bhp at 3,000 rpm. The Beetle was continuously improved, the heating system perfected, and fuel consumption slightly reduced. The VW 1303 of 1975 had a 1,285 cc engine with output of 44 bhp that could achieve 34 miles per gallon (8.8 litres per 100 km) if driven at a steady non too fast a speed on the motorway.

The Kharmann-Ghia was built between 1955-1974 on a Beetle chassis. It was designed by Ghia and built by Karmann. A total of 364,401 coupés and 80,899 convertibles were made.

Volkswagen cars

VW Beetle

*The first pre-war prototypes had no rear windows.
The first post-war cars had two small windows, like
spectacles.*

*The VW Cabriolet appeared in 1949 and was built by
Karmann in Osnabrück.*

Model year: 1946-present day

Number made: Unknown (in excess of
20,000,000,000)

Special remarks: The first Beetles were
rather primitive cars. The gearbox was not synchronised and the engine was noisy, used a lot
of petrol, an no great power source at 25 bhp.

*The British Colonel Radclyffe permitted Hebmüller to build a convertible which went into production in 1949.
Up to 1953, 696 of them were sold.*

The VW 1500 and 1600 were available as saloon, coupé, and estate car.

The 1500/1600 formed the basis for the Karmann-Ghia. Between 1961-1973, 42,505 coupés and 17 cabriolets were sold.

VW 1500/1600

MODEL YEAR: 1961-1973

NUMBER MADE: 2,584,904

SPECIAL REMARKS: The boxer engines in these cars was so flat it could be fitted under the boot space. The engines were 1.5 and 1.6 litre units.

VW 411/412

MODEL YEAR: 1968-1974

NUMBER MADE: 355,163

SPECIAL REMARKS: Until the 411, Volkswagen had not built a car with four doors. The cars built in 1972 had a 1,795 cc engine with output of 85 bhp.

VW K70

MODEL YEAR: 1970-1975

NUMBER MADE: 211,127

SPECIAL REMARKS: The K70 was a five-seater with a fine engine with overhead camshaft and twin Solex carburettors. The power output of the 1,605 cc engine in the K70 S was 90 instead of the standard 75 bhp.

VW 181

MODEL YEAR: 1969-1978

NUMBER MADE: 90,883

The VW 181 was a replica of the war-time Kübelwagen. It was sold to the army and the public.

SPECIAL REMARKS: The 1,584 cc engine in the 181 produced 44 bhp. When the 1,584 cc four-cylinder engine was used, power increased to 54 bhp.

Volvo

Assar Gabrielsson, the sales director of the Swedish ball-bearing maker SKF met the engineer Gustav Larson in 1924. Both of them dreamed of a Swedish car industry and they quickly realised their dreams. Gabrielssohn had studied economics and took on the business side while Larson was responsible for production. The first test drive of their car occurred in 1926. The first Volvo ÖV 4, better known as Jakob, rolled out of the factory on 14 April 1927. The pre-war Volvo cars looked much like the output of Detroit, except that they were adapted to the harsh Swedish climate and poor, unmetalled roads.

The first post-war models were already driving on Swedish roads in 1944. These were type PV 444, with PV for Personvagn or private car, the first 4 represented 4-seats, and 44 the model year of 1944. This was an attractive car and when it was shown at an exhibition in Stockholm 2,300 orders were placed immediately. Post-war production got under way with the PV 60 of 1939. The 444 did not roll off the line until 1947. Only 2,000 were built in that year because trucks and tractors had priority. The 444 had a 1,414 cc four-cylinder engine that delivered 40 bhp. In 1950 the output was increased to 44 bhp and in 1955 the engine's output rose to 55 bhp.

The Volvo Amazone was introduced in 1957 to provide the backbone to the range. There was a 1,582 cc overhead valve engine under the bonnet that produced 60 bhp in the standard version but 76 bhp in the "S" model. The cylinder capacity was increased to 1,985 cc in 1968 and power output rose to 82 bhp. This engine was also installed in the PV 544

Assar Gabriëlsson (1891-1962).

The Volvo PV 444's wheelbase is 2,600 mm (102 in), length 4,350 mm (171 in) and top speed 69 mph (110 kph).

Safety has always been of prime importance for Volvo. They were one of the first with a "safety" dashboard.

which succeeded the 444. The PV 544 closely resembled its forerunner but could be recognised by the different grille and one piece windscreen.

There were also sporting convertibles and coupé built on the basis of three 444 and 544. The P 1900 of 1956 was a 2+2 convertible with a polyester body. This car was never cured of its teething problems and never truly went into series production. The P1800 was much more successful. This was built using PV 544 parts. The body was designed by Per Petterson. When the car was ageing and need of replacement the solution was found by just remodelling the rear end to create the 1800 ES. This car was nicknamed "Snow White's hearse"

The Amazone was an attractive car and still looks so today. The people at Volvo thought differently and produced a replacement in 1966. The 140 series had an entirely new body but retained the old 1,778 cc engine, replaced in 1968 with a 1,985 cc unit. Volvo's top-of-the-range car to compete with

The PV 544 can be recognised by its new grille and single piece windscreen.

Volvo PV444

MODEL YEAR: 1947-1958

NUMBER MADE: 196,005

The first PV444's had two small rear windows. A single window was fitted from 1955.

Mercedes-Benz and BMW was the Volvo 164, introduced in August 1968. This had a 2,978 cc six-cylinder engine and power output of 145 bhp. Standard equipment included leather upholstery, power steering and servo-assisted brakes, and an electrical overdrive, although most of the cars were supplied with an automatic gearbox. When the engine finally got fuel injection the power rose to 175 bhp at 5,500 rpm.

There was a new range in 1974 known as 240 and 260 to replace the 140 series. The 240 had a 1,985 cc four-cylinder engine with an overhead camshaft and output of 82 bhp. It was also available with a 2,127 cc engine of 97 bhp. The 260 had a new 2,664 cc six-cylinder engine developed jointly with Renault and Peugeot.
This had power output of 140 bhp at 6,000 rpm. The P1900 and P1800 were not really sports cars but should be seen as more in the class of Renault Dauphine and VW Karmann Ghia.

SPECIAL REMARKS: The PV444 had a monocoque body, independent front suspension, and an engine with overhead valves.

Volvo P1900

MODEL YEAR: 1956-1957

NUMBER MADE: 67

SPECIAL REMARKS: This two-seater had a developed version of the PV444 engine. The bodies for the early examples were produced in the USA by Glasspar.

The Volvo Amazone, like this 122 S, is still a fine-looking car.

Volvo cars

COUNTRY OF ORIGIN: Sweden

276

The engine of the 122 S had twin carburettors and five-bearing crankshaft to increase life expectancy.

Volvo 120

MODEL YEAR: 1957-1970

NUMBER MADE: 667,323

SPECIAL REMARKS: The Volvo 120 was initially built using PV544 parts. The Amazone was primarily a two-door saloon but was later also available as four-door saloon and estate car.

Volvo P1800

MODEL YEAR: 1961-1972

NUMBER MADE: 39,406

SPECIAL REMARKS: At its introduction, the

The p1800 "Snow White's hearse" was designed by Jan Wilsgaard.

The character of Simon Templar made the P1800 world-famous by driving it in the television series "The Saint".

P1800 was sold with the new 1,780 cc B18 engine with its output of 90 bhp. In 1964 this four-cylinder unit was enlarged to 1,985 cc. When fuel injection was added to this larger engine power increased from 105 to 120 bhp.

The Volvo 140 series appearance altered little in it 8 years.

The P1800 was not a sports car, more a sporty-looking coupé that was ideal for long journeys.

Volvo 140

MODEL YEAR: 1966-1974

NUMBER MADE: 1,205,111

SPECIAL REMARKS: The 1,778 cc engine produced power of 75 bhp of 96 with twin carburettors and higher compression. The engine was enlarged in 1968 to 1,985 cc with power of either 82 or 105 bhp. The 164 was the first Volvo six-cylinder engine since the

1930s. This engine was a 2,978 cc capacity unit with power output of 130 bhp at 5,000 rpm.

Volvo 240

MODEL YEAR: 1974-1993

NUMBER MADE: Unknown

SPECIAL REMARKS: Only the front suspension and engine were new in this model. The rest was virtually the same as the 140 series.

The Volvo 164 was designed to compete with Mercedes-Benz and BMW. This is a 1970 example. The early car had especially large grilles.

The 240 series can be recognised by its heavy and unfortunately rather ugly bumpers.

The 140 and 160 series were built on the same chassis. Only the striking nameplate "164" gave the game away.

Wartburg

Wartburg

When the German Democratic Republic (East Germany) came into existence in October 1949, the car industry centres of Chemnitz, Eisenach, and Zwickau suddenly found themselves behind the "Iron Curtain". The Russians annexed most of the factories and

An interesting version of the Wartburg 311/312 was the Camping Limousine that was built between 1957-1963 in small numbers.

The 353 had an old chassis but new body. The final examples had a VW engine.

removed many of the machines but left enough to be able to make cars once more. Hence EMW cars rolled out of the former BMW works at Eisenach. There were also the IFA cars that were merely East German versions of pre-war DKW cars. In 1956, an entirely new make was created, the Wartburg. This was an improved version of the IFA and hence was powered by a three-cylinder two-stroke engine. The Wartburg was available in various versions, even as coupé and convertible. During the mid 1960s and during the 1970s the cars regularly had new bodies. Thus the Wartburg 353 was created but still with the smelly two-stroke engine under the bonnet. This model was built until 1991. The two-stroke engine though was replaced after 1988 by a Volkswagen Golf engine.

Wartburg cars

COUNTRY OF ORIGIN: Former German Democratic Republic (East Germany).

Wartburg 311

MODEL YEAR: 1956-1962

NUMBER MADE: Unknown

SPECIAL REMARKS: The three-cylinder two-stroke engine had a capacity of 900 cc and delivered 37 bhp to the front wheels. The car's top speed was 72 mph (115 kph).

The Wartburg 311 like this 4-door saloon, was a dream for the East Germans. In 1962 the car got a 991 cc engine and became the 312.

Willys

The Allies won the war with the help of the Jeep. This strange-looking vehicle really was an all-terrain vehicle. It could leap if necessary and even swim. Many regard Willys-Overland as the inventor of the Jeep and the Jeep-Eagle brand that now forms part of Chrysler are the last people to deny this. The reality is that the small-scale American Bantam Company, that built a small Bantam car under licence from Austin of England, created the concept. In any event, Willys became world-famous for the Jeep of which they have made more than 360,000. Ford built 277,896 of them and Bantam a mere 2,500. Willys-Overland also had the foresight in 1950 to register the name Jeep as their trademark.

Only Willys continued to build Jeeps after World War II, both for the military and for civil purposes. Farmers in particular found it an excellent general purpose vehicle. An entirely new market was created in 1946 with the introduction of the Station Wagon, which was the first all-steel American estate car. At first these had rear-wheel drive only but in 1949 a true 4x4 could also be ordered. Up to 1950 the Station Wagon had a four-cylinder Go-Devil engine but after this date was fitted with the Hurricane motor.

The most interesting post-war Jeep though was probably the Jeepster, which became a real fashion statement in its day, which film stars were pleased to be seen in. This vehicle was only available as a convertible. The roof and side panels were attached by poppers to the body. The Jeepster shared mechanicals with the Station Wagon but was never made as a four-wheel drive. Customers could choose between the four-cylinder Go-Devil or six-cylinder Lightning Six power units. When the Station Wagon got the Hurricane engine and a new grille in 1950, the Speedster was launched at the same time. Of the more than 19,000 Jeepsters that were built, 2,431 of them were fitted with the six-cylinder engine.

Willys was less successful though with building family cars after World War II. The Willys Aero Wing appeared in 1951 with a two-door monocoque body and room for six persons. By American standards this was a small car to fill the gap between the Nash Rambler and the larger American cars. A slimmed down version followed the next year as the Willys Aero Lark with six-cylinder side-valve engine from the Station Wagon. The cars were also available with four doors from 1953. There

The post-war Station Wagon provided plenty of space, go-anywhere ability and was virtually indestructible.

was also an Willys Aero 2600 with mono-coque body and similar engine to the Jeep. In 1953, Willys Corporation became part of Kaiser.

This meant an end to production of Willys cars. From 1955 only Jeeps were produced. A new factory was built in Sao Paulo, Brazil in 1960 specially for the construction of Jeeps.

Willys vehicles

COUNTRY OF ORIGIN: USA

Willys Aero Wing

MODEL YEAR: 1951-1955

NUMBER MADE: Unknown

SPECIAL REMARKS: This car had a 2,638 cc six-cylinder engine with the inlet valves in the cylinder head and exhaust valves in the cylinder block. The motor produced power of 91 bhp at 4,200 rpm.

Willys Aero 2600

MODEL YEAR: 1960-1970

NUMBER MADE: Unknown

SPECIAL REMARKS: The engine was a replica of the Jeep motor with overhead tappet-oper-ated inlet valves and push-rod operated exhaust valves. The 2,638 cc six-cylinder en-gine produced 110 bhp at 4,400 rpm. Power to the rear wheels was controlled via a col-umn-operated gear-lever to the three-speed gearbox.

Willys Station Wagon

MODEL YEAR: 1946-1963

NUMBER MADE: Unknown

SPECIAL REMARKS: The Jeep Station Wagon was an extremely practical car despite its three doors. Those with four-wheel drive could be taken almost anywhere but it looked more like a car than a Jeep.

Willys Jeepster

MODEL YEAR: 1948-1950

NUMBER MADE: 19,130

SPECIAL REMARKS: The Jeepster was a fash-ionable vehicle as the Range Rover was to be-come many years later. With is removable side windows it was intended for fine weather.

A 1949 Jeepster. In 1950 it got the same grille as the Station Wagon.

This Willys Aero 2600 was built in Brazil in 1968. The factory also produce Renault cars under licence.

The hood and sides were fastened with zips and poppers.

Wolseley

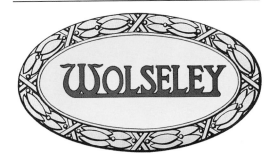

The boss of the Wolseley Sheep Shearing Machine Company Ltd in Birmingham was Herbert Austin. Despite his good job, Austin was more interested in cars than shearing machines which led to him building a tri-car that was an obvious copy of Léon Bollée's "automobile". The most interesting aspect of this car was the engine with its twin horizontal cylinders, which had an overhead camshaft. The prototypes were sufficiently advanced in 1899 to consider commercial production. Wolseley produced all manner of cars from small runabouts to enormous cars with 12-litre four-cylinder engines.

The Wolseley company got into financial difficulties in 1927 so that Sir William Morris (later Lord Nuffield) was able to buy it for a small consideration and make it part of his Nuffield Group. Herbert Austin had left Wolseley many years earlier to start up his own successful car business in 1905. Wolseley was the quality marque within the Nuffield Group and the cars could be recognised from 1933 onwards by the illuminated emblem on the radiator.

The Wolseley 6/110 was a 6/99 with engine uprated to 120 bhp. It was built from 1961-1968 and succeeded the 6/99.

After World War II, Wolseley introduced several models. There was the cheaper Eight and slightly more expensive Ten, 12/48, 14/60, and 18/85. The first three of these had four-cylinder engines of respectively 918, 1,140, and 1,548 cc. The latter two had six-cylinder units of 1,818 and 2,321 cc. All the engines had overhead valves and they were all fitted to four-door bodies with leather upholstery and wooden trim. The Wolseley 4/50 and 6/80 were introduced at the 1948 London motor show. These were the deluxe versions of the Morris Oxford and Morris Six.
The cars now had monocoque bodies and independent front suspension.

Austin merged with the Nuffield Group in 1952 to form the British Motor Corporation. Under this BMC mantel the Wolseley 4/44 came into being. This was a luxury car with the body and 1,250 cc engine from the MG Magnette. When a 1,489 cc engine was developed for the MGA this was also fitted to the 4/44 which changed its name to 15/50.

The concept of "badge engineering" had been well-known in the Nuffield Group for some time. Marques such as Wolseley steadily lost their individuality. The 6/90 of 1954 was in reality a Riley Pathfinder with an illuminated Wolseley emblem on its radiator grille. The Wolseley 1500 for the "common man" in 1957 was a cross between a Morris Minor and a Morris Oxford.

The final examples of the 15/50 were sold in 1958 as 15/60 or 16/60 depending on whether they had the 1,489 or 1,622 cc engine. These cars had a new body designed for BMC in Turin by Pininfarina. The following year Pininfarina created bodies for the Austin Westminster, Vanden Plas Princess, Wolseley 6/99, and 6/110. These cars were equipped once more with a six-cylinder 2,912 cc engine of 102 or 120 bhp. These were the top-of-the-line models of BMC. As counterpart to the successful Mini, Riley built the Riley Elf and Wolseley produced the Hornet on the same body as the Elf. These cars had an 848 cc engine that was later increased to 998 cc.

There were also Wolseley versions of the Morris 1100 and 1300. The Wolseley versions had a typical Wolseley grille and engine with twin carburettors that produced either 55 or 70 bhp. The Wolseley 18/85 was also not a real Wolseley but an Austin/Morris 1800 with a few more extras and the famous grille of course. The final car to be sold as a Wolseley was the Six in 1972 with a 2,227 cc six-cylinder engine.

This same car was also available as an Austin or Vanden Plas Princess. The Wolseley era was over and yet another famous marque had vanished.

Wolseley cars

COUNTRY OF ORIGIN: United Kingdom

Wolseley 12/48

MODEL YEAR: 1946-1948

NUMBER MADE: 5,602

SPECIAL REMARKS: The 1,548 cc engine with output of 44 bhp was the biggest and most powerful four-cylinder engine available from the factory immediately after World War II.

The 12/48 was the only small Wolseley with a sun-roof. There were also hydraulic jacks at each corner of the car.

Wolseley 15/50

MODEL YEAR: 1956-1958

NUMBER MADE: 12,353

SPECIAL REMARKS: When BMC developed the new 1,489 cc engine for the MGA this was fitted to the 15/50. The engine produced 56 bhp and gave a top speed of 81 mph (130 kph).

Wolseley 6/90

MODEL YEAR: 1954-1959

NUMBER MADE: 11,852

SPECIAL REMARKS: The six-cylinder engine had a cylinder capacity of 2,215 cc and produced 80 bhp at 4,800 rpm. The Wolseley body was identical to that of the Riley Pathfinder.

Wolseley 1500

MODEL YEAR: 1957-1965

NUMBER MADE: 103,394

SPECIAL REMARKS: The 1500 had a top speed

This 1961 Wolseley 1500 is a regular sight on racing circuits where it competes in races for historical cars.

The small 1,489 cc ohv engine produced 50 bhp at 4,200 rpm in its standard version.

of 81 mph (130 kph) with its 50 bhp engine. It was 151$^1/_2$ in (3,850 mm) long and had a 86 in (2,190 mm) wheelbase.

Wolseley 6/99

MODEL YEAR: 1959-1961

NUMBER MADE: 13,108

A 2,912 cc six-cylinder engine throbbed in the 6/99. Its air/petrol mixture was derived from twin SI-HD4 carburettors.

SPECIAL REMARKS: The 6/99 was a luxury car with a 2,912 cc six-cylinder engine producing 102 bhp. The car had disc brakes on the front wheels and an electrically-operated overdrive for its three-speed gearbox.

Wolseley Hornet

MODEL YEAR: 1961-1969

NUMBER MADE: 28,455

SPECIAL REMARKS: A Mini with a better-looking body? This car benefited from all the changes and improvements that were made to the Mini. Its engine grew from 848 cc to 998 cc and power increased from 35 to 39 bhp.

A Mk III Wolseley Hornet with proper wind-up windows.

The imposing appearance of the Wolseley 6/99 was designed by Pininfarina.

The boot looked better on the Wolseley Hornet than on the Mini and had a volume of 230 litres instead of 155 litres with the Mini.

Zündapp

Some time after both Heinkel and Messerschmitt had introduced their midget bubble cars, Dornier in 1955 also created such a car as the third German former aircraft company to enter this market. In Dornier's case the production rights were sold by Claudius Dornier to Zündapp and production started in 1956.

Zündapp had established a name for motorcycles and had built the big four-cylinder machines with sidecars that saw such wide-scale service with the Wehrmacht. Zündapp scooters formed a large part of the post-war street scene in Germany. The Dornier Delta was taken in hand by Zündapp and emerged as the Janus. The name from the Roman god with two faces who could look both forwards and to the rear was chosen because the car was almost symmetrical front and back and only discernible from the lights. The driver and passengers also sat back to back in the car.

Unlike other bubble cars they did not have to step into the car but could walk in thanks to the large front and rear doors. The Janus was no speed freak. Without a passenger the car

The front of the Zündapp Janus is recognisable from the headlights.

could eventually reach 50 mph (80 kph) but took 35 seconds to do so with the foot flat on the floor on the accelerator.

Zündapp cars

COUNTRY OF ORIGIN: Germany

Zündapp Janus

MODEL YEAR: 1957-1958

NUMBER MADE: 6,902

SPECIAL REMARKS: The rear wheels were powered by a 248 cc single-cylinder two-stroke engine that output 14 bhp. This engine was mounted amidships beneath the seats.

And this is what the back looked like. The front and back doors were the same size.

Index

Dashboard of the Kleinschnittger with the once popular column gear-change.

Contemporary publicity material for the Mk II MG Magnette.

Morris celebrated its 50th anniversary in 1962 and also launched the Morris 1100.

The 412 is a spacious 5-seater estate. Its 1.8-litre engine gave it a top speed of 100 mph (160 kph).

Author's and Photographic acknowledgements

The author and publishers wish to thank the following persons who provided photographs for their help in compiling this book. They are acknowledged in alphabetical order.

Tom W. Barett II, Scottsdale, Arizona, USA
Gunnel Ekberg, Saab, Sweden
Ford Motor Company, Dearborn, USA
Ford Motor Company, United Kingdom
Albrecht Guggisberg Oldtimer Garage, Toffen/Bern, Switzerland
Dieter Gunther. Hamburg. Germany
Ferdi Hediger, Lenzburg, Germany
Lukas Huni, Zürich, Switzerland
Jan Janssen, Ressen, Switzerland
Hans Karl Lange, Villach Austria
Rick Lenz. Bloomington, California USA

Reinhard Lintelmann, Espelkamp, Germany
Klaus-Peter Martin, Opel, Germany
Christian Monnier, Peugeot Museum, France
Ylva Peer, Volvo, Sweden
Anne Pezant, Renault, France
Peter Rau, Touring Garage, Zürich, Switzerland
Mary Jo Ring, Oldsmobile, Detroit, USA
Alex Rüber, Zürich, Switzerland
Wolfgang Schmel, Greiling, Germany
Reinhhard Schmidlin Oldtimer Gallery Toffen/Bern, Switzerland
Ernst Scheidegger, Schwyz, Switzerland
Ron Smit, Nijkerk, The Netherlands
Mat Stone. Glendale. California, USA
Max Stoop. Langnau/Zürich, Switzerland
Belinda Werner, Cadillac, Detroit, USA
Donald E. Williams, San Ramon, California, USA